BIBLICAL PORN

JESSICA JOHNSON

Biblical Porn

Affect, Labor, and

Pastor Mark Driscoll's

Evangelical Empire

DUKE UNIVERSITY PRESS | *Durham and London* | 2018

Typeset in ArnoPro by Westchester Publishing
Services

Library of Congress Cataloging-in-Publication Data
Names: Johnson, Jessica, [date] author.
Title: Biblical porn : affect, labor, and pastor Mark
Driscoll's evangelical empire / Jessica Johnson.
Description: Durham : Duke University Press, 2018. |
Includes bibliographical references and index.
Identifiers: LCCN 2017046939 (print) |
LCCN 2017051059 (ebook)
ISBN 9780822371601 (ebook)
ISBN 9780822371366 (hardcover : alk. paper)
ISBN 9780822371533 (pbk. : alk. paper)
Subjects: LCSH: Mars Hill Church (Seattle, Wash.)—
History. | Big churches—Corrupt practices—
United States. | Fundamentalist churches—
Clergy—Conduct of life. | Driscoll, Mark, 1970–
Classification: LCC BX7800.F8634 (ebook) | LCC
BX7800.F8634 S43 2018 (print) | DDC 280/.4—dc23
LC record available at https://lccn.loc.gov/2017046939

Cover art: Mark Driscoll preaching at the Mars Hill
Ballard Campus, 2008. © Lauren Greenfield.
Courtesy of Lauren Greenfield/INSTITUTE.

Contents

Acknowledgments

I would like to thank the people of Mars Hill Church who invited me into their homes and visited my neighborhood, sharing stories, lives, and friendship. Their vulnerability was a risk and a responsibility for which I am forever appreciative.

From the outset, I encountered institutional barriers to this research, obstacles that shifted in form as my position within the academy grew increasingly insecure. From 2012–2017, the period during which I did much of the interviewing and writing that comprises this book, I was lecturing at the University of Washington as a contingent faculty member in the Department of Anthropology; the Department of Gender, Women and Sexuality Studies; and the Comparative Religion Program. I would like to thank the students with whom I worked in various classrooms covering a wide range of subjects. Whether we were discussing books I was thinking through for research purposes or whatever I was writing at the time, their intellectual curiosity and engagement was a great support.

I have had the good fortune of meeting many wonderful colleagues on the road. A particularly generative space for taking risks was the Religion, Affect and Emotion group within the American Academy of Religion. I would like to thank Gail M. Hamner and Donovan Schaefer for organizing stimulating panels and including my work in the mix. Donovan also offered trenchant critique as a reader of this manuscript, pushing my thinking in productive directions, encouraging nerve on the page.

My deep gratitude goes to Sean McCloud for offering, insisting, to read chapters of this manuscript before I even thought to ask. I am thankful for his generosity in providing feedback throughout various stages of writing with such a perceptive and kind editorial voice. Sean also introduced me to Jason Bivins, another scholar of American religion, who was a wonderful conversational partner and invaluable set of eyes as I revised this manuscript.

Jason's suggestions facilitated improvisation, his commentary affording both insight and freedom. I am thankful for his generous spirit as a scholar.

Kathryn Lofton and John Modern invested in this project at a critical juncture. Katie's fierce encouragement was an incredible gift. My thanks also go to Joseph Masco and Kevin Lewis O'Neill for their thoughtful comments on early paper presentations, as I began playing with the concepts that generated the arguments of this book. I am grateful to Gregory Seigworth for organizing the Worldings/Tensions/Futures Affect Theory Conference in 2015, which provided an exciting venue for talking research. I would particularly like to thank Lawrence Grossberg, Gillian Harkins, Jason Read, and Tony Sampson for conversation and collegiality, as well as the organizers of the panel to which I contributed, Sophie Bjork-James and Yunus Dogan Telliel.

Finally, I wish to thank Miriam Angress and Sara Leone for their dedicated editorial support at Duke University Press. In addition, I would like to thank the editors and anonymous reviewers for journals and collections in which sections of this manuscript have previously appeared. Passages from the Introduction were published in the volume *Feeling Religion*; sections of chapter 1 appeared in *Feminist Studies* Vol. 43 (1) and *Political and Legal Anthropology Review* Vol. 33 (2); passages from chapter 3 appeared in the collection *New Views on Pornography*; sections from chapter 4 were published in the third edition of *Religion and Popular Culture in America*. I would also like to thank the Wenner-Gren Foundation for supporting the initial stages of this research, as I was investigating the politics of gay marriage legalization in Washington State for my dissertation on that subject.

Although it is highly unusual for Christians to publicly demonstrate outside a church against the mishandling of administrative and spiritual matters, it was not my first experience standing among protestors a stone's throw from Mars Hill's parking lot. While the issues cleverly summarized in protest slogans on placards raised important questions through which to engage passers-by on their way to worship, it was a thirty-minute video posted to the church website that inspired ex-members to rally behind the cry, "We Are Not Anonymous." That video began with Pastor Mark Driscoll sitting down in a simple wooden chair in the imposing Bellevue sanctuary, his figure flanked by rows of empty seats rather than large screens, the pulpit lectern onstage out of focus behind his left shoulder. The camera angle was such that it felt as though he was facing me from where I sat with laptop open at my desk. His complexion was ruddy but grizzled with salt-and-pepper stubble. The only prop that appeared throughout his delivery was a leather-bound Bible, which he physically and verbally gestured with and to in the video's opening moments:

> Hi, Mars Hill, Pastor Mark here. I wanted to give you a bit of an update on the season that we have been in and continue to be in. I was thinking about it and when I was seventeen years of age Jesus gave me this Bible through a gal named Grace who is of course now my wife, and Jesus saved me when I was nineteen, in college as a freshman, reading this Bible, and I started opening this Bible when I was twenty-five and Grace and I were a young married couple in our rental home. We felt called to start Mars Hill Church and so we would have some people over for a Bible study and there was not a lot of people so we didn't have a full service, instead I would sit in this chair and I would open this Bible and just teach a handful of people, or a few handfuls of people that would show up in our living room, and that grew to be Mars Hill Church. Now that I'm forty-three, almost forty-four, looking back it's, it's overwhelming if I'm honest, it's

shocking and amazing and staggering and wonderful. What Jesus has done has far exceeded even what I was praying for or hoping for or dreaming of.[1]

After this introduction littered with references to the Bible in his hands, a material manifestation of God's hand in Mars Hill's successful growth as well as his own spiritual authority, Driscoll explained that the purpose of this video was to communicate "in a way that is godly," by "directly" addressing congregants in a manner that was intended "as a means of loving you and informing you."[2] Within the first five minutes of this performance publicly disseminated online yet purportedly broadcast for a particular audience of intimates, Driscoll made the statement that many I spoke with attributed with triggering the protest:

> During this season as well, I have been rather silent and there are some reasons for that. First of all, we, including myself, needed to determine what exactly was happening. If I'm real honest with you, at first it was just a little overwhelming and a bit confusing. . . . As well, one of the things that has been complex is the fact that a lot of the people we are dealing with in this season remain anonymous. And so we don't know how to reconcile, or how to work things out with people because we're not entirely sure who they are, and so that has, that has made things a little more complex and difficult as well.[3]

Stunned, I looked at my browser loaded with tabs open to sites with names such as Joyful Exiles, Mars Hill Refuge, Repentant Pastor, and We Love Mars Hill, where multiple testimonies to spiritual, emotional, and financial exploitation were posted with the authors' names clearly identified. My initial sense of betrayal seemed unreasonable given I had no personal attachment to any of the people in these stories, had not seen Driscoll preach live for years, and had never considered him an authority figure given I did not and never have self-identified as a Christian.[4] I was not the video's intended audience; there was no rationalization, let alone words, for how I felt. I was not physically shaking as I watched Driscoll lie to my face through the computer screen, but my agitation was palpable and did not recede during the entirety of his message. Even more disconcertingly, I found myself not only hoping but also believing that he was going to change course and repent of his sin, as he had admonished audiences repeatedly and vehemently to do. I kept waiting for an acknowledgement of the specific charges of abuse, and the suffering that abuse had done to those who had the courage to openly testify to its prolonged spiritual and psychological toll, including the inability to trust religious authority or step foot into a church. When that did not happen, instead of doubting Driscoll, I started wondering if I had misheard or misunderstood. In a sense, I kept the faith alive until the final minutes of his message:

> Lastly, many of you have asked myself and other leaders, how can we be in prayer? I genuinely appreciate that. I would say, pray for your local leaders, they're dealing with things that, that I'm not dealing with . . . and, ah, there are some things in this season that are just, they're just, they're strange . . . ahh . . . unique. For example, at one of our churches, someone is folding up pornography and putting it in our pew Bibles. Just, all kinds of things in this strange season, so that when the lead pastor gets up and says, "Hey, if you're new or not a Christian, we've got some free Bibles in the pew, feel free to pick one up and go to page whatever for the sermon," and they open it up and they're exposed to pornography, and this can be adults or children, and so now there's a team having to go through our Bibles and take the pornography out to make sure their Bibles are clean on Sundays.[5]

The working title of my book on the church had been *Biblical Porn* for a couple of years. I was also in the process of writing a chapter on spiritual warfare, and never was my sense of it so keen as when I unexpectedly burst out laughing at this story's end. It was a full body laugh that erupted from my gut and lasted a long time, but not because I found the act of vandalism described particularly funny. After all the lies I had listened to, I highly doubted the authenticity of this anecdote, but that did not make it any less affective.

"Affect" is widely theorized across disciplines within the humanities and social sciences, but rarely ethnographically investigated as intersubjective intensities with political effects that traverse time and space. In this light, the empirical examination of affect complicates distinctions between macro- and micropower, what Gilles Deleuze and Felix Guattari call the "molar" and the "molecular"—a becoming-other that they describe as the "microphysics of desire."[6] The definition of affect offered by Spinoza and taken up by many political theorists, among them Brian Massumi, is "the power 'to affect and be affected.'"[7] Massumi writes, "Thinking *through* affect is not just reflecting on it. It is thought taking the plunge," a process of change that is "the first stirrings of the political, flush with the felt intensities of life."[8] Massumi describes affect on the whole as a "virtual co-presence of potentials" through which "power comes up into us from the field of potential. It 'in-forms' us."[9] The clunky hyphenate used by anthropologists to describe ethnographic fieldwork, "participant-observation," becomes usefully troubled in the examination of affect—participant-observation does not occur *in* the field, it is *of* the field.

Laughter is such a field. Philosopher William E. Connolly describes laughter as "a manifestation of surplus affect," which can inspire "side perceptions at odds with the dominant drift of perception and interpretation" such that the flow of thought is interrupted to "open a window of creativity."[10] Massumi states that laughter is one of the most powerful affective expressions because it interrupts a situation.[11] It was not what Mark said that had made me laugh, but the sense that we were sharing an inside joke. This surplus affective value did not register in his rhetoric, reside in a commodity, or remain self-contained, but manifested as conviction so unfocused that it emitted both within and without me. After the video ended, I sought to interpret and identify what I was feeling in emotional terms and settled on paranoia, figuring this irrational response would quickly subside. After all, Mark's employ of hyperbole and humor to excite and seduce audiences were renowned and considered among his gifts and strengths as a communicator. However, rather than fading, the intensity and unpredictability of sensations impossible to pin down kept me awake nights and indoors at my desk scanning the Internet for the unknown and unknowable. Information? Affirmation? Safety? And from whom or what, exactly?

At first, I rationalized my feelings in terms that I could understand and articulate as a feminist anthropologist—social justice. Put simply, I desired recognition for those whose suffering went unacknowledged. Despite its good intentions, such an explanation was no excuse for the disturbing and overpowering need I had to do something without knowing what that could be, other than endlessly tracking the explosion of media coverage surrounding Driscoll and the church. A few days after the anonymous video's release,

Mark began blogging on the topic of spiritual warfare, a six-part series that ended the same week in late August when he preached what would be his last sermon from the Mars Hill pulpit.[12]

While his opening posture and closing story provided the perfect tactile validation for my book's title beyond anything I could ever dream or script, it was not until I asked for permission to join the protest with former Mars Hill members via a public Facebook page entitled "We Are Not Anonymous" that its affective value became clearer. I had come "under conviction," but not of my own sinful nature and need for salvation. I did not become born-again in Christian terms, but I had to confront the troubling reality that I had desired to believe in "Pastor Mark." This was a desire that I did not feel I deserved, nor frankly wished to own, given I had never sacrificed for the church nor ideologically seen eye-to-eye with Driscoll. That video haunted me with surplus affect, both possessed and inhabited, that was not truly mine.

Anthropologist Susan Harding notes that when social scientists have investigated why people convert to Christianity, they inevitably deduce individuals have good reason to be "susceptible, vulnerable, and in need of something, so the question becomes 'Why? What's wrong? What's unsettling?' Or, 'what's setting them up? How have they been predisposed to convert?'"[13] In turn, accounts of various ritual practices and psychological techniques that catalyze transformation from one worldview to another posit conversion as a kind of brainwashing.[14] Harding describes her own experience of coming under conviction in terms of being "caught up in the Reverend Campbell's stories—I had 'caught' his language—enough to hear God speak to me when I almost collided with another car that afternoon. Indeed, the near-accident did not seem like an accident at all, for there is no such thing as a coincidence in born-again culture."[15]

By contrast, Driscoll was not witnessing to me personally in the video, nor was he using a biblical grammar that opened narrative gaps through which to insert myself as unbelieving listener. Rather than a sacred rite of passage, his concluding remarks conjured the folding of pornography into pew Bibles—a profane joke that complicated our subject positions of speaker/ listener and believer/nonbeliever, given its ambiguity. I could not be certain whether the prank was *on* or *by* him. Semiotics was an unhelpful tool of analysis, as this affective process was unnecessarily dialogical and therefore porously open-ended; mediation occurred bodily without becoming meaningful. Harding describes coming under conviction as chronological and spatial—a crossing from the terrain of disbelief into a liminal space of suspension or limbo that precedes the (potential) conversion from non-Christian into born-again believer. Clearly defined, preordained subject positions of speaker-saved and listener-lost are acknowledged by individuals who choose to enter into a relationship situated through a specific lexicon with a particular motive. Instead, I experienced conviction as irreducibly social while sitting alone at my desk.

I had no language for what I was experiencing, nor had I "caught" Pastor Mark's. I could not discern divine providence or impose self-will in explanations for what was bodily unfolding. I did not ask *why* I wanted to believe Mark would repent to the extent that I even doubted myself, as there were no religious or personal reasons for such an investment; instead, I kept asking *how*. This experience of conviction was akin to what William Connolly describes as belief that confounds cognitive understanding, belies agentive autonomy, and disrupts the individual's prerogative to judge what is true— "spiritual dispositions to action that both flow below epistemic beliefs and well up into them . . . the tightening of the gut, coldness of the skin, contraction of the pupils, and hunching of the back that arise when an epistemic belief in which you are invested has been challenged."[16] In this study, I examine conviction as surplus affective value which troubles felt distinctions between the sinner and saved, profane and sacred, subject and object, and spiritual and worldly. While I could not have articulated it at the time or during the many months that I sought the fellowship of former Mars Hill members over longtime friends, the disjuncture that I experienced was not a matter of worldview but the matter of worlding.[17] Anthropologist Kathleen Stewart suggests that writing culture is "an attunement, a response, a vigilant protection of a worlding."[18] In this mode, the ethnographer is instrument rather than authority.

SUBJECT AND ARGUMENT: BIBLICAL PORN

From 1996–2014, Mars Hill Church of Seattle multiplied into fifteen facilities in five U.S. states, serving approximately 13,000 attendees as Pastor Mark Driscoll's preaching on "biblical oral sex"[19] earned him international celebrity: "Men, I am glad to report to you that oral sex is biblical. . . .

Ladies, your husbands appreciate oral sex. So, serve them, love them well."[20] In sermons such as "The Porn Path"[21] and an e-book called *Porn Again Christian* (2008),[22] Driscoll stated in no uncertain terms that "free and frequent"[23] sex between a husband and wife is necessary to assure fidelity within Christian marriages and secure masculine leadership within evangelical churches. "Our world assaults men with images of beautiful women," he warned. "Male brains house an ever-growing repository of lustful snapshots always on random shuffle. . . . The temptation to sin by viewing porn and other visual lures is an everyday war."[24] As Driscoll claimed, "sometimes pornography is in an image, sometimes it is in your imagination,"[25] his sexualized hermeneutic revealed women's body parts cloaked in biblical metaphor.[26] Meanwhile, question-and-answer sessions during services encouraged congregants to text queries that materialized as sound-bite confessions to sins and desires on large screens surrounding Mars Hill's sanctuary. The church's employ of visual and digital media served to amplify Driscoll's sermonizing on sex by conscripting audience participation in animating a pornographic imaginary, legitimizing his spiritual authority.

Biblical Porn: Affect, Labor, and Pastor Mark Driscoll's Evangelical Empire examines how Driscoll's audiences were affectively recruited into sexualized and militarized dynamics of power through the mobilization of what I call *biblical porn*. By *biblical porn*, I mean the affective labor of mediating, branding, and embodying Driscoll's teaching on "biblical" masculinity, femininity, and sexuality as a social imaginary,[27] marketing strategy, and biopolitical instrument. My use of *affective labor* builds upon Michael Hardt and Antonio Negri's theorization: "contact that can be either actual or virtual . . . [care] entirely immersed in the corporeal [while] the effects it produces are immaterial . . . social networks, forms of community, biopower."[28] In theorizing biblical porn as affective labor, I signal the critical potential of examining "porn" not simply as image or text, but also as imaginary and industry—or, more precisely, imaginary *as* industry. This industry is not interpretive but affective; it consists of material and immaterial labor that is social and embodied, producing surplus affective value that can be manipulated and exploited—the "carnal resonance" of conviction. In repurposing the term *carnal resonance* as used by porn studies scholar Susanna Paasonen, I play with the notion of resonance as a concept that she employs to "[make] sense of the movement between porn and its users."[29] In her formulation, carnal resonance "describes the force and grab of porn—its visceral appeal and power to disturb," as well as "how users attach themselves to porn sites, images, videos, and texts and recognize some of the carnal sensations depicted on the screen."[30] She states that her project is "to tackle the interactive nature of such attachments, for the central question is pornography's power to touch and move us, to arouse our senses and interest alike."[31] In a similar if distinct manner, I wish to examine the affective entanglements, attachments, and labor of biblical porn by theorizing conviction as social and in process, visceral and disturbing, of bodily sensation and collective desire.

"Porn" in this instance is not cinematically portrayed onscreen or online through sexually explicit imagery such that clear distinctions can be drawn between producer and consumer. However, biblical porn is usefully considered in light of what porn studies scholar Stephen Maddison calls "immaterial sex"—the "creative and affective energies commodified in porn production."[32] Maddison examines how immaterial sex constitutes "the entrepreneurial voyeur" such that "porn consumption, sexual subjectification and enterprise culture mutually reinforce one another."[33] This immaterial-entrepreneurial dynamic produces forms of sex and sexual agency through neoliberal "free market" logics of governmentality that regulate sexual autonomy and exploit immaterial labor while proliferating sexual variation and "altporn" for the sake of capital.[34] In contrast, biblical porn is not generated through sexual performances per se, though it does function on an affective register with entrepreneurial drive as a tool of promotion and evangelizing. By framing "porn" as "biblical," I wish to decenter representational, discursive, and ideological modes for thinking and feeling sexual imaginaries, their bodily expression, affects and effects. In the immaterial sex of biblical porn, "emotional and physiological energies, desires, and sensations" are created and capitalized on during the affective labor of its cultural production and mediation as a social imaginary, marketing strategy, and biopolitical instrument.[35]

Pornography is typically considered in terms of the surveillance of pleasure—in Michel Foucault's language "knowledge of pleasure: a pleasure that comes of knowing pleasure."[36] Foucault argues that the pleasures of the body are socially and historically constructed and contextualized through discourse; changeable and politically put to use to constitute subjects and desires and to regulate bodies and populations. Biblical porn does this work too, constituting Mars Hill congregants as gender-specific sexual agents and sinners who are trained to normatively embody masculinity, femininity, and sexuality. However, the affective labor of biblical porn also recruits and perpetuates visceral, virtual, and visual processes that are non-intentional, animating conviction in calibrated yet uncontrollable ways that are not always pleasurable or intelligible. I reassess conviction in terms of gut feeling which signals desires and passions simultaneously biological and social, examining how they activate and contaminate habits of the everyday. In response to political theorist Wendy Brown's dismissal of conviction as a "performative speech act of discursive subjection" that renders individuals "unfree to act,"[37] I argue that the political valence of conviction lies in its affective capacity to register as a belief that feels like one's own, but may be steered toward inspiring voluntary and involuntary affective labor. At Mars Hill, such affective labor entailed a variety of service opportunities that primed the church's atmosphere and fostered networks of care, such as worship band, media production, security team, and children's ministry. In addition, affective labor was enlisted through inadvertent yet habituated bodily responses of the nervous system—gut feelings, belly laughs, glances, and gestures—that excited, agitated, and exploited a desire to believe.

The orchestration of this affective labor was articulated in terms of "air war" and "ground war," with the aim to "rally one thousand churches behind one pulpit."[38] As Mars Hill's facilities multiplied, imperatives to support the church's propagation were framed in violent terms of combat-readiness and the sexualized embodiment of "visual generosity" and "sexual freedom" by Christian wives. The theology of sex proscribed by Driscoll as "biblical" generated an evangelical genre of "social pornography"[39] that was contingent on the "free" industry of congregants who contributed to its production, distribution, and diffusion. Practices of confession and processes of imagination were bodily and virtually mediated and networked via nervous systems and fiber optics. In turn, fear, shame, and paranoia circulated within and well beyond Mars Hill's facilities as political and economic affective value.

This religiously inflected form of biopower directed a collective sense of conviction in support of Driscoll's vision for Mars Hill's empire, a strategy of biopolitical control that reverberated throughout the church's ministry, including sermon study in small group settings, social media forums, men and women's "training days," church leadership "boot camps," and "military missions" that gifted *Porn Again Christian* to troops in Iraq and Afghanistan. In Foucault's theorization of "biopower," he discusses a "power over life" that invests "life through and through" via two poles—one that disciplines the body to increase its usefulness, efficiency, and docility; and one that invests in biological processes such as propagation, health, and housing—to further systems of economy.[40] Biopower includes myriad techniques for the subjugation of bodies via institutions such as the family, army, hospital, and school—mechanisms of surveillance and regulation that become internalized to inspire self-governance—while "biopolitics" includes "regulations of the population," such as "the harnessing, intensification, and distribution of forces, the adjustments and economy of energies."[41] Sex is a primary instrument through which this political technology of life functions, "deployments of power" that are "directly connected to . . . bodies, functions, physiological processes, and pleasures."[42] In my examination, biopower is operationalized through what I call an *affective ecology* of "Evangelical Empire"—an assemblage of agency that includes nonhuman bodies such as media technologies, collective moods, and invisible demons—through which relations and strategies of power excite and contaminate, rather than strictly police or regulate. This form of biopower is regenerative of populations, what cultural theorist Jasbir K. Puar calls "systems of unleashed circuitry," which are "exuberant and fertile."[43] Writing on Deleuze and Guattari's concept of "assemblage," Puar notes, "Assemblage is actually an awkward translation—the original term in Deleuze and Guattari's work is not the French word assemblage, but actually Agencement, a term which means design, layout, organization, arrangement, and relations—the focus being not on content but on relations, relations of patterns. . . . Assemblages do not privilege bodies as human, nor as residing within a human/animal binary. Along with a de-exceptionalizing of human bodies, multiple forms of matter can be bodies—bodies of water, cities, institutions, and so on. Matter is an actor."[44]

The affective political and economic value of biblical porn extended beyond the monitoring and management of normatively "biblical" gender and sexuality, generating the social conviction and self-sacrifice necessary for Mars Hill's ongoing expansion beyond reason or resources—against the moral conscience of leaders, financial capacity of the church, and "man-power" available at local facilities. Precarity intensified as locations multiplied and congregants were increasingly exposed to risk in spiritual, emotional, and material ways, a constant sense of insecurity that infused the very constitution of work.[45] Servitude was fought for as though it were salvation at the church via an affective ecology of fear tinged with hope. I call this affective ecology "Evangelical Empire" to signal a dynamic of biopower through which the circulation and amplification of affect via social processes of media(tion) agitated and infected Mars Hill congregants across its multiple facilities and within their homes. In linking "Evangelical" to "Empire," I index not only Driscoll's vision for the church's multigenerational legacy, or its model of entrepreneurial enterprise in the style of multinational corporations, but also how the affective ecology of Mars Hill inspired processes of militarization and sexualization that enlisted affective labor and self-sacrifice. In this sense, empire is not a totalizing, global form of domination, but a globally directed microphysics of desire that conflates freedom and control, perpetuating and exploiting conviction as bodily affect to political and economic effect. The affective ecology of Evangelical Empire is an assemblage of human and nonhuman bodily encounter that involves voice, tone, mood, atmosphere, image, imagination, demons, and technologies in ways that importantly transgress representational, discursive, or ideological systems to generate and network conviction as surplus affective value.[46]

Thus, this dynamic of biopower is less predicated on technologies of self—the disciplinary forms of self-governance and self-care that factor into Foucault's formulation. In the affective orchestration of Evangelical Empire, church discipline was a distinct mechanism through which biopower operated, priming a perpetual sense of impending threat (e.g., for "gossiping" or "divisiveness"), as well as inspiring and extracting as much affective labor as possible in order to "plant churches" and "make disciples."[47] For Foucault, the deployment of sexuality "engenders a continual extension of areas and forms of control," particularly "the sensations of the body, the quality of pleasures, and the nature of impressions, however tenuous or imperceptible they may be."[48] In theorizing biopower, he turns to a *history of sexuality* in order to show how "this idea of sex took form in the different strategies of power," such as the "hysterization of women" or "psychiatrization of perversions."[49] By shifting this discussion to the *biopolitics of sex*, rethinking the deployment of sexuality in relation to the affective labor of biblical porn, I critically reassess the political impact of bodily sensation, tenuous pleasure, and imperceptible impression as vital materialities[50] in this "globalized" age of media convergences. Brian Massumi suggests the necessity for such reexamination when he states, "An American president can deploy troops overseas because it makes a population feel good about their country or feel secure, not because the leader is able to present well-honed arguments that convince the population that it is a justified use of force. And the media are not mediating any more—they become direct mechanisms of control by their ability to modulate the affective dimension."[51] Biblical porn was affectively networked and biopolitically disseminated, penetrating what Massumi calls the "micropolitical realm," where "mass affect" proliferates and becomes more diffuse, distributed, and insidious.[52] For years, scandal and controversy surrounding Driscoll and the church only served to circulate and amplify the affective value of fear and hope, shame and pride, and paranoia and conviction.

Within the field of porn studies, there is scholarly attention paid to what is called *sexualized culture*, a term with myriad uses that can mean anything from "a contemporary preoccupation with sexualized values, practices, and identities; the public shift to more permissive sexual attitudes; the proliferation of sexual texts; the emergence of new forms of sexual experience; the apparent breakdown of rules, categories, and regulations designed to keep the obscene at bay; our fondness for scandals, controversies, and panics about sex."[53] At Mars Hill, these various facets of sexualized culture converged in productively troubling ways. "Social media" (including screens, glances, texts, amps, laughter, and gut feeling) generated biblical porn as an imaginary of surveillance, strategy of branding, and biopolitical technology of contagion. Through sermon vodcasts, audio downloads, and church blogs, the practice of confession was commodified for public consumption. This industry proliferated and intensified congregants' sense of sin, affectively convicting them via a feedback loop that simultaneously validated Driscoll's spiritual authority. The affective labor of biblical porn gleaned website downloads that advertised Driscoll's charisma, popularity, and books, while his sexualized hermeneutic garnered media headlines, cultural influence, and market value as he became a key player in, and money maker for, a celebrity-driven "evangelical industrial complex."[54] In her groundbreaking study of hardcore pornography, Linda Williams writes, "I had begun with what I thought to be an invulnerability, even a disdain for the texts of pornography, but was then surprised to find myself 'moved' by some works. What was the place of this vulnerability in writing about the genre?"[55] I felt similarly about my field site and found myself moved by its space and people in unexpected ways. However, the vulnerability I experience in writing about biblical porn is distinctly affective—I can repeat Driscoll's jokes verbatim and hear his voice as I do.

Digital media and communication studies scholar Tony Sampson writes that pornography serves as a cultural amplifier that, among other objects, generates a world "awash with hormones and consumer goods," in which "affects are significantly passed on, via suggestions made by others, more and more through networks."[56] In her examination of how power operates through couplings of freedom and control via the Internet, digital culture scholar Wendy Hui Kyong Chun speaks of this conflation as a response to the Cold War and the successes and failures of containment.[57] She discusses the Internet as a site of moral panic whose intensity far surpassed the actual viewing of cyberporn in the mid-1990s. It was the fear and paranoia that children would glimpse online pornography that made it "hypervisible," not the number of images themselves.[58] In examining the affective labor of biblical porn, I demonstrate how biopolitical control has gone viral through affective networks of suggestion that supersede institutional regulation or jurisdiction of the state, as the surplus value of conviction is incited and exploited across religious and secular divides.

METHODOLOGY: ETHNOGRAPHY AND AFFECT

This study is based on a decade (2006–2016) of gathering ethnographic evidence. From 2006–2008, I conducted fieldwork at Mars Hill's headquarters in Ballard, a centrally located Seattle neighborhood, as the church began multiplying into satellite campuses throughout the city and its suburbs. I regularly attended not only sermons but also gospel classes required for membership; seminars on how to embody biblical gender and sexuality; a women's "training day" called *Christian Womanhood in a Feminist Culture*; and Film and Theology Nights, when Hollywood movies were screened and discussed. Over the span of my fieldwork from 2006–2008, I was unable to receive the permission from Driscoll required by the Institutional

Review Board (IRB) at the University of Washington to conduct formal interviews. However, I was afforded the opportunity to attend any public events open to nonmembers. During the time that I attempted to receive Driscoll's consent, I informally met with several pastors and a deacon in women's ministry to discuss the church's theology, gender and sexuality doctrine, and engagement with popular culture.[59] I also visited a community group gathering in my neighborhood. All of these events were open to non-members, and those I spoke with were aware that I was an anthropologist at the University of Washington attending the church to better understand its teaching on marriage for research purposes, given I was investigating the politics of gay marriage legalization in Seattle for my dissertation. Most of the teaching events on gender and sexuality I attended were women-only, while larger gatherings included couples and families.

In the ensuing years as I finished my dissertation, I continued to follow what was happening at the church through local and national media, watched sermons online, and attended a 2011 Easter service held at Qwest Field (where the Seahawks football team plays). In 2012, after teaching at a university in Miami for one year, I returned to Seattle to find that Pastor Paul Petry, one of the leaders fired during my initial fieldwork, had inaugurated the website Joyful Exiles. On this portal, he archived primary documents (e.g., emails with leadership; internal church memos) that detailed his termination and shunning. Although returning to Seattle was not my plan, and re-embarking on fieldwork was not my aim, as the public testimonies to financial, emotional, and spiritual abuse mounted during and after 2012, a sense of urgency took hold. I did not hear God, but I did feel His hand.

Mars Hill's facilities steadily replicated until 2014, when a deluge of evidence surfaced online supporting several accusations against Driscoll. These charges included the surreptitious use of a marketing ploy to cull the buyers' lists necessary to achieve bestselling status for Driscoll's book *Real Marriage: The Truth About Sex, Friendship, and Life Together* (2012).[60] They also identified bullying, micromanagement, and tactics of intimidation and social isolation used to suppress information and stifle dissent.[61] After numerous former leaders posted confessions seeking repentance for sinning as—and being sinned against—church administration, a protest was organized outside the main facility in August 2014, which had shifted from

Seattle to suburban Bellevue.[62] From 2014–2016, in the aftermath of attending this protest, I spoke with former leaders and members who worked for the church during the stages of its foundation, expansion, and dissolution. These conversations and interviews suggested that I was neither immune from, nor had left behind, affective entanglements and labor that I was not privy to during my initial years of fieldwork.

Initially, my requests for interviews among those who began going public with their stories went unanswered, and I did not push. However, as the scandals continued and leaders began leaving the church in increasing numbers, publishing confessions on personal blogs and sites such as Repentant Pastor, media attention paved the way for more opportunities to speak with those I had once only seen from a distance onstage. I did not arrive at Mars Hill Bellevue and walk down the line of protestors holding signs passing out business cards; I stood with them and held one myself.[63] After the protest, I had the opportunity to meet with people formally and informally, including a long-standing weekly gathering of former male members who sat around a bonfire and talked through their experiences in the aftermath of leaving Mars Hill; a women's event for former members who wished to testify to their ongoing experiences of living with the affects and effects of spiritual abuse; and at dining room tables during holidays and neighborhood potlucks. My interviews with individuals and couples were in coffee shops, homes, and breweries; conversations were had after music shows and films. Since my field site was my home, people from Mars Hill quickly became an integral part of my social circle and we developed intimate friendships born out of shared sensibilities rather than aligned ideologies.

My analysis includes interview material and is also informed by casual conversations with former leaders and members, church documents leaked and curated on the Internet, and online confessions and testimonies by former leaders and members. Some of those I spoke with said that their names could be used, but many preferred to remain anonymous or "off the record," aside from written documents publicly accessible. For this reason, I have eliminated all personally identifying information from dialogue and interview material. The only exception to this rule is Pastor Mark, given his public stature. Often, those I spoke with had already released testimonies and confessions online and specifically asked that I use material from those sources; thus, when names were attached to these documents, such identifiers remain. At the time of this book's publication, websites full of online testimonies are disappearing as Driscoll gains a new platform for his teaching, much of it recycled from his time preaching at Mars Hill, as a blogger on the faith forum Patheos. While some of this material is edited out of necessity due to length, I keep much of it intact in order to convey the mood, actions, and atmosphere of particular situations and scenes, as well as to reestablish an archive of labor and events erased or elided. I formally interviewed men and women, as well as met with couples in their homes. On the whole, I met with more men than women on an individual basis, but participated in several gender-segregated groups, achieving a balance in my interactions. I also attended larger informal gatherings by explicit invitation. During this stage of the research process, I received exemption from the IRB because the church was dissolving and so much information was publicly available online. In addition to this testimony, I analyze sermons and other audiovisual teaching material produced by Mars Hill spanning the years of 1997–2014; Driscoll's books (electronic and print); media coverage; audio recordings, blog posts, and other teaching and promotional material publicly distributed by the church.

While de-emphasizing the meaning of Driscoll's language, I examine how its onstage, onscreen, and online performance agitated and exploited affective processes during which the space and medium of communication conflated. When I examine texts, films, sermons or speech, I am not strictly doing so in ideological, discursive, or representational frames but as social, embodied processes of communication and mediation. Driscoll's voice, image, expressions, gestures and their affective impact in terms of rhythm, humor, tenor and inflection are a critical focus of my investigation, and I am purposefully promiscuous in my use of affect theory in their analysis. I use *mediation* to signal subjectivity as always already social, a transsubjective encounter of human and nonhuman bodies. As a concept, mediation is particularly useful to the analysis of empirical evidence grounded in the reflexive practice of autoethnography, wherever the "field" may be or might consist of—my laptop, the church sanctuary, or laughter. This approach aligns with what affect theorist Lisa Blackman describes as "processes, practices and affects that move through bodies in ways that are difficult to see, understand and investigate."[64] Blackman suggests that instead of talking about bodies, we should speak of "brain-body-world entanglements" that entail haptic, or affective, communication.[65] She writes that such processes of mediation do not "require a human subject governed by psychic dynamics of subjectivity or sociality, but a nervous attunement or synchronizing of the body with technology."[66] According to Blackman, practices of suggestion are enacted through brain-body-technology entanglements such that they produce certain effects and affects. In this Introduction's opening moment, despite the space, time and screen between us, Driscoll and I were affectively entangled, but it took an uncontrollable, disturbing laugh to show me how.

In anthropological theory, affect has been described by William Mazzarella as carrying "tactile, sensuous, and perhaps even involuntary connotations," implying "a way of apprehending social life that does not start with the bounded, intentional subject while at the same time foregrounding embodiment and sensuous life."[67] Rather than an emotional state that can be named and is "always already semiotically mediated," according to this definition affect is precognitive, prelinguistic, and prepersonal.[68] As Mazzarella's formulation suggests, affect is difficult to analyze by conventional discursive methods given it is radically grounded in the body to the extent that it cannot be articulated or rendered immediately intelligible in language. Theorizing what he calls "affective space," anthropologist Kevin Lewis O'Neill writes, "Affect as a religiously managed and politically manipulated sensation makes legible a series of spaces that are not necessarily territorial but that are nonetheless deeply political. These include, for example, the felt distance that exists between *us* and *them*."[69] I concur with O'Neill's suggestion that such "broken space" between the profane and sacred, sinner and saved, and local and global must be critically examined in studies of American religion, rather than analytically assumed.

Thus, I examine how fear, hope, conviction, shame, and paranoia circulated to generate what feminist affect theorist Sara Ahmed calls an "affective economy," whereby "emotions play a crucial role in the 'surfacing' of individual and collective bodies through the way in which emotions circulate between bodies and signs."[70] Ahmed's formulation contests the notion that emotions are psychological dispositions or private property—that they come from within a person and then move outward. Instead, "emotions *do things*, and they align individuals with communities—or bodily space with social space, through the very intensity of their attachments."[71] According to Ahmed, emotions work to mediate the relationships between psychic and social or individual and collective—it is their circulation and capacity to "stick" that creates bonds, involving subjects and objects without residing positively within them.[72] The affective labor of biblical porn came at spiritual, emotional, and bodily cost—immaterial yet visceral processes described to me by former members in terms of a "theology of rape," "spiritual abuse," and a "culture of fear."

Relations of affect and power have been theorized in ethnographic monographs by drawing attention to circuits of everyday sociality embodied in the ordinary, and tracing historical and contemporary performances and policies of the state that intensify a sense of emergent threat in the name of national security.[73] My analysis takes up anthropologist Kathleen Stewart's suggestion that terms such as neoliberalism which serve as shorthand for totalizing systems of politics and economy are insufficient to describe their force in everyday life, whereby "the political" and "the economic" affectively surface as shock, habit and resonance.[74] In his book *Religious Affects* (2015), religious studies scholar Donovan Schaefer provides a useful genealogy of affect theory, which examines tensions between what he calls the Deleuzian and phenomenological branches.[75] His research develops the materialist shift in religious studies by using affect theory to map power relations beyond language and through bodies in order to postulate that animals have religion and religion itself may be considered animal. Schaefer aims to trouble human exceptionalism as a framework uncritically adopted in the study of religion, a commitment that my project also advances insofar as I use ethnographic field methods to examine relationships and experiences that occur between persons and other vital materialities.

Biblical Porn also complicates accounts of evangelical cultural performances and the politics of affect that only consider the aim of conversion.[76] I investigate processes and relations of power that cannot be summarized by hegemonic notions concerning evangelical cultural politics. Anthropologist Susan Harding's ethnographic study of the cultural politics of Jerry Falwell's Moral Majority shows her methodologically "standing in the gaps" between the subject positions of believer and nonbeliever—a "paradoxical space of overlap [that] is also the space of ethnography."[77] Harding's linguistic analysis focuses on rhetoric rather than affect, yet her ethnographic practice of listening "actively and uncritically" to a reverend's witnessing opens a door whereby she hears God speak.[78] She writes, "Preachers construct such contexts verbally, and life presents them virtually every day—those gaps in the ordinary, when the seams split apart and you encounter the unknown, the unexpected, the uncontrollable, the irrational, the uncanny, the miraculous."[79] I argue that anthropological research into the lived practice of evangelical concepts such as conviction or repentance demonstrates how their political dimensions surpass self-contained "religious" publics and identities, while offering potential for rethinking so-called secular political concepts such as freedom, or formations such as empire.

Joel Robbins called for an anthropology of Christianity in and for itself while positing such research as a risk: "Anyone who has been told in the course of fieldwork that to understand is to convert has a visceral sense of the force of such Christian challenges to the modernist tradition."[80] My ethnographic investigation complicates this notion of risk by privileging vulnerability and uncertainty over researcher control and reflexivity. Through ethnographic engagement with the study of affect and its embodied sociopolitical effect, I demonstrate the critical potential and ethical necessity of reflecting on what anthropologists Peter Benson and Kevin Lewis O'Neill call the "phenomenology of 'doing' fieldwork . . . embedded in the contingency and risk of human relationships."[81] Utilizing ethnographic methods and empirical evidence to analyze dynamics of power animated through circuits of affect suggests underexplored ethical potential and relations of sociality. *Biblical Porn* shows how "ethnography's ethical possibilities are *actualized* when ethnographers change . . . not simply for the self and its interests, but rather for the sake of new kinds of collective affiliations across interpersonal and intercultural boundaries."[82] My examination not only analyzes the affective labor of biblical porn as it impacted the lives of Mars Hill congregants, but also how it unpredictably affected my positionality and stakes as an anthropologist.

When I described my experience of coming under conviction during the "anonymous" video to a former leader—how I trusted Mark would repent to the extent that I questioned myself—he emphatically gestured to my phone on the table as it was recording our conversation and exclaimed, "Put that down! Get that in!"[83] At the wooden table where we sat, I was not the only one taking notes. I used pen and paper; he used a tablet. I had asked permission to record our time together, an interview that lasted nearly six hours, and whenever there needed to be a pause, he would double-check to see if "we" were recording again.

Many of those I spoke with did not want to be recorded or have their names used. I understood. It was risky. I was asking people who had been socially isolated out of fear of being labeled "gossips" or "divisive" to discuss events that could be read as indictments of themselves and/or others, some of whom were family members or friends that remained connected to Mars Hill after they left. I asked people where they wanted to meet so that they could choose whether they would be more comfortable talking at home or in public. In one Seattle coffee shop in the vicinity of a Mars Hill facility before the church officially disbanded, a former pastor spent much of our thirty minutes together glancing around the premises, informing me when someone associated with the church walked in, eyes darting and brow lightly beaded with sweat. In one home, tears surfaced in the eyes of an ex-pastor as soon as we sat down; later during our conversation, tears welled up in mine. Many confessed that they felt duped and betrayed as well as culpable. There was tension between what was attributable to human will and what was attributable to divine will, individual agency and God's sovereignty. People were not only looking to answer, but also to find answers themselves. None of my "interviews" with former church staff were a one-way affair.

I played informant, too, describing the arguments of my book, experiences at Mars Hill, and fluctuating feelings in the aftermath of its dissolution. In the frantic days after watching the video, I found a link to the public Facebook group We Are Not Anonymous. Without forethought or script, I woke up one morning and wrote a former church leader that I had not met. That lengthy email message is truncated below: "I'm writing for your thoughts on the question of whether my presence would be welcome at the protest this Sunday. . . . I have been reluctant to join anything that would make anyone uncomfortable, especially as I'm a non-Christian. . . . I'm in a strange limbo state where I'm not an 'insider' but not really an 'outsider' either, and it's hard for me to simply watch from the sidelines with all that's happened."[84]

I never omitted that I was not a Christian or pretended to be anything but a feminist anthropologist. Openly informing those I spoke with of my identity was ethical according to my methodological training, yet "positionality" was inadequate to the task of explaining my prolonged experience of liminality and displacement—a process through which I came to affectively, if not theologically, resonate with former church members. To claim any positionality in my case was feeble—a hollow gesture and ideological fiction in the face of sociality generated out of a disaggregation of self.

Coming under conviction online compelled inquiry into distinctions between the human and nonhuman, matter and language, as well as the boundaries constituted and policed by the categories "religious" and "secular." Language was not the catalyst for a religious conversion; instead, there was a "conversion of the materiality of the body into an event."[85] An intensification of my body's relation to itself occurred in an event-encounter with other bodies—an assemblage that included Driscoll, his Bible, my laptop, tabs open to websites dedicated to former congregants' testimonies, the (supposed) prankster putting pornography into pew Bibles, and Satan. All of these bodies were affective conductors, rendering fault nonsensical and my positionality arbitrary. Rather than ask, "who is to blame?" for Mars Hill's decline, better to ask, "what were the affective conditions necessary for the event-space to unfold?"[86] In other words, how did the church recruit affective labor and mobilize an affective ecology such that fear, hope, conviction, shame, and paranoia circulated to spiritual, economic, and political effect? Ethnographic fieldwork elicits attunement to ecological and phenomenological processes of worlding that signal an ethical dimension to the movement of bodies as they are moved together. By examining my affective entanglements and attachments with the space and to the people of Mars Hill Church, I suggest that the ethical promise of ethnography, and political potential of ethical action, lies in the bodily risks, vulnerabilities, and transformations of the field, an encounter of precarity.

FIELDWORK AND SETTING: MARK DRISCOLL AND MARS HILL CHURCH

As pastors left the church for various reasons, their names were excised from the Mars Hill archive without comment. Thus, the creation story of Mars Hill Church has dramatically changed over the years. In a 2005 visitor's guide, its history was told as such:

> Mars Hill Church began with 12 people studying the Bible and worshipping together in a living room, the shared vision of Pastors Mark Driscoll,

Lief Moi, and Mike Gunn. The goal was to create a healthy body of believers in what was, at the time, the least-churched city in the least-churched state. The outreach began primarily to the least-churched demographic as well—college men and women in their late teens and early twenties. In October 1996, the growing core launched as an official church with about 100 regular attendees, and numbers increased steadily through word-of-mouth.[87]

It was said that Driscoll "grew up amid the strip clubs, tarmacs, and turf wars of south Seattle, where his family moved from North Dakota a few years after he was born."[88] He was raised a Catholic, but did not consider himself a Christian until his first year at Washington State University, where he majored in communication. His wife, Grace, was his "high school sweetheart," and they married in 1992. In 1996, after leading youth group at another church, Mark felt called to "preach the Bible, plant churches, and train men."[89] I often heard him refer to the earliest days of Mars Hill—when he was twenty-five years old and its size was that of "a small Mormon family"—as meeting in a Seattle rental house where he lived with his wife Grace and their growing family (eventually of three boys and two girls). As more people showed up, the church moved near the University of Washington campus, with offices in what was known as the Earl Building. During this period in the mid- to late 1990s, a didgeridoo might serve as worship music before evening sermons lit by candles, and there was a rotation of preaching pastors; however, Driscoll's voice would soon rise over the others. In 2000, he cofounded the Acts 29 Church Planting Network, which trained and offered seed money to men who felt called to build congregations in the United States and around the world. In 2001, Mars Hill moved to a smaller building in Ballard and launched its first Sunday morning service. In 2003, after nine years of bouncing around Seattle, the church relocated to the repurposed hardware warehouse in Ballard that became known as "central," where I attended my first service. During my ethnographic fieldwork from 2006–2008, I met people who drove from the suburbs to the city in order to attend Mars Hill, a reversal of the stereotypical megachurch model whereby congregants flock to large stadium-sized facilities outside of urban centers. I often met members or nonmembers who drove more than an hour, sometimes two or three times a week, to participate in sermons and other church events.

I began attending Mars Hill when it was known as theologically hardline but culturally hip, appealing to arty urbanites in their twenties and thirties with its raucous music, savvy employ of visual and digital media, and edgy sermons delivered in the sarcastic patter of a stand-up comedian by a brash pastor who was generationally and culturally aligned with his congregation. The man I quickly became accustomed to calling "Pastor Mark" preached live from a stage loaded with high-end sound equipment and beat up guitars. While Driscoll's personalized tag line became "a nobody trying to tell everybody about Somebody," and Mars Hill's publicity proclaimed the church was "All About Jesus," the flat screen TVs projecting Pastor Mark's image throughout the amphitheater seating over 1,200 belied this humble posture. The church's cream-colored lobby, which featured members' artwork, well-stocked bookshelves, and canisters of free coffee, affected the contemplative ambience of a gallery, in stark contrast to its black box exterior and the buzz of the crowd before services. Young guys lingered in the parking lot at all hours beyond an entryway announcing "meaning, beauty, truth, community" within, while worship music thundering outside during band practice in the sanctuary testified to the authenticity of this promise.

In the local press, Driscoll described Mars Hill as theologically conservative but culturally liberal, an anomaly among a growing movement of "emerging churches" attracting a young demographic in U.S. city centers while responding to a "new crisis in American culture fueled by the emergence of a postmodern, post-Christian, neo-pagan culture and the global war on terrorism."[90] Mars Hill was far more orthodox than smaller emerging churches in Seattle: Quest Church, whose Pastor Eugene Cho, a former youth-group leader at the Korean church Onnuri, attracted a more ethnically diverse audience; at the Church of the Apostles (known as COTA), pastored by a black woman named Karen Ward, hands-on arts and crafts and discussion-focused worship commingled with Episcopalian liturgy.

Mars Hill's name came from the Book of Acts, where the apostle Paul stands up in a meeting of Athenians at Areopagus (Mars Hill) and proclaims the gospel. The visitor's guide that I picked up at the information desk stated, "Mars Hill Church seeks to embody [Paul's] mission here in Seattle, a city that prides itself on art, education, culture. . . . To connect relevantly with this time and place we know it is crucial not only to be in contact with popular thought and culture, but to engage it directly."[91] Thus, the church targeted young Christians and nonbelievers by emphasizing the importance of engaging the natural and creative expressions of the Seattle environment and culture.

When I initially began attending, the church had a vaguely "liberal" reputation among locals, due to its well-advertised acceptance of congregants with tattoos and piercings who liked to drink beer and enjoyed indie music in the style of Seattle bands like Modest Mouse. Mars Hill volunteers also booked bands at the Paradox, one of the only all-ages music venues in Seattle in the late 1990s and early 2000s, where acts transgressed religious and secular divides, flouting stereotypical Christian rock. The Paradox provided an important opportunity for "organic evangelism," or "the patient work of building relationships and looking for natural opportunities." Members were discouraged from "verbally dispensing the gospel" or "confrontationally or propositionally" proselytizing, and the Paradox proved to be a useful space for attracting musicians and artists to Mars Hill services.[92] Film and Theology Nights, where Hollywood films were screened and discussed by way of a lecture, purposefully trained congregants how to critically and biblically engage popular culture, given "movie theaters are modern day techno-pulpits."[93] For young Christians raised in Baptist, Fundamentalist, or Pentecostal churches, Mars Hill offered previously unknown freedom for creative and personal expression. Meanwhile, Pastor Mark preached in the verse-by-verse style of systematic theology, cleaving to a "literal" reading of the Bible and a conservative social doctrine that was communicated with enough fire and brimstone to feel familiar and authoritative.

Mars Hill's website demonstrated that the church aspired to be cutting edge in communicating the gospel within a digital context. The visitor's guide proclaimed that "the Internet is the Greek Marketplace of Acts 17: the place in which people gather to dialogue thoughts, philosophies, opinions."[94] The church's website popped with flashy graphics, was highly trafficked and user-friendly. Its media library included vodcasts of sermons; audio recordings of worship music; film and theology commentary, gender seminar recordings, and other teaching material; interviews with Driscoll; and (positive) media coverage on the church. Mars Hill benefited from its location in the Pacific Northwest, "an open religious field" where "sectarian entrepreneurial churches" could flourish due to the city's infotech labor pool and the preponderance of volunteer interns eager to gain experience in this growing industry, with Microsoft and Amazon nearby.[95] The church garnered much success and positive press in the early to mid-2000s; in 2006, a survey distributed among 2,000 (non-Catholic) Christian leaders to assess the "50 Most Influential Churches" ranked Mars Hill 22nd.[96]

Four sermon times—9:00 a.m., 11:15 a.m., 5:00 p.m., and 7:15 p.m.—were displayed in large block numerals on a sign at the top corner of the plain black building whose façade remained true to its previous incarnation as a hardware storeroom. Upon entering the main doors, there were no religious symbols in sight. On the side opposite the main lobby was a children's ministry, where parents dropped off their kids (up to age nine) for Bible study during sermons. In the back and off to another side of the sanctuary was a corridor of smaller rooms, where Bible classes were held on Wednesday evenings. The visitor's guide said, "Instead of acting like an institution, Mars Hill Church seeks to be a family," and the feeling in the lobby resonated with this sentiment.[97] During my first visit, it struck me that many people knew each other. The church functioned as a social center well beyond Sunday services and the spatial circumference of its amphitheater. Conversations were neither hushed nor hurried prior to sermons. To-go cups of coffee were common accessories as people looked for friends and stood talking in the spacious lobby or aisles. I spied many undergraduates in Seattle Pacific University and University of Washington sweatshirts who looked like they had just rolled out of bed, exchanging stories about their weekends as they would on campus Monday morning.

Entering Mars Hill's sanctuary felt like walking into a nightclub. The dimly lit lamps cast a dark glow from high-beamed ceilings that bore traces of the warehouse that it used to be, exposing guts of large tubes piping in data, electricity, and air. The black outer walls and dusky hue of the open amphitheater added breadth to its cavernous layout absent any widows or structural cushion to soften tone or image. An iron-wrought cross cast a large shadow against dark-red curtains behind the stage that served as a pulpit. There was a large sound and light board system in the middle of the room, where two DJs in headphones twisted knobs and muted the lighting still more, creating a cool ambience of expectancy. The atmosphere of Mars Hill on Sundays felt like an extension of Saturday night. There were several mikes, two guitars, an electric bass, drum kit, and keyboards on stage. Announcements flashed on the large screens flanking the pulpit and hovering over aisles, including calls for volunteers to help with facility cleanup and expansion efforts. A schedule of upcoming events also came into view, which varied according to the time of year. During my fieldwork, Mars Hill hosted weekly climbing excursions, Wednesday evening Gasworks Park picnics, a Fourth of July party, a New Year's Eve party, film and theology screenings of movies such as *X-Men 3*, *Grizzly Man*, and *Stranger than Fiction*, and, in August, public baptisms taking place at Golden Gardens Park, not far from Mars Hill's Ballard location.

It was difficult to precisely assess the ratio of women to men, but the crowd was predominantly white, and the number of twenty- to thirty-year-old men in attendance was definitely high. Even at 11:15 a.m., the sanctuary had the vibe of a singles scene. There were a lot of people in their teens and twenties in pairs or small groups. As I walked along the back wall to get a sense of the space, a man in his mid-twenties dressed in long, baggy shorts greeted me with a "Good morning" and smiled. As I moved up to find a seat closer to the stage, a woman wearing jeans who also looked to be in her twenties wished me another good morning. There were no ties or jackets to be found. I noticed many young couples, some with small children. Next to me a woman was introducing her parents to Mars Hill for the first time (I noticed that her father filled out the visitor's information card). The worship band entered and struck the strident chords that signaled people should take their seats, and after a few songs, the amphitheater filled.

To my surprise, there was a baptism onstage. A gangly nineteen-year-old college student stood before the congregation, his face slightly flushed. He wore a rugby shirt and his hair hung down to his shoulders. Speaking slowly and clearly, he explained that he had never known a "rock-and-roll" lifestyle; he had given his life to Christ at an early age, but had never really known what that promise entailed. Now that he had a clearer understanding of this commitment, he felt compelled to demonstrate his true devotion and faithfulness to Jesus by being baptized and born again (again). He stepped down into a wooden tub stage left, was fully dunked under the water by a pastor, and then escorted to the wings as the congregation applauded. I came to understand that baptisms were one of the many metrics used by Mars Hill to prove its success; however, during my fieldwork, I rarely met people who converted at Mars Hill. Mark often referred to "the non-Christians in the room" during his sermons, and purposefully distinguished us from Christians when it was time for communion and the offering, "if you're not a Christian, or you're a first time visitor, we don't want your money, but if you feel moved to join us today in communion and meet Jesus. . . ." Every time I listened to this refusal-invitation, I wondered how many non-Christians there actually were in attendance. Driscoll also claimed that the political partisanship of the church was split fifty-fifty between Republicans and Democrats, but that was impossible to judge. While abortion was never directly referenced from the pulpit, there were "recovery groups" for people with postabortion trauma (as well as for those "struggling with same-sex attraction"). I read pro-life blog posts by leaders other than Driscoll. Homeschooling children before college was a common denominator among some.

After the baptism, the room went black and the large screens surrounding the stage lit up with a short film produced in-house. The first sermon I attended was the opening night of the 2006 *Vintage Jesus* series, a title animated by a montage of the Seattle skyline, shot from a car at night superimposed with Jesus represented in classical, kitschy, and pop cultural forms. The droning static of guitar that served as the video's soundtrack was echoed in the fuzzy shifting images that blurred the biblical, modern and postmodern—a neon Jesus hanging on the cross; plastic and porcelain figurines of Jesus bearing goofy and somber expressions; the cartoon Jesus of *The Simpsons* and *South Park*. Throughout the sermon series, this visual introduction was laced with voices culled through closing interview segments with the likes of Dustin Kensrue, lead singer and guitarist of the band Thrice (who would later become an elder); stoned visitors to Seattle's annual hemp fest; and James Wellman, Professor of Comparative Religion at the University of Washington, who provided commentary that punctuated the video's soundscape. Wellman's language was edited to supply the exclamation point that suggested a need to take up arms and rally the troops, "Christians who say they're right . . . I think they're fools." This phrase reverberated as the screen went black and the Mars Hill logo, a large M inside a circle, appeared on mock stock footage that started to burn as though lit by a match. The clicking sound of a film reel wound down to a stuttering halt as the logo smoldered. While the affect of this film on me—a graduate student in the initial stages of her dissertation fieldwork of the politics of gay marriage in Washington State—could have been alienation or disgust, I was drawn in.

I couldn't see the reactions of those around me; the Mars Hill sanctuary was dimmer than a movie theater, without prominent exit signs or footlights up the aisles.

When Driscoll entered stage left in dark jeans and a black T-shirt with "Jesus is my Homeboy" stenciled in white, he looked less like a pastor and more like a rock star. The opening of his sermon conflated biblical and local idioms, much like the video:

> Well, we'll talk about Jesus Christ tonight. The name Jesus Christ is actually very indicative of his ministry, a derivative of the Old Testament name Joshua, which means Yahweh God saves. And, ah, Christ means the anointed of God, the anointed one of God come to save God's people. And when we're speaking of Jesus Christ, we're speaking of someone who was born roughly two thousand years ago, in a dumpy, rural hick town . . . like Kent, essentially, is what we say at Mars Hill.[98]

His pacing just right, Pastor Mark grinned to give his audience a chance to laugh at the inside joke only those living in the Seattle area would understand. He was making fun of "rural hicks" in a church purposefully planted in a city, creating an advantageous urban/rural divide such that the former was clearly the superior while situating biblical stories in a present day context that made them timely and relatable. But it was his stand-up shtick, caustically humorous and aggressively confrontational, that struck me. As I watched, his preaching lived up to interviews in which he professed to be a "smart-ass" who taught "straight from the Bible."[99] These sentiments were echoed by attendees and elders who called him a "gifted" speaker who "tells it straight," a pastor who spoke in the voice of "a persuasive friend, cajoling, chiding, throwing in sarcastic jabs" such that the Bible became "understandable."[100] His sermons typically lasted over an hour and were interspersed with personal details and stories that contextualized Scripture in terms of present-day life in Seattle and Mark's experiences as a pastor, husband, and father. Just as the baptismal waters at Mars Hill were not meant to assuage, there was no sugarcoating of the Word in Sunday sermons to make people feel good. Driscoll claimed this style was natural yet deliberate: "It's way more Chris Rock than Puritan. That's just the way I am. When it comes down to culture, a lot of it comes down to humor and rhythm and pace.

One of the most important things I can do is agitate people to the point they want to investigate. Otherwise, they're indifferent."[101] A little later in his sermon, the visceral force of this tactic became clear:

> You may also have seen Jesus in various movies. He's appeared in more than a hundred movies . . . and one of the funniest is *Talladega Nights: The Ballad of Ricky Bobby*. I love the fact that Will Ferrell plays the character, he does a good job and it's funny. And he repeatedly prays to baby Jesus . . . he keeps praying, "Thank you, baby Jesus, for my smoking hot wife." And that's become a sort of recurring theme in our house, when my wife, for example, came out the other day and said, "How do I look in these jeans?" I said, "Thank you, Jesus, for my smoking hot wife.' "[102]

At the end of this statement, Mark pulled back his arm with a gloating grin and glint to his eye, then slowly swung it forward, hand open, as though slapping his wife's ass. Hearing the laughter around me, I was convicted; I would write my first book on Mars Hill.

In addition to analogizing his sermon patter to stand-up comedy, Driscoll had a penchant for self-identifying as a "Biblicist" while calling attention to Mars Hill's success through statistics that provided empirical proof of the Holy Spirit at work. This habit reflects a strain of Evangelicalism that sociologist Christian Smith calls "the church-growth movement":

> American evangelicals—especially those shaped by the church-growth movement—assume that numerical growth in a congregation indicates spiritual strength and vitality, which, in turn, indicates possession of the truth. Numerical growth, the assumption suggests, can be taken as an empirical indicator that the Holy Spirit is present and working and leading a congregation into the right beliefs. God must be "blessing" such a spiritually vibrant and faithful church with increased numbers of visitors and members. . . . Understood in this way, then, Biblicism may represent a particular effort to prevent what Biblicists perceive to be ever-menacing external and internal threats to order, security, and certainty.[103]

Driscoll regularly framed talking points with statistics that advertised blessings and asserted authority. In his book on how to mobilize congregants and grow a church called *Confessions of a Reformission Rev.: Hard Lessons from an Emerging Missional Church* (2006), each chapter title has a number beneath indexing how many people were in attendance during the period of expansion discussed. By chapter 5, "Jesus, Why Am I Getting Fatter and Meaner," the statistic below reads "350–1,000 people," which increased to "1,000–4,000 people" in chapter 6 and "4,000–10,000 people" in chapter 7.[104] Mars Hill also publicized an annual report each year that mapped God's witness through metrics concerning real estate purchases, the local and national multiplication of facilities, the global planting of churches, Easter service attendees (typically the biggest Sunday draw), baptisms at Easter service, baptisms per campus, tithing per campus, attendees per campus, website hits, sermon downloads . . . the list goes on and on.

Driscoll became known as the bad boy of Neo-Calvinism in the United States, featured in articles with titles such as "Young, Restless, Reformed" and "Who Would Jesus Smack Down?"[105] However, in the collection *Listening to the Beliefs of Emerging Churches* (2007), he contributed the first chapter entitled, "The Emerging Church and Biblicist Theology." Editor Robert Webber writes, "[Driscoll] refers to himself as a 'devoted biblicist' and notes, to prove his point, that he supports his theology with more than seven hundred verses of Scripture."[106] Indeed, all 176 footnotes from his chapter but the last two reference the Bible; those remaining point the reader to the websites of Mars Hill Church and the global church planting network he cofounded, Acts 29. By structuring the entirety of his chapter with numeric references to the Bible rather than actual verse—page after page and comma after comma—Driscoll forecloses any interpretation beyond his own while defending this hyperbolic annotation by exclaiming that it is his way of being "faithful" to Scripture.[107] The authenticity of his exegesis becomes measured in a size queen way as he assaults the reader with numbers signifying, rather than engaging, the Word. When I first read this chapter in *Listening*, I took it for an immature prank—a *Punk'd* hermeneutic.

Advances in audiovisual and new media in the late 1990s bolstered Driscoll's ability to communicate a missional message for evangelical pastors eager to engage in "Generation X ministry" by capitalizing on elements of postmodern culture. Driscoll describes the publicity he received after his first message on this topic at a conference hosted by Leadership Network, an organization that was shaping what was then called the "emerging conversation":

> Because I was familiar with the growing curiosity about postmodernism, I spoke on these subjects. I titled my session "The Flight from God," which I stole from existential philosopher Max Picard's book by the same name. That message reportedly outsold any conference tape . . . and it shifted the conversation from reaching Generation X to the emerging mission of reaching postmodern culture. I was not prepared for the media onslaught that came shortly thereafter. Before I knew it, National Public Radio was interviewing me. *Mother Jones* magazine did a feature on our church [and] Pat Robertson's *700 Club* gave me a plaque for being America's "Church of the Week."[108]

While listening to the audiocassette recording of this talk, I was struck by how this "flight" was specifically identified by Driscoll as a "flight against the fear of God"—a spiritual crisis signaled by the popularity of Islam in U.S. cities as Christians worshipped in suburban churches that lived in yesterday.[109] Furthermore, cities were identified as the "epicenter" of "culture wars" whose "tremors are felt underground," which Christians could not sense the reality of because "our faith has become about thoughts, not feelings, moods."[110] Therefore, the church had to attract "artists, mystics, poets, and philosophers" to engage postmodern culture through emotional and affective means that touched the heart, increased the pulse rate, and primed the collective mood. In this way, true faith could be reignited and spread against the rise of Islam while combating the ineffectualness of consumer-driven megachurches to "expose people's hearts" and "command them to repent of sin," affording missional Evangelicals "the authority to proclaim a gospel of freedom."[111] In his admonishment to appeal to feeling rather than thought by emphasizing fear, sin, conviction and repentance (without mention of grace, love, forgiveness or reconciliation), Driscoll laid the groundwork for testimonies to spiritual abuse by ex-staff and congregants.

One former Mars Hill member describes spiritual abuse as "when one narrative voice controls the emotional power of the narrative."[112] In a blog post on this topic he states, "A skeptic, a rationalist, an agnostic, [or] an atheist will not concede that there is a 'spirit' in the 'spiritual abuse' [but it] can be considered emotional abuse that plays out at an interpersonal, even social level . . . with religious rationalizations."[113] Driscoll's best-selling talk at Leadership Network signaled his affective capacity to control the emotional power of Mars Hill's narrative. He was invested in exposing and manipulating the heart on a collective scale by calls to conviction that would habituate confessions to sin and leverage repentance as a weapon. In turn, as Mars Hill and Acts 29 multiplied facilities on local, national, and global scales, innovations in media technologies audio, visual, and digital bolstered this physical expansion. In effect, Pastor Mark's voice was secured as the space and medium of spiritual authority on mission to Evangelical Empire. In "The Flight [from fear] of God," Driscoll commandeered "freedom" as the "emerging" and "missional" emotional narrative; he also knew that to amplify its bodily affect and extend its political effect, he needed to attract and exploit artists and entrepreneurs with the same atmosphere and buzz that they played roles in affectively priming and globally marketing.

The invitation to speak at the Leadership Network conference came on the heels of Driscoll's mention in what became a canonical text for emerging Christians, Donald Miller's *Blue Like Jazz* (2003), as "Mark the cussing pastor."[114] It also followed a verse-by-verse sermon series on the Song of Songs during which Driscoll routinely preached for over an hour while he "extolled the virtues of marriage, foreplay, oral sex, sacred stripping, and sex outdoors, just as the book teaches, because all Scripture is indeed profitable."[115] Later, he would attribute his "frank but not crass" approach to sermonizing on sex with congregational growth and cultural reformation: "apparently a pastor using words like 'penis' and 'oral sex' is unusual, and before you could say 'aluminum pole in the bedroom,' attendance began to climb steadily to more than two hundred people a week . . . A lot of people got engaged, and young wives started showing up with big baby bellies, a trend that has continued unabated ever since."[116] According to Driscoll, this success generated a buzz to the extent that Christian leaders from around the country began to visit in order to see how Mars Hill was achieving such popularity.

On June 6, 2005, the morning of the Gay Pride Parade in the Capitol Hill neighborhood of Seattle, Driscoll gave a sermon on Genesis 38 in which his primary theme was fear of God. As supporters and gay marriage activists marched down Broadway, Capitol Hill's main drag, he told the congregation, "God is supposed to scare you. . . . He will kill sinners, He is meant to scare you into repentance. It is a myth that God is all about love, that's the God up on Broadway for the parade . . . the fairy, hippy God . . . the pansy Jesus in a purple G-string."[117] As an example of God's wrath, Driscoll proceeded to tell a story in which a church member came to him for counsel. The young man's father had taken his family on a mission to the Philippines. While there, his father met a man in a chat room who became an Internet sex partner. After much success converting people and planting a church in the community, the father emptied his family's bank account and left to be with his lover in New York City without a word. As a result, new converts left the church. Eventually, after much suffering, the rest of the family left the Philippines. Driscoll asked the young man to kneel with him and pray for the repentance or death of his father. Two weeks after their prayer, although he was in good health and had no prior history of heart trouble, the young man's father died suddenly of a heart attack. Driscoll's message during the sermon that day was: "Sin leads to death and fear of the Lord is the beginning of wisdom. . . . Our culture has no moral high ground when it comes to sexuality, marriage, or women. At the Gay Pride parade, they are talking about sex, gender, marriage, relationships. . . . We need to talk about this as Christians. Sex and marriage don't go together in our culture."[118]

Although I heard disclaimers from the pulpit that distinguished Driscoll from "culture war" stalwarts like Jerry Falwell or James Dobson, he regularly drew analogies between the sins of homosexuality and murder without skipping a beat, distancing Mars Hill from old school moral value politics by sermonizing on sin as equal opportunity. At the same time, he repeatedly insisted that the greatest obstacle facing institutional Christianity was its dearth of masculine, entrepreneurial leaders, a crisis exacerbated by Evangelicals who did not view Jesus' death on the cross as a penal substitution for human sin; resisted openly denouncing homosexual acts as sinful; questioned the existence of hell; and, rejected "biblically defined gender roles, thereby contributing to the 'mantropy' epidemic among young guys now fretting over the best kind of loofah for their skin type and the number of women in the military dying to save their Bed, Bath, and Beyond from terrorist attacks."[119]

This comment posted to a thread on *Leadership Journal* was my introduction to Driscoll's response to the "Homosexual Question" beyond Mars

Hill's sanctuary, and my initiation into his way of utilizing controversial topics and online forums to draw attention to Mars Hill's success in one of the "least-churched" U.S. cities:

> Before I begin my rant, let me first defend myself. Lastly, don't just rant that I'm yet another angry fundamentalist who does not understand. First, the guy who was among the first to share the gospel with me was a gay guy who was a friend. Second, I planted a church in my 20's in one of America's least churched cities where the gay pride parade is much bigger than the march for Jesus. Third, my church is filled with people struggling with same sex attraction and gay couples do attend and we tell them about the transforming power of Jesus. Fourth, I am not a religious right wingnut. In fact, when James Dobson came to town to hold the anti-gay rally we took a lot of heat for being among the biggest churches in the state, the largest evangelical church in our city, and not promoting the event in our church because we felt it would come off as unloving to the gay community. The men who hosted the event are all godly men and good friends and I've taken a few blows for not standing with them on this issue. Fifth, I am myself a devoted heterosexual male lesbian who has been in a monogamous marriage with my high school sweetheart since I was 21 and personally know the pain of being a marginalized sexual minority as a male lesbian.[120]

While Driscoll bluntly preempts the criticism he is well aware his choice of words will invite—he can rant, but you cannot—he asserts his authority to speak on the "homosexual question" based on his own balls, aggressively playing offense while on the defense, knowing that what he is about to say will and should offend, but giving the reader reason to think otherwise. Once his renunciations are established, he freely channels the *Jackass* humor he quickly became famous for. While his stance from the pulpit appeared more balanced than "anti-gay" protester James Dobson, his rhetoric on virtual channels overtly signaled not only a less tolerant position than his sermons would suggest, but an affinity for using digital culture to popularize his voice and actualize his image as a rebel with a cause and vision for legacy in Jesus' name and fame.

In 2006, accelerated growth warranted Mars Hill's transition into a multisite structure whereby videos of Driscoll's sermons were projected onto flat screens hovering over pulpits throughout the city and its suburbs. A facility in suburban Shoreline was an experiment to see if congregants would flock to watch Mark preach via video rather than live. As that satellite campus grew, the Resurgence was launched as an online ministry of the church, serving as a platform for Driscoll's blog posts and an archive of teaching material produced by Mars Hill and Acts 29 pastors, as a way to connect and train young male leaders. While church facilities and community group cells replicated like Starbucks coffee shops within Seattle, its suburbs, and Washington State (including a location in the capital of Olympia that opened in 2008), innovations in visual and digital technology were employed to advance Driscoll's cultural influence within and beyond Christian audiences. Concurrently, increasing demands were placed on members to provide voluntary labor and submit to church authority, as self-sacrifice became embedded in a hierarchical reorganization through bylaw changes that consolidated executive power and enforced shunning procedures against "divisive" staff and congregants. During this upheaval in 2007, all members were required to resign their old membership covenant with the church, then re-sign a new membership contract agreeing to the new bylaws and in turn submitting to stricter forms of church discipline. During this process, three pastors were fired or marginalized to the extent that they eventually resigned, while roughly a thousand members left. Despite this upheaval and the negative press surrounding it, the church continued to replicate and attendance numbers grew. In 2009, Mars Hill launched its first location outside of Washington State, in Albuquerque, New Mexico. Later, facilities in Orange County, California, and Portland, Oregon would follow.

However, by 2014, the scandals surrounding Driscoll and the church were rapidly mounting amid intense turnover in staff as pastors began steadily resigning, and attendance numbers dropped from roughly 13,000 to 7,000 that summer. Evidence had surfaced online that supported several accusations against Driscoll, including plagiarism, the surreptitious use of the marketing firm ResultSource to achieve best-selling author status on a variety of book lists, the misappropriation of tithes intended as a "global fund" for churches in Ethiopia and India, and formal charges of bullying and micromanagement lodged by twenty-one former pastors.[121] This escalation in controversy was preceded by prior episodes that suggested Driscoll's use of social media was becoming increasingly offensive to an ever-larger audience, given his regularly caustic use of Twitter and Facebook. For example, on Inauguration Day in 2013, as President Obama was being sworn in for his second term, Driscoll tweeted: "Praying for our president, who today will place his hands on a Bible he does not believe to take an oath to a God he likely does not know." The *Christian Post* reported, "The tweet has since gained a great deal of controversy; it has been retweeted 3,181 times as of Tuesday morning, and been 'liked' nearly 10,000 times when it was posted on Facebook."[122] In the same article, it was said that blogger Hemant Mehta from the *Friendly Atheist* responded, "I can't tell if that's more or less demeaning than flat-out calling him a Muslim."[123]

In March 2014, Driscoll publicly apologized for his scandalous use of social media in a letter to his congregation that received national coverage. In this message, he said that his "angry-young-prophet days [were] over" and that he would take steps to become "a helpful, Bible-teaching spiritual father."[124] As reported in the evangelical publication WORLD, "Among the steps Driscoll planned to take included refraining from posting on social media until 'at least the end of the year' and to doing few, if any, media interviews."[125] However, weeks later, the Executive Elders—Driscoll, Sutton Turner, and Dave Bruskas—announced a new document retention policy that would destroy all staff emails more than three months old. The plan was dropped only after the group's attorney, Brian Fahling, asked the church to "preserve electronically stored information that may contain evidence" for legal action in which the church, Driscoll, and others in church leadership "will be named as defendants."[126] The letter lists anticipated litigation in the areas of "RICO [Racketeer Influenced and Corrupt Organizations Act], Fraud, Conspiracy, Libel, Slander, Intentional Infliction of Emotional Distress."[127] One example of such treatment against a staff member publicly surfaced in late May 2014, when Mars Hill elder Phil Smidt refused to sign a noncompete agreement, which by then had become a requirement for all departing church employees who wished to receive severance benefits. This contract prevented anyone from serving in a church leadership position within ten miles of a Mars Hill location. Given the expanse of the church's facilities, this noncompete agreement made it difficult for ex-staff to find pastoral work in western Washington. Nondisclosure agreements were also required, and the threat of legal action invoked distress that haunted leaders long after their employ was terminated. In gathering material for their coverage on the controversy surrounding these agreements, WORLD contacted at least a dozen elders and former Mars Hill employees who refused to talk on the record because they feared retribution from the church; one pastor in Charlotte, North Carolina, stated that while it was common for churches to require departing staff to sign nondisclosure agreements, "noncompete agreements cross[ed] over into paranoia."[128]

In the summer of 2014, amid accusations of financial, emotional, and spiritual abuse leveraged against leadership, Mars Hill continued advertising expansion that it could no longer actualize, leading one *Forbes* reporter to call it "the Enron of American churches."[129] After a six-week hiatus from the pulpit while these charges were formally investigated, Pastor Mark resigned from the eldership of Mars Hill Church on October 14, 2014, although he was not deemed disqualified or removed by the board of overseers evaluating his fitness to pastor. At that time, well-respected evangelical author and leader Timothy Keller credited Driscoll with building up "the evangelical movement enormously," even as he admitted, "the brashness and the arrogance and the rudeness in personal relationships—which [Driscoll] himself has confessed repeatedly—was obvious to many from the earliest days, and he has definitely now disillusioned quite a lot of people."[130] However, given he left without any judgment of illegal or immoral activity, Driscoll soon established a website under his name through which to release sermons preached at Mars Hill. He also planted a new church within two years of turning in his resignation, The Trinity Church located in Scottsdale, Arizona, which opened its doors in August 2016. Meanwhile, in Pastor Mark's absence, Mars Hill quickly fell apart, and officially dissolved as a corporate body on December 31, 2014.

CHAPTERS

Chapter 1, "Arousing Empire," investigates how sexualized and militarized dynamics of power were structurally embedded and bodily networked through visual and digital media as the church went multisite and framed its ecclesiology in terms of air war and ground war. I analyze Mars Hill's approach to ongoing expansion in tandem with teaching on entrepreneurial leadership that promoted "authentic" embodiments of biblical masculinity and sexuality. Specifically, I examine how spiritual and military warfare were conflated and conjured in the name of security; Driscoll's use of a public online forum to rant on the social ills of a "pussified nation" in order to agitate a masculine reformation within the church; how *Fight Club* became a motivational tool of men's ministry; teaching on biblical masculinity articulated in military terms against the rise of Islam in U.S. cities; the short film *A Good Soldier*, which was produced by staff as teaching material for a global church planting conference; and a blog post by Driscoll labeled misogynistic that triggered the first protest I attended outside the church. In this chapter, I analyze how congregants' affective labor on behalf of Mars Hill's security, legacy and growth primed an atmosphere of combat readiness, circulating fear and animating a pornographic imaginary.

Chapter 2, "Under Conviction," theorizes conviction in relation to biopower. Specifically, I analyze events surrounding the firing of a pastor who questioned bylaw changes, and the subsequent shunning of his family, in relation to Driscoll's lecture series *Spiritual Warfare* (2008). In particular, I consider Driscoll's self-proclaimed "spiritual gift of discernment"—through which he could identify insurgent "wolves" and visualize sexual sin—in tandem with procedures of containment, isolation, church discipline, and demon trials. In so doing, I analyze testimony by congregants and leaders exiled for being "unrepentant" and not submitting to the "spiritual authority" of church leadership. I also examine how soldiers' testimonies, battle imagery, and a Film and Theology discussion of *The Hurt Locker* capitalized on logics of U.S. militarism and processes of militarization shaped by the global war on terror to leverage confession, conviction, and repentance as instruments of biopolitical control.

In chapter 3—"Porn Again Christian?"—I concentrate on particular interactive technologies and tropes of social media as they were developed and repurposed by the church to further its cultural influence within and beyond evangelical audiences. While analyzing how digital culture was used to incite, habituate, and proliferate confessions to sexual fantasies and sin, I theorize how a pornographic imaginary was produced through affective labor to circulate paranoia as political and economic value. Specifically, I examine the multimedia production of Driscoll's controversial yet popular sermon series *The Peasant Princess* (2008) to analyze how feminized sin went viral within and beyond the church's facilities. I consider Driscoll's teaching on the imperative that wives embody visual generosity and sexual freedom in his e-book *Porn Again Christian* (2008) alongside confessions to premarital sex, the withholding of sex, and spiritual/physical adultery narrated onstage and online by Mars Hill women. Finally, I consider how paranoia affectively materialized as a bodily force of habit while discussing my experiences at a women's training day.

In chapter 4, "The Porn Path," I analyze Driscoll's gambit to rebrand his image as authentic to elevate his celebrity. To do so, I consider how baptisms were performed in public parks, before sermons, and in large-scale productions on Easter for marketing in music videos of MTV-quality. This evidence is examined in tandem with a sermon series event—*Porn Again: Pastor Mark and a Former Porn Star Discuss Pornography*—which Driscoll used to promote the book cowritten with his wife Grace entitled *Real Marriage: The Truth about Sex, Friendship and Life Together* (2012). I investigate this media strategy in relation to the financial manipulation that earned Driscoll *New York Times* number one best-selling author status on its How-To/Advice list. Specifically, I consider Driscoll's teaching on porn addiction, during which he discusses neurobiological research regarding "mirror neurons" that cultivate a "porn path," as resonant with the church's misappropriation of tithes to cull the buyers' lists necessary to achieve Driscoll best-selling author stature. In turn, I consider how Driscoll performs expertise in neuro-marketing while selling authenticity in order to augment the affective value, monetary profit, and celebrity pull of "Pastor Mark." I also analyze testimonies by women and men that describe the emotional, spiritual, and affective costs of "the harmful teaching of wives as their husbands' porn stars."[131] In this chapter, I argue that "Pastor Mark" the brand name not only supported the expansion of Mars Hill's empire but also an "evangelical industrial complex"[132] that intensified the affective capacity and value of his performances. Thus, this chapter analyzes the virality of joyful encounter and emotional entanglements of shame-interest to consider how the sacrament of baptism and contagion of the porn path were exploited to excite affective labor that amplified Driscoll's authority and trademark.

In chapter 5, "Campaigning for Empire," I examine how the affective infrastructure and atmosphere of the air war–ground war was networked within and beyond Mars Hill facilities to channel teaching, worship, and community engagement through Driscoll's voice and image. In the e-book *Campaigns* (2012), Driscoll describes his vision and strategy for Evangelical Empire by globally marketing materials and locally training disciples through calibrations of affective labor, technology, and mood. I analyze the cultural production, material effects, and spiritual affects of Campaigns as they facilitated the networking of violence-care among leaders and congregants, examining public confessions and online testimonies that detail tactics of bullying and micromanagement resulting in PTSD-like symptoms. While considering how Campaigns fostered claims of spiritual abuse by church members, this chapter analyzes the visual and affective strategies used to promote tithing for Mars Hill Global, a ministry dubiously linked to congregations in Ethiopia and India.

The conclusion, "Godly Sorrow, Worldly Sorrow," discusses my participation in the protest outside of Mars Hill in August 2014, analyzing empirical and discursive evidence leading up to and in the aftermath of Driscoll's unrepentant retirement from the Mars Hill pulpit. In light of his virtually reclaiming that pulpit by redistributing Mars Hill sermons through his self-titled online ministry while preaching at a new church in Arizona, I consider the spiritual, political, and ethical valences of repentance. I also reflect on the affective labor of my fieldwork and writing process to argue for ethnography's ethical potential beyond its applied virtues and anthropocentric values. In this discussion, I analyze theoretical debates concerning the political possibilities of love and vulnerability, taking into account the affects and effects of the 2016 election and Mars Hill's fall, concluding with thoughts on Foucault's conceptualization of biopower as it relates to freedom and resistance.

The first and only time I met Pastor Mark was during the gospel class series required of church members. After months of trying to get his approval to conduct formal interviews with members as required by the IRB, I was surprised and glad to see him during the first lecture. He announced that he would be available for questions after his talk, and would stay as long as it took. The documents that I had emailed to another pastor several weeks earlier detailing the questions that I would ask church leaders and congregants, and the rules of consent and confidentiality that I would follow, had been unacknowledged by Driscoll. Getting his permission was no easy task for a host of reasons. A journalist named Lauren Sandler had recently published a book called *Righteous* (2006), which included a scathing chapter on Mars Hill. Sandler was granted access to men and women who she condescended to and fully identified in writing. It was heavy-handed investigative journalism and, from an anthropological perspective, unethical; she betrayed her subjects without a care. Women who were named in the book sounded as though they were wistful for days of independence and freedom pre-Mars Hill, downtrodden by their wifely duties and responsibilities of motherhood, and represented as stereotypical victims brainwashed by church leadership. Although these women publicly condemned their portrayals in *Righteous*, the fallout from the book's publication was still fresh.

When I attended the gospel class, I was taught that the majority of the elders subscribed to a "soft Calvinist" approach, which entailed belief in: God's absolute sovereignty (salvation is given from God alone, not through good works); man's total depravity (we are all born with a sinful nature); predestination or elect salvation (God chooses who is saved by electing them before time began); and penal substitutionary atonement (Jesus died in the place of sinners). The eight-week course culminated in an invitation to sign a Mars Hill Membership Covenant. There was a list of declarations for the incoming member to agree to: "I commit myself to the Mars Hill church family and agree to aid in fulfilling its missional purpose to both be and bring the gospel to Seattle by being a doer of the Word"; "I covenant to practice the humility and sacrificial attitude of Christ by considering the needs of others and by not gossiping"; "I covenant to follow the biblical procedures of church discipline regarding my brothers and sisters in Christ, and submit myself to church discipline if the need should ever arise"; and last, "I covenant to submit to the authority of Scripture as the final arbiter on all issues. *God enabling me, I will strive to consider my commitment to this Membership Covenant on a yearly basis. I understand that it is an evaluative tool, as well as an affirmation of my continuing conviction and purpose.*"[133] This covenant, and my experiences on the first day of the gospel class, were my initiation into how the church "made disciples."

During his lecture consisting of power point slides on the subject of Scripture, Driscoll gave yet another rendition of the metaphorical imagery in the Song of Songs. By then, I had heard more than one mention of how the fawns in this book of the Bible represented women's breasts, and that "all men are breast men except for three kinds, dead, gay, or blind. . . . It's Biblical." There were about fifty people in attendance, and I willingly waited at the end of the line to speak with Driscoll afterwards. I took the opportunity to watch him interact with people from a respectable distance while

talking to the two young men in front of me. They were both in their early-
to midtwenties and told me that they were living with six other guys who
also attended Mars Hill. During the class, Mark mentioned that when you
covenanted with the church, a community group or service leader needed
to vouch for you, which made them sound like gatekeepers who measured
commitment in terms of volunteer hours. When I remarked that I did not
know such an endorsement was necessary, one of the young men quickly
said, "well, it's good to give to your church and community groups are
important to connect with people."

Watching Mark, I noticed that he never looked distracted, always made
eye contact, spoke softly, and appeared willing to help. Several people used
hushed tones while conversing with him. The young man who was very
chatty and comfortable while speaking with me stammered while talking to
him. In response, Mark was kind; I overheard him say that he "didn't know
what went on at the big man's house," but that the young man should let
him know if he had any problems. Mark also showed a surprising degree
of familiarity with the house itself, asking the guys which rooms they were
in, as though he knew the property well. Then, after waiting an hour, it was
my turn.

By the time Mark and I spoke, it was 9:30 p.m. I mentioned my research
and explained that I was speaking to both conservative and liberal Christian
groups. Mark gently interrupted: "Yeah, being in Seattle as liberal as it is, we
come across as more conservative than we are. It's like being a jockey on top
of a horse, the jockey's short but on top of the horse he appears to be really
tall." Suddenly, all the lights cut out. The room went black and turned awkward. We both laughed and Mark shouted into the dark, "Still talking here,"
and the lights quickly returned, although we appeared to be alone.

He asked where I was getting my master's degree, a common assump-
tion at the church, and I routinely corrected him by stating that I was working toward a doctorate then asked for an interview. Initially, he said that it
was no problem, and then mentioned another pastor as a valuable resource
given he was a biblical counselor. He added, "So many daughters are molested by their fathers, sexual abuse is a huge issue. It's amazing how many
people we have come in here who need help," emphasizing that Mars Hill
recovery groups for victims of sexual abuse were "packed." I asked Mark
how to make an appointment with him. He passed along the name of his

assistant who did all of his scheduling between speaking engagements then said, "I'm not going to lie to ya, it's going to be tough to see me." I acknowledged that I knew how busy he was, thanked him for his time, and walked away impressed by his ability to make those he spoke with feel cared for, while steering them away from asking more of him.

The second Mars Hill sermon I attended, in October 2006, was part 2 of the *Vintage Jesus* series, "How Human Was Jesus?" Pastor Mark summed up his response to this theological query in one sentence, "The first thing that I want to tell you is that Jesus was a dude."[1] As he continued to speak on how "normal" a dude Jesus was, Driscoll offered speculation concerning his appearance to make his case: "He was a carpenter, so he may have been in fairly decent shape, callouses on his hands for swinging a hammer, there were no power tools in that day so he was a manual laborer, he walked a lot so he may have been lean and thin and rugged."[2] He contrasted this "biblical" image of Jesus with representations found in popular culture, "If you've seen the pictures of drag queen Jesus [audience laughter], um, it's very troubling to be honest with you. He tends to have very long hair with product, wears a dress and open-toed sandals. Listens to a lot of Elton John, that kind of thing [audience laughter]. Um, and it's hard to worship him, 'cause you could beat him up even if you're a girl [louder laughter]."[3] Then, Driscoll showed off a T-shirt peeking out from underneath his dark blazer; it was white and had a close-up of "drag queen Jesus" with "very long, beautiful curly hair, nice features, a little rouge on his cheeks" that underneath read "Jesus watches you download porn."[4] While comparing Jesus' humanity to his own, Mark added that he is Lord over his "little kingdom" of five children: "two daughters that I love and they're very girly, so we go out shoe shopping and to tea," and three sons who "want to wrestle, pee in the yard, eat meat, or make everything into a gun [audience laughter]. . . . The first thing my boys want to do [when I come home] is have an ultimate fight, 'cause we watch a lot of ultimate fighting at the Driscoll house, and that's how it goes [audience laughter]."[5]

Pastor Mark appeared to have his audience in the palm of his hand, inspiring laughter such that his portraits of "manly" Jesus resonated. However, when Jesus' humanity became figured through a sense of humor, interference irrupted.

I'll tell you some aspects of Jesus you may not have known. The first is that he was funny. OK? Now some of you have never heard this, you've been in the wrong church. You've been told that Jesus was not funny. He was very religious, and serious [Driscoll's eyes bug out and he grimaces], and I think [his face relaxes and eyes glint with a smart-aleck grin] that's funny [burst of audience laughter]. Jesus had a sense of humor. . . . Do you really think that Jesus went camping with twelve guys for three years and never told a joke [chuckles from audience]? Any of you guys ever been camping with other guys? That's basically what they did [laughter builds]. You ever been fishing with your buddies, no women around? You have the pull-my-finger marathon [loud laughter], you know what I'm talking about? Some of you are saying, are you really saying Jesus played pull my finger [loud laughter]. . . . I'm just sayin,' it's possible. Ah . . . [6]

At that moment, I noticed a man standing in the center aisle. He pointed at Driscoll onstage and shouted, "I disagree!" In the dim light, it was difficult to see or hear him well. Driscoll did not visibly register the man's cry, and no one close to me reacted. He appeared to be thin, with long gray hair, and he was moving forward, but slowly. His voice and stance were confrontational, but hardly menacing. He did not get very far, if reaching Driscoll was his goal, disappearing as quickly as he appeared, smothered and dragged out by phantom men. Pastor Mark continued his patter without skipping a beat:

How do you hang out with twelve guys, mainly blue collar, for three years and not tell a joke or laugh at one? Can you imagine telling a joke and Jesus saying [he points with an angry face at the crowd], you knock it off, we are religious men [audience laughter], this is *serious business*, and I will not tolerate shenanigans [loud burst of prolonged laughter]. I believe that Jesus had a perfect sense of humor, and a perfect sense of comedic timing.[7]

It was clear that Driscoll thought the same of himself. After that Sunday, there was no word from the pulpit concerning any disturbance, but the sight of security guards monitoring the Mars Hill Ballard entryway with the impassive self-importance of club bouncers became routine. Before sermons, service opportunities flashed onscreen, including the need for male volunteers to "protect the body." While Pastor Mark preached, two unsmiling men wearing Bluetooth headgear and black T-shirts embossed with the Mars Hill logo and "security" etched in white flanked the stage, surveying the audience like a private militia ready to pounce. Years later, after Mars Hill received criticism for its surveillance tactics, Director of Security Nathan Finn responded: "On Sundays, we keep watch on the premises, mostly in an effort to deter any potential threats by being proactive not just reactive."[8] In his post, Finn makes no reference to a particular antagonist, rationalizing the presence of Mars Hill's security team according to a preemptive logic, which Brian Massumi argues "takes threat, which has no actual referent, as its object."[9] As Finn explains why Mars Hill's security team was hypervisible in specific spaces, we glean insight into how the affective reality of future threat was cultivated by and at the church.

> If you are saying to yourself, "aren't they exaggerating this whole thing? I didn't see or hear of anything," it is because our security teams are doing a fantastic job mitigating threats we see regularly throughout the year. . . . Ever wonder why there are two security team members who sit at the front of the sanctuary while Pastor Mark preaches? Because several years ago, a man charged the stage with a large knife while Pastor Mark was preaching. In general, there is a higher potential of threats when the sermon topic is on spiritual warfare.[10]

The security team spectrally haunted rather than strictly policed the sanctuary. While physically protecting Driscoll's body from faceless assailants, they materialized spiritual warfare in the emergent present, a duty that involved but also surpassed their stance of surveillance. In the most basic terms, spiritual warfare is understood as an ongoing worldly battle between Satan and God, demons and angels, and good and evil. Scholar of American religion Sean McCloud, writing on contemporary Third Wave Evangelicalism in the United States, says, "Spiritual warfare entails fighting real demons who occupy physical spaces—including human bodies, objects, places of residence, tracts of land, even entire cities and countries."[11] At Mars Hill, the terrain of spiritual warfare was a social imaginary of visceral tenor—not located in objects or territories per se, but nevertheless tangible, embodied, and real. While the story of the man rushing at Pastor Mark with a knife became Mars Hill folklore sutured to his preaching on spiritual warfare, it was an affect-event precipitated by a joke about Jesus' humor and no more than a minor glitch at the time. Years later, when I read mention of this demonic dissenter in a local media source, he was said to be wielding a "machete" as he "charged the pulpit" with a "heart full of rage."[12] While my sightline was not optimal, I never saw a weapon in the man's hand, nor registered rage in his tone. When I spoke with a member about this incident, I was told that the so-called machete was no larger than a Swiss Army pocketknife.

The security team flanking either side of the stage served as more than a reminder of the man who supposedly rushed the pulpit with a knife; they conjured the felt reality of future threat while bodily conscripting Driscoll's audience into a past event with prophetic reverberation. Although Finn linked a state of alarm to services during which Driscoll preached on spiritual warfare, the actual presence of the security team on any given Sunday normalized the perception and cultivated the affective reality of emergent threat regardless of the sermon topic. Thus, spiritual enemies could take myriad demonic forms as religious, racialized, and sexualized "others," infecting porous bodies within and outside the congregation. Driscoll considered teaching on spiritual warfare "incredibly controversial," but also "incredibly vital," "because there's an enemy who hates God, hates you, and has set his army against you because you're a citizen and servant of Jesus' Kingdom . . . every Christian is a soldier in this war."[13] This teaching was reinforced through the church's use of military rhetoric and militarized imagery, particularly in its men's ministry, conflating spiritual and worldly warfare while affectively animating amorphous yet immediate enemies. Collective yet embodied processes of militarization went viral via a social imaginary that networked menace potential, converging the demonic with antagonists such as "Islam," Christian leaders who transgressed Driscoll's "biblical" theology, sexualized single women, and effeminate men putting the church and nation at risk.

The church's priming of a mood of unending battle agitated what anthropologist Kathleen Stewart calls "atmospheric attunements," which "attend to the quickening of nascent forms, marking their significance in sounds and sights and the feel of something's touch or something penetrating."[14] At Mars Hill, fear, in the words of Sara Ahmed, "play[ed] a crucial role in the 'surfacing' of individual and collective bodies."[15] Such uneven immaterial circulation overrides self-monitoring and exceeds the intentional subject, bodily networking emotion as affective value. Nebulous yet urgent threat manifested through the mobilization of what affect theorist Jasbir Puar calls a "terrorist assemblage."[16] This social imaginary propelled nonwhite "foreign" and hypersexualized "domestic" terrorist-bodies into phenomenological and ecological relation as congregants became "affective and affected entities that create fear but also feel the fear they create."[17] Unbeknownst to me at the time, I was affecting and affected by the vitality of this atmosphere; despite myself, I laughed.

PROTECTING AND INFECTING THE BODY

In 2007, as the church re-architected to accommodate its plans for further physical expansion, Driscoll preached through the Book of Nehemiah, a sermon series that ran for twenty-two weeks. The series was assigned a tagline, "Building a City within a City," that in typical fashion blended biblical and local idioms such that Seattle became Jerusalem and Driscoll an amalgamation of Ezra and Nehemiah as they built walls and preached to fifty thousand. Nehemiah, as Driscoll often portrayed himself, endured "great opposition," including "death threats."[18] However, due to perseverance and God's grace, Nehemiah succeeds in rebuilding the walls that fortified the city and organizes its first church service. After this introduction to the story unfolding in Scripture, Pastor Mark contemporizes it to suit his purposes circa 2007, dubbing the church's ecclesiological architecture the air war and ground war:

> And so what you'll see this week is two things we like to call at Mars Hill, the air war and the ground war. The air war is going to be the preaching of a six-hour sermon. . . . In addition to that, then you'll see a ground war, where one-on-one and in small groups, leaders meet with people and follow up with their questions. . . . Churches need to have both. . . . In the air war, you're dealing with the masses. That's what I do. That's what the bands do. That's what the media technology opportunities we have do. Sermons go out to four thousand, five thousand, six thousand people on a Sunday, and then podcasts, vodcasts, tens of thousands more. . . . What we see is that the air war leads. It goes first, and the ground war follows. And the air war is very visible. This is a very visible event.[19]

I attended the *Nehemiah* sermon series throughout that spring and summer into early fall, and noticed a difference in Mark's preaching. He was yelling a lot more. There was also a lot more laughter and affirmation by way of "amens" from the audience. The color scheme onstage set a somber, angry tone of deep red and black. The video introduction for the series began with a grainy view of an industrial plant pumping smoke into the sky. This shot jumped to a sidelong angle of the glass exoskeleton of the Seattle Downtown Library, scanning over gray city streets until flushing out to a helicopter view of skyscrapers overlooking Puget Sound, their lights glowering in the dusk as the density of buildings took the shape of a fortress. During this montage Mark intoned, "The hope of Mars Hill since the beginning is that Seattle is a great city and what it needs is a great city within that city. A city that loves Jesus, a city that believes Scriptures, a city that lives for the good of the whole city and not just its own self-interest."[20] *Nehemiah* was stark and stridently militant in its presentation of a city under siege and in need of defense. According to Driscoll, what Seattle needed most of all was to hear the Word as preached by him. Ezra may have been the "Billy Graham of the Old Testament," but Pastor Mark was the Billy Graham of today: "I like to open the Bible and preach God's Word . . . what God historically uses to change people's hearts, minds, lives, to transform cities and nations and bring about revival."[21]

It was during this sermon series that I was suddenly overcome by waves of nausea during a service. As my discomfort intensified, I broke into a cold sweat. Sitting in the middle of a long row of chairs at the center of the sanctuary made it difficult to leave. Eventually, Driscoll's sermon wound down and the people in my row stood in order to receive communion. I quickly headed for the back entrance, opened the door, and immediately threw up. While the reasonable next move was to alert someone at the help desk and apologize for the mess, I went with my first instinct, which was to flee the scene of the crime. The flu symptoms that I was convinced would surface never did. When I repeat this story, I am often asked what Driscoll said that prompted me to feel ill, the presumption being that there was a cause and effect relation between the content of his sermon and my nausea. I have no satisfactory reply. When I look over my field notes nothing screams, "I was really angered/saddened/confused (or otherwise oppressively interpellated)." No identifiable moment or message caused me to feel sick that day.

Though I could not articulate it at that time, the atmosphere of spiritual warfare had infected me in ways that I could not make intelligible. I was participating in and contributing to collective affective labor beyond my ken. Interpreting "my" vomit as a sign of disgust did not do it social justice or register its affective dimension. Instead, this physiological repulsion signaled what anthropologist Kathleen Stewart describes as an "intimacy with a world [that] is every bit about that world's imperative," such that "the things in it have a force and a say. We sense out what affects us, and the sentience of a situation is filled with tracks of labor and attunement."[22] I was not the only one who sensed an ominous shift in mood during the *Nehemiah* series. Years later, as former members spiritually and emotionally harmed by church administration posted their stories online, one of the first women to openly testify to such abuse, and her contrition in its contagiousness, was Jonna Petry: "Mark was preaching through the book of Nehemiah, utilizing it to promote his future vision for the church. And now, into summer, an oppressive heaviness began to overshadow everything. There was a real sense of spiritual warfare and I fasted and prayed under the burden on multiple occasions."[23]

Driscoll wound down his sermon on the air war–ground war with a story in which a "Muslim friend" who carefully placed the sacred Quran at the top of an otherwise messy stack of books had convicted him that "We should at least do that with the Scriptures that tell us about the real Jesus," since "[the Quran] is a book written by a guy inspired of demons that sends people to Hell."[24] As his audience took that comment in, Pastor Mark made a joke of it: "Did he say that?"

"Yeah, I think he did."

"So he's not a Muslim?"

"I don't think so. I think he's a Christian."

"Is there really a difference?"

"Yeah, there's a huge difference."

"Isn't somebody gonna get mad?"

"Oh yeah, definitely."[25] Staging this conversation in mockingly muffled tones to much hooting, hollering and applause from the congregation, Driscoll then concluded with a quip known to any familiar with his sermonizing: "Just trying to put the fun back into fundamentalism."

While Mark claimed to be just horsing around for the sake of fun and his audience roared their approval, he used this opportunity to posit "Islam" as demonic-terrorist potential. Massumi remarks, "Now policing works more and more . . . through gatekeeping—detection, registration and feedback," such that "the threat will still be there of something getting through that shouldn't. Terrorism is the perfect example."[26] The affective labor of the security team contributed to a gatekeeping-feedback mechanism that stoked and spread the felt reality of menace potential, conjuring a militarized imaginary that affectively registered "Muslim friends" as future threats. Jasbir Puar observes, "The materialization of the feared body occurs through a visual racial regime as well as the impossibility of containment of feared bodies. The anxiety of this impossibility of containment subtends the relegation of fear to a distinct object, producing the falsity of a feared object . . . it is precisely the nonresidence of emotions, their circulation between bodies, that binds subjects together, creating pools of suspicious bodies."[27] During a politically incorrect joke that generated yelps of jubilation, fear circulated below the radar of cognition as a social process of embodied conviction that resonated with Pastor Mark's preaching on the perils of effeminate men predominating U.S. Christianity and the nation.

TROLLING ON MISSION TO SAVE A "PUSSIFIED NATION"

Mars Hill's foray into online ministry became a media spectacle fifteen years after Driscoll's trolling under a pseudonym on a thread he dubbed "Pussified Nation." In his book *Confessions of a Reformission Rev: Hard Lessons from an Emerging Missional Church* (2006), Driscoll skips over the content of his posts while highlighting their pugilistic affect and effect—what was described to me by one former congregant as "midrashing it out" like Paul in the Athenian square of Mars Hill.[28]

> Our church . . . started an unmoderated discussion board on our website, called Midrash, and it was being inundated with postings by emerging-church-type feminists and liberals. I went onto the site and posted as William Wallace II, after the great Scottish man portrayed in the movie *Braveheart*, and attacked those who were posting. It got insane, and thousands of posts were being made each day until it was discovered that it

was me raging like a madman under the guise of a movie character. One guy got so mad he actually showed up at my house to fight me one night around 3:00am.[29]

While Driscoll claims to attack "emerging-church-type feminists and liberals" as William Wallace II in *Confessions*, his first post indexes enemies more pervasive and enduring. Throughout the thread, his voice vulgarly echoes poet Robert Bly, one of the leaders of the "men's movement" of the early 1990s, which organized retreats designed to help men reclaim their "deep manhood" and "warrior within."[30]

> We live in a completely pussified nation. We could get every man, real man as opposed to pussified James Dobson knock-off crying Promise Keeping homoerotic worship loving mama's boy sensitive emasculated neutered exact male replica evangellyfish, and have a conference in a phone booth. It all began with Adam, the first of the pussified nation, who kept his mouth shut and watched everything fall headlong down the slippery slide of hell/feminism when he shut his mouth and listened to his wife who thought Satan was a good theologian when he should have lead [*sic*] her and exercised his delegated authority as king of the planet. As a result, he was cursed for listening to his wife and every man since has been pussified sit[ting] quietly by and watch[ing] a nation of men be raised by bitter penis envying burned feministed single mothers who make sure that Johnny grows up to be a very nice woman who sits down to pee.[31]

The publication of such passages in a 140-page PDF distributed online by former members led to accusations of misogyny lodged against Driscoll in colorful terms that matched his penchant for derision. One former staff member who worked in information technology at Mars Hill told me that Driscoll excitedly and repeatedly stopped by his office soon after this post and exclaimed, "I dropped the bomb man, you gotta read it." After doing so, this staff member asked himself, "Is this theater? What is theater? Is theater OK?" and concluded that Driscoll's trolling was "hyperbole"—an "experiment" to see "how far he could push dudes to get their shit together."[32] As these gestures to the performative suggest, Driscoll's embodiment of William Wallace II online could be construed as that of a bully in drag, whereby hyberbolic gender norms are "reidealized."[33] However, what is most powerfully enacted throughout "Pussifed Nation" is not a discourse of hegemonic masculinity. In Driscoll's terms, the affective value of his voice reverberated with the thunder of bombs.

One former congregant named Zach Malm who attended Mars Hill for nine years, from its early stages until it grew to multiple locations, made a query to an online forum whose stated purpose was the opportunity to "Ask Mark Anything": "I explained that Mark's various inflammatory statements were making me weary, as I'd much rather defend Christ than have to defend my church all the time. I asked if the statements were intentional, if Mark was inviting controversy as a way to market the church, raise its profile, and bring in more people."[34] The response he received? Leave:

> Find a different church? I'd been there since I was 18. I helped build the community, I met my wife there, all my closest friends who I'd poured my life into for 7 years were there, and [the Lead Pastor's] advice was that I just leave? I couldn't bring myself to do it, and more importantly, after hearing so many anecdotes from the pulpit about the unnamed theological nutjobs running rampant in the leadership of Seattle churches, I flat-out didn't trust that there was another church here that was safe to attend. . . . Oh, and that question I asked that resulted in being advised to leave, the one about whether Mark says controversial stuff on purpose? Mark wrote a whole blog post about the technique a few months ago. He calls it "riot evangelism." Essentially, I asked, "Why does Mark keep stepping on landmines?" and 6 years later, his answer was, "I'm not stepping on landmines. I'm throwing bombs."[35]

Malm describes the circulation of fear as a strategy of containment. By persuading members that leadership in other churches was suspect and demonically inspired—"theological nutjobs" who could not be trusted to discern biblical truth and from whom Mars Hill congregants needed spiritual defense—Driscoll's "riot evangelism" not only policed but also terrorized the network-body of the church during a prolonged period of physical and virtual expansion by "throwing bombs" to avoid "stepping on landmines."

As Driscoll's first "Pussified" post builds to its conclusion, what it means to be a "real man" and enact "biblical masculinity" becomes sutured to an aggressive sexual drive that should be freely expressed for the sake of spiritual salvation:

> So, Johnny hits youth group one day to hear from his pussified youth pastor that he should perfect his virginity and dating skills. So Johnny tries to be a loving and patient man who looks for a nice woman like mom who will whip him into shape and beat him into submission so that he can one day join a men's accountability group and learn how to keep his urges under control, which just causes him to earn a B.A. in masturbation, M.A. in porno, and PhD in knuckleheadology as Johnny is now so terrified of women and his own penis that he sits in his room alone each night on the internet hoping to get some. . . . I know many of the women will disagree, and they like Eve should not speak on this matter. And, many men will also disagree, which is further proof of the pussified epidemic having now become air born and universal. Pussified men are inarguably legion. Nothing short of an exorcism is needed.[36]

Writing on the word *malediction*, anthropologist Thomas Csordas focuses on the physical properties of "diction" to emphasize the curse's material aspects as rhetorical performance, which may be seen in a phenomenological sense as "opening the door" to demonic activity, such that "malediction is understood to have a real and negative spiritual effect that transcends the realm of human emotion or agency."[37] Rather than simply mapping Csordas's argument onto Driscoll's virtual embodiment of William Wallace II, I take up his claim concerning the necessity for anthropologists to wrestle with the question of evil in human being to argue that reading "Pussified Nation" in a spiritual as well as political grammar usefully shifts its diction from the realm of the polemical to the ontological. Driscoll's voice may then be read as religiously managed and politically manipulated sensation that opens the door to demonic activity without personifying evil per se. Driscoll's trolling on mission to cast out "pussified" men from the (white, Christian) nation is reformed into an act of spiritual warfare against a global terror that is pervasive, ambiguous, and infectious.

The next Wallace post begins, "Todays rant is in response to the insanities paining me today in this very moment of my inner *Fight Club*."[38] Allusions to this film are scattered throughout the thread by Driscoll and others, including a contributor called "Rev. Tyler Durden." One of the ex-members who helped recover "Pussified Nation" for public dissemination after the church's attempt to scrub all evidence of its existence years prior shared my view that Driscoll's online persona resonated with Brad Pitt's character in *Fight Club* more so than the Scottish warrior of *Braveheart*: "I'd been there for two months at the time. . . . [Mike Gunn and James Harleman, who ran Film and Theology Nights,] they'd show *Fight Club*. It wasn't William Wallace, it was Tyler Durden that he [Driscoll] was being. . . . The reason that we leaked [Pussified] is 'cause, in reading it we thought, um, yeah, he kinda is that guy."[39]

In an early scene of *Fight Club*, the Narrator, played by Edward Norton, is making copies of the bottom of a Starbucks to-go cup that is metaphorically connected to the exhausted haze of his insomnia—a state in which he is never really awake or asleep and everything seems to be "a copy of a copy of a copy." He muses that "when deep space explorations ramp up it will be the corporations that name everything—the IBM Stella sphere, the Microsoft Galaxy, Planet Starbucks." While this scene gestures at critiquing materialism and corporate culture, it is a fleeting attempt that resonates with Mars Hill's paradoxical relationship to neoliberal dynamics of political economy. While the church elders disparaged those "consumers" who merely attended sermons without contributing their talents to the church in the form of volunteer labor, Mars Hill's multisite network increasingly operated according to the logic of multinational corporations like Starbucks, replicating throughout Seattle and beyond Washington State. When Mars Hill celebrated its ten-year anniversary, in October 2006, they announced this milestone with a pamphlet that read,

> We thank God for taking us from a Bible study to a church of 5,000 in one of America's least churched cities and a church planting network that has planted over a hundred churches in the US and more internationally. What God has done through the people of Mars Hill is nothing less than a miracle, and a recent survey ranks us as one of the twenty-five

most influential churches in the nation. Another survey ranked us as one of the sixty-fastest growing churches in the nation. Are we boasting? Yes. . . . We are thrilled to be recipients of His grace and participants on His mission to Seattle and beyond.[40]

This Neo-Calvinist discourse has neoliberal and missional overtones, logics of economy are privileged metrics linked to spiritual authority, evangelistic purpose, and God's grace. However, rather than preaching that individuals will reap sanctified rewards from sacrificial giving in the manner of a prosperity gospel more closely aligned with neoliberal principles of self-interest, Mars Hill tithes were purposefully used to culturally amplify its influence in Seattle and beyond, as the church continually rearchitected in order to transmit Pastor Mark's preaching to its multiplying locations via video.[41] This ongoing reorganization and expansion required affective labor and self-sacrifice of congregants beyond monetary donations: volunteering time and energy to ready new facilities, changing church homes in order to support the larger mission, and the uprooting of families in order to plant churches throughout and outside of Washington State. From 2006–2008, Mars Hill grew to seven autonomous campuses, a feat which gleaned them press and admiration (or envy) among Christian leaders throughout the country.

The church filmed a thirty-minute lecture by Driscoll for distribution on the Mars Hill website called *Videology* (2008),[42] to describe how its innovative employ of visual and digital technology invited active participation rather than passive consumption on the part of audiences. Throughout his talk, Driscoll couches the "information age" in terms of an "experience economy" based on "various distribution channels for the communication and articulation of ideas" that create three stages: observation (watching a video); participation (responding through prayer, the taking of communion, getting to know other congregants); and immersion (helping to create the experience).[43] Driscoll depicts Mars Hill's "videology" as a worship practice and community-building process through which audiences become producers of content that is framed not only in language or text but also by mood, sensation, and feeling—a labor that, as it is integrated and networked to serve the church, is both personally and collectively transformative. As he explains the connections between observation, participation, and immersion, Driscoll distinguishes Mars Hill from traditional megachurches that convene followers en masse. He also claims that the church's model of physical and virtual multiplication is distinct in the way it elicits audience participation via forms of mobile communication, differently constituting and configuring "live" and "remote" congregants to and through the Mars Hill experience as mediated via his voice and image.

In the closing segments of *Fight Club*, Tyler Durden flies around the country franchising fight clubs from city to city as the Narrator snidely remarks, "Planet Tyler." These branches soon "evolve" into the terrorist organization "Project Mayhem." Driscoll's ranting as William Wallace II was not hate speech but a malediction that signaled the affective value of trolling in bad faith, as anonymous cage fighting online became a methodology of "globalizing" men's ministry such that masculine evangelical identity was not shaped or regulated but bodily triggered as social habit. His brand of riot Evangelicalism sutured "authentic" embodiments of gender and spirituality such that the felt reality of future threat became a copy of a copy of a copy. The few critical voices that chimed in on "Pussified Nation" over the span of 140 pages nevertheless maintained that Wallace raised some excellent points, and far more frequent than challenges were chants of affirmation and cheers of glee. Early in the thread, Driscoll announced,

> Inspired by Peter 3:1–7, *Fight Club*, *Braveheart*, and *American Beauty*, I have compiled the rules for a secret men's organization that will not be publicly known for I fear that, like the Elks, one day women will sue us and demand that they come to play with our cards, eat our wings, drink our ale, smoke our pipes, and thereby ruin our lives. We will meet monthly at undisclosed locations and no man will be able to speak about it to anyone, and newcomers are only permitted to attend if they are sponsored by a member. Our charter members are coming together quickly and we will convene after the new year. We are not a self-help group, accountability group, Bible study, or men's ministry. We are a revolution.[44]

This unmoderated discussion board served as an unruly body through which to affectively network combat readiness *as* masculine evangelical social subjectivity. Rather than use the language of reformation to promote his masculinist version of evangelical revolution, Driscoll referenced Hollywood films such as *Fight Club* and *Braveheart*. Meanwhile, he adamantly pushed against the parlance of self-care and aims of self-esteem so often assumed as the default discourse and hegemonic objectives of evangelical ministries in lieu of calling on his brothers-in-arms to foment a movement not unlike Project Mayhem.

In *Confessions*, Driscoll demonstrates the importance of putting down porn and taking up arms to secure personal transformation, cultural reformation, and affective labor on behalf of the church:

> Things were starting to get out of hand with the men, so I called a meeting and demanded that all of the men in our church attend. I preached for more than two hours about manhood and basically gave the dad talk to my men for looking at porno, sleeping with young women, not serving Christ, not working hard at their jobs, and so on. I demanded that the men who were with me on our mission to change the city stay and the rest leave the church and stop getting in the way because you can't charge hell with your pants around your ankles, a bottle of lotion in one hand, and a Kleenex in the other. On their way out of the meeting, I handed each man two stones and told them that on this day God was giving them their balls back to get the courage to do kingdom work. Guys put them on their monitors at work or glued them to the dash of their truck and kept them like stones of remembrance from the Old Testament. (129)

Every male congregant that I spoke with about this event remembered Mark's chastisement as pivotal in their decision to become church members who rose in Mars Hill's ranks. One man I spoke to described Driscoll's two-hour admonishment in glowing terms and concluded, "Mark ripped us all a new asshole." A couple that had misgivings about joining the church in the early 2000s told me that this talk was what led them to stay, while a former pastor I spoke with remarked that the sense of conviction in the room was "palpable." Mark proclaimed his haranguing of the men a widespread spiritual and practical success, "The next week the offering doubled and the men caught fire. It was a surreal time, since I was basically fathering guys my own age and treating them more like a military unit than a church. The life change was unreal. We had guys getting saved en masse. We had gay guys going straight. We had guys tossing out porn, getting jobs, tithing, taking wives, buying homes, making babies."[45]

Once Driscoll addressed his male congregants as a military unit, they transformed (seemingly overnight) from perverted sinners into Christian citizen-soldiers, a normalizing of the population (apparently) achieved. Same-sex attraction, porn addiction, singleness, unemployment, lack of property ownership, and other signs of "unproductive" behavior became opportunities to secure wives, jobs, and homes, not to mention procreate children and facilities for the sake of the church's legacy. Whether or not this masculine reformation happened on the scale or at the rate that Driscoll implied, commitments to marriage, family, fiscal autonomy, and property ownership figured prominently in his depiction of church stability. Familial responsibility was also rendered critical to young white males' socio-economic empowerment and integrity as Christians. Thus, as Mars Hill offered events like "men's training days" or "boot camps" to afford male congregants a collective space for mobilization, Driscoll also preached a "privatized notion of agency" consistent with neoliberal cultural and economic values whereby "success is simply a matter of getting off one's back and forging ahead."[46]

In *Confessions of a Reformission Reverend*, the coda to this story reads like a biblical *Fight Club* in which the men of Mars Hill spar over gospel acumen in theological cockfights:

> There were too many guys to fight individually, and I needed a way to fight with them all at once. So in an effort to clean up the mess, I started a weekly men-only meeting, which I named "Dead Men" and which ran for a few months. I paired guys up to debate an assigned theological issue, and other guys in the audience would chuck things at them and mock them if their study was not good or their argument not cogent. At the end of the debate, we would vote, declare a winner, and give him a mock prize and crown him with a Viking helmet. The men liked the competition and got into studying and debating theology.[47]

One member who attended Dead Men debates told me: "It was basically an ad hoc initiation process for the men [who] Mark [Driscoll] and [cofounding pastors] Mike [Gunn] and Lief [Moi] considered productive enough to contribute to the cause. . . . He convinced us all the Dead Men initiation process would establish which guys were on mission. I went to at least a third or half of them, and it seemed pretty clear the aim was to figure out who was going to be the new core of men the leadership could depend on."[48] According to this logic, Driscoll's stint as William Wallace II was a test to see which men would rise to his challenge to "man up." Dead Men events were theological competitions to sift out those too "pussified" to lead the church on mission, a form of ritual combat defined in terms of sacrifice. Such violence in "play," according to anthropologist Clifford Geertz, becomes "dangerously and entrancingly close to the expression of open and direct interpersonal and intergroup aggression . . . but not quite, because, after all, it is 'only a cockfight.' "[49] If pedagogy is about transforming the way the world feels such that bodies learn by switching affections,[50] Driscoll's bomb throwing while trolling online to save a "pussified nation" was a crusade of shock and awe.

MENGINEERING 101

Driscoll's preaching on evangelical masculinity at the turn of the twenty-first century at a time of deindustrialization in the United States echoed the preaching of revivalist Billy Sunday at the turn of the twentieth century, when the impact of industrialization, exponential growth in immigration, and the rapid expansion of cities precipitated a sense of national crisis disrupting white heteropatriarchy.[51] As neoliberal dynamics of "free" trade and market deregulation rapidly outsourced blue-collar work in the 1990s-2000s, this shift in political economy increased unemployment among working-class white men, Driscoll's target audience. Like Sunday, he spoke to his times, capitalizing on economic precarity and an all-volunteer armed forces overtaxed by the ongoing war on terror. According to Driscoll, feminism was to blame for the disempowerment of men at work, war, and home, not structural transformations in political economy and military policy. During a series on Proverbs in 2001, Driscoll preached on the destructive power of a cultural "gender war" that needlessly posits women and men as enemies, "If you don't know that we are made in the image of God and we are equal male and female because of God's image and likeness, then you create something called a gender war, which means that for years chauvinists won and now feminists are winning, and we're trying to figure out who should win and who should lose. When Scripture says basically they should be holding hands and participating in the same work as allies, not as adversaries."[52]

"Complementarianism," the organizational logic of the gender doctrine taught at Mars Hill as well as at many theologically conservative evangelical churches, espouses that men and women are "equal but different." To further my understanding of this doctrine's scriptural basis and practical application, I attended Mars Hill's annual women's "training day" in 2007, *Christian Womanhood in a Feminist Culture*. In preparation, I was asked to read Alexander Strauch's complementarian primer entitled *Men and Women, Equal Yet Different: A Brief Study of the Biblical Passages on Gender* (1999). Within the opening pages of this book, a quote from the United Nation's Human Development Report of 1993 was sidebarred: "No country treats its women as well as it treats its men."[53] The passages that followed constructed a narrative of injustice against women that drew distinctions between so-called modern, developed societies and less developed countries. Although the book's arguments and evidence were structured and supplied by biblical passages, Strauch also included secular studies and statistics to verify the global inequality of women. Whether this data was articulated from the perspective of a universal liberalism or a conservative Christian paradigm, it confirmed, in the words of anthropologist Talal Asad, "modernity as a political-economic project . . . constructs categories of the secular and the religious in terms of which modern living is required to take place, and non-modern peoples are invited to assess their adequacy."[54] Strauch's text portrays representations of "the secular" and "the religious" as mutually constituting yet separate domains by which citizen-subjects in "modern, developed societies" mediate their identities in relation to a free market and civilized (predominantly Christian) culture. By extension, "less developed" countries are figured as uncivilized, poverty-stricken, and ruled by tyrannically outdated (non-Christian) forms of power. Secular conceptions of universalized human rights are rendered enlightened and analogous to deployments of gender equality in complementarian theology. This neoliberal articulation of women's equality provides a contiguity or bridge between progressive liberals championing multicultural civil rights and moral conservatives preoccupied with the defense of marriage and national borders. By framing gender roles in equal yet different terms, Mars Hill reconciled its culturally liberal position with its conservative theology.

As Strauch's book continues, he lists crimes against women specific to the Philippines, Thailand, India, Africa, Afghanistan, and China, including minors forced into prostitution, wife burning, female circumcision, refusal of health care and education, and female infanticide. By contrast, he mentions only one crime against women of the Western world: harmful divorces that leave them without financial support for their children. A discourse of equality that renders women of "less developed" societies victims of uncivilized cultures, premodern states, or patriarchal religions deflects attention from the effects of disparate socioeconomic conditions wrought by uneven distributions of global capital, as well as from complementarianism's resonance with the gender hierarchy perpetuated in "patriarchal religions." Furthermore, he ignores economic inequities women suffer in "modern, developed societies," instead focusing on individual harms and responsibility for social ills perpetuated by divorces. In the liberalist and complementarian frameworks offered by *Women and Men, Equal Yet Different*, equality and agency are tethered in a relationship constrained by notions of choice and resistance relegated to autonomous modern (white, heterosexual, middle-class) subjects afforded the privilege of traversing distinct public and private spheres.

Driscoll spoke to the need to "remasculinize" the Christian nation and church using the doctrine of complementarianism inflected through a military lexicon.[55] This language resonated with the military metaphors used by Promise Keepers, founded in 1990 by the University of Colorado football coach Bill Bright, to encourage men to be "holy warriors."[56] In 1997, Promise Keepers hosted a Stand in the Gap event in Washington, D.C., where hundreds of thousands of men gathered on the Mall "to atone for their sins, reassert their beleaguered masculinity, and pray for the 'deliverance of the nation.' "[57] Like Promise Keepers, Mars Hill "joined the religious war with an approach that utilized the language and symbols of the military."[58] However, Driscoll's sermons did not follow a "jeremiad pattern of crisis and renewal": a delineation of sins, a warning of God's awful judgment, and an offer of renewed hope for the nation.[59] Mars Hill primed an atmosphere of spiritual warfare with global, rather than strictly national, implications; meanwhile, Driscoll's use of militarized language had affective impact that surpassed discursive appropriation, to incite combat readiness out of fear. In fact, the men's ministry at Mars Hill derisively criticized Promise Keepers prayer circles and stadium events in which men bought merchandise and cried together. Such a collective outpouring of shopping therapy and emotional catharsis was "unmanly" according to Mars Hill leadership, a belief that was also taken up by members.

According to a congregant named Grant, the gender doctrine of biblical masculinity preached at Mars Hill defined itself *against* a Promise Keeper ethos of "benign patriarchy."[60] In a post to the Mars Hill website, Grant describes his participation at a men's "basic training" event called "Mengineering 101," a daylong workshop in anticipation of a subsequent three-day retreat, Men's Advance 2007: Reborn on the Battlefield. Grant begins his account by mockingly revisiting an experience he had with Promise Keepers.

> Anybody ever been to Promise Keepers? Well, I have. I recall with nausea and trepidation the memories of holding hands with not only men, but also complete strangers. The odor of dudes and repetitive corporate "praise" tunes haunts and frightens me to this very day. I'm sure many a man's life was reclaimed for Jesus at these events, but Promise Keepers was most definitely not for me. Nearly 700 men attended [Mars Hill's] basic training. . . . To my joy this event smelled nothing of Promise Keepers—just straight up worship through singing, Biblical teaching, and authentic conversation with earnest and God-fearing men. There were no frills and definitely no gimmicks.[61]

This post describes an intense feeling of disgust at a Promise Keepers event, in stark contrast to the joy experienced in "straight up" worship and "authentic" conversation with the "God-fearing men" of Mars Hill. To authentically embody biblical masculinity, the men of Mars Hill took responsibility not only for the propagation and legacy of their immediate families, but also of the church. A global church planting war organized in accordance with "technologies of citizenship"[62] was agitated by an atmosphere of spiritual warfare that drafted men as Christian citizen-soldiers into affective labor on behalf of Evangelical Empire.

A GOOD SOLDIER

Mars Hill was asked to present a short film at a 2007 church planting conference due to its successful multisite expansion in the Seattle area, the extensive national and global outreach of Acts 29, and Driscoll's subsequent rising position of influence among evangelical entrepreneurs. *A Good Soldier: A Conversation with Pastor Mark Driscoll*, begins with heavy metal guitar chords, raucous and strident, and the close-up of a cross on a white military headstone. With each subsequent punch of sound, a statue's clenched fist comes closer into view. Flashes of daylight cast staccato shadows as clouds move in fast-forward motion behind the statue. The third close-up is of a shotgun barrel and the fourth shows another angle of the fist, as the editing speeds up in synch with the dissonant chords. The fifth close-up is of a gun's muzzle pointing at the sky, and the sixth shot is of the graveyard at a greater distance. Rows of white headstones fill the frame as the camera pans over them. The film fast-forwards and rewinds at increasing speed, until the rows of graves are mere blurs before finally halting on the fully revealed statue of a soldier.

The film's "conversation" begins with Pastor Mark pacing over graves in profile to the camera, his head slightly bowed, as he speaks of a "church planting war" that Christians are losing. He sports an untucked black flannel shirt and looks up to face the camera as he speaks:

> Paul uses some interesting language in the New Testament to talk about pastoral ministry in general and church planting in particular. [The view shifts from Driscoll to the soldier's gun.] He tells Timothy on a few occasions to fight a good fight; he uses soldier language. [When the camera cuts back to Driscoll, the film is a bit grainier, highlighting his beard stubble; a necklace of thick, woven cord comes into better view, as his pace of speaking slows for emphasis as he looks straight into the lens.] Now when you think about pastoral ministry, you tend to think of, ah, a really nice guy who can sing prom songs to Jesus, who's really good at settin' up chairs and puttin' up with B.S., and you don't think of a guy who can fight, you don't think of a guy who is a scrapper, you don't think of a guy who can hold his ground, fight heretics, nutjobs, weirdos, tell the lady with the tambourine who shows up for church to park it. The body count is really high in the church planting war, some say upwards of eighty percent of church plants fail. If church trends continue, by the year twenty-fifty, there will only be half the number of Christians in America that there is at present. [As the camera zooms in, we see a heart,

a miniature replica of the organ with arteries exposed, hanging from the thick cord around Driscoll's neck.][63]

In this film recorded for an audience of evangelical leaders, Driscoll blames the "body count" in the church planting war on effeminate Christian men who sing prom songs to Jesus instead of aggressively taking control in the church. The effect of this crisis of masculinity in U.S. Evangelicalism means losing male leaders to the "enemy" of "Islam." In a lecture titled "The Ox," given to an audience of potential church planters at a 2008 Acts 29 "boot camp" Driscoll states,

> We hold masculine male leadership in the highest esteem, yet the church is almost completely effeminate in America. There has been a wholesale departure from masculine leadership in the home and church. Women and children go to church, men do not, and those men who do go to the church are effeminate, worthless men. Christianity is not doing well in this country. That is why young men in urban centers are attracted to Islam; they want a masculine religion, a powerful God, something that gives them truth and that calls them as a team.[64]

Thus, according to Driscoll, "pussified" insurgents must be replaced by "masculine" citizen-soldiers in order for Christianity to thrive in the United States, win the global church planting war, and protect the country from demonic Muslim terrorists. Without a masculine reformation among white Evangelicals, the urban centers vital for success in a transnational economy and tantamount to national security during a global war on terror would be lost.

In a lecture entitled "Reborn on the Battlefield," given by Pastor James Harleman at a 2007 Men's Advance retreat, processes of militarization took an affective, ecological cast that exceeded the mere use of military metaphor: "Real men are at war. . . . We got ripped from our Father, we're still on the battlefield, we're not in heaven, and we're not at home. . . . Most of us are a bloody newborn mess. . . . We worship creature comforts but not our threats. . . . We don't think about the spiritual war we're in. . . . Real men are exiles."[65] Due to this exile, Christian citizen-soldiers needed Pastor Mark to keep them battle-ready.

In March 2009, Al Lobaina's "Biography of a Christian Soldier" appeared in a two-part blog post on Mars Hill's online ministry, the Resurgence. In this message, Lobaina states that he "would have felt like a wuss" had he not joined the military after "watching the Twin Towers crumble to the ground like a couple of Jenga towers."[66] Soon after finishing college, he enlisted and was deployed to Afghanistan. His routine entailed conducting missions during the day, reading the Bible at night, and watching porn before drifting off to sleep. Then, he writes, "I started to listen to some sermons on my iPod that I had randomly downloaded off of iTunes from this guy from a church in Seattle called Mark Driscoll. . . . As soon as Pastor Mark made some comment about butch ladies and bucking authority, I was hooked on this guy's teaching."[67] Driscoll's sermons became accessible and popular on bases located in Afghanistan and Iraq, as women's presence increased in the all-volunteer forces (AVF). In an AVF that is classed, raced, and gendered along stratified lines unlike any time since the end of conscription in the United States,[68] it is helpful to reduce "a crisis of capitalism . . . to a crisis of masculinity."[69] As *The Atlantic* slyly announced "The End of Men" in a 2010 cover story that suggested women would take over from men in a postindustrial society,[70] Driscoll's sermons preempted such news, couching women's potential socioeconomic empowerment as not only a threat to (white, heterosexual) men, but also to national security and the future of Christianity.

Individual soldiers invested in a relationship with the church as they circulated Driscoll's sermons and volunteered for a Mars Hill ministry called Military Missions. Lobaina describes how Driscoll's sermons had an enormous impact on the moral instruction of his company:

> My wife started burning anything she could get her hands on from Mars Hill, from audio sermons to video sermons, and mailing them out to me in Iraq. We started rounding up the guys and showing at least one sermon a week on a laptop through a projector with speakers hooked up to it, and this was our Sunday church service. There were nights when we would just chill, drink some coffee, and go through a few sermons. The flood-gates opened with the guys as we worked through porn, masturbating, beer, Calvinism, the exclusivity of Christ, being a husband and daddy, and war. . . . One of the coolest things I got to experience was seeing guys borrow external hard drives from one another, not to get the latest porn, but rather to make sure they had all of the vodcasts posted by

Mars Hill. . . . Instead of filling their brains with endless hours of garbage, they were watching Pastor Mark preach through the Word.[71]

In the 1980s, connections between moral and warfare instruction were strengthened when the military supported evangelical proselytizing and worship among troops. Additionally, conservative evangelical leaders such as Paul Weyrich advocated for an increased military presence in inner city school districts to provide discipline and moral instruction so as to "save" the poor and, ostensibly, the nation.[72] By contrast, Driscoll was unconcerned with saving economically impoverished inner city populations in lieu of attracting white, college-educated, entrepreneurial men looking for a sense of purpose, a job, and a wife, so as to secure Mars Hill's expansion and legacy.

A Good Soldier climaxes with a tirade:

> Most churches are struggling, dying, and failing, and most church planters will just be part of the rising body count of failed church plants, if they are unable to gather, to inspire, to correct, to discipline, to instruct men, and this is particularly important for young men. The least likely person to go to church in the United States of America is a young man in his twenties, guys banging their girlfriends, blowin' all their money, staying up all night playing World of Warcraft, finding free porn on the internet, and trying to figure out how to get a bigger subwoofer into their retarded car. Those are the guys who must get a swift kick in the rear, need a good run through boot camp, need to be told that Jesus Christ is not a gay hippie in a dress and that they're dealing with the king of kings and lord of lords, and that there's a mission that he's called them to.[73]

A punch of guitar chords accompanies a close-up of the clenched fist of the soldier statue, then a close-up of Driscoll's face:

> In addition to the man, and the mission, is the message . . . the ascension of Jesus back into Heaven like a triumphant and victorious warrior, who after a long season of battle and defeat of his foe has returned home. Tragically, the word has gotten out about Jesus that somehow he's a marginalized Galilean peasant hippie in a dress, rockin' out to the Spice Girls, driving around in the Middle East in a Cabriolet, hoping to meet nice people to do aromatherapy with while drinking herbal tea. That's not

the guy we're talkin' about, we're talkin' about Jesus in his glory having returned home as a triumphant warrior and victor [music begins to pound in the background] over Satan, sin, death, and demons, because the victory of the Lord Jesus is applied to the mission and the men who lead it.[74]

To the full onslaught of guitars Driscoll bows his head, turns, and walks toward the graves with hands in his pockets as the camera pans to a bird's eye view of the soldier statue.

This video was vehemently criticized; Christian leaders discussed their theological objections to Driscoll's definition of what it means to be a man, his cursory dismissal of women, and his use of military lexicon to frame the church planter's mission. However, Mars Hill deployed more than a normative masculine worldview couched in military metaphor as it successfully expanded its empire. *A Good Solider* assaults its audience; the camera never rests and the fast-forward motion of the clouds and graves against violent bursts of guitar allow little recourse to a frame of reference aside from Driscoll. The scene of this film is relentlessly fragmented rather than set. In such instances, perception is turned back upon the body of the perceiver such that it affects and alters that body,[75] a strategic animation of visual culture that was pronounced throughout Mars Hill's ministries, with military films and imagery particularly prominent during men's training days and retreats.

The affective ecology of Evangelical Empire and its practical embodiment on mission was not only brought to life during seminars led by elders, but also cultivated through the use of cinematic clips and screenings. While writing on a scene in *Jesus Camp*, religious studies scholar Donovan Schaefer notes: "The meaning of the word war indexes a global sedimentation of affective attachments rather than a dictionary definition. It turns into an affective invocation that is then creatively—even playfully—redeployed in new contexts."[76] The frequency and effectiveness with which war movies and videos evoking battle were used to engender and intensify affective attachments during the 2007 Men's Advance: Reborn on the Battlefield retreat was reflected in one young congregant's account: "My squad, being me, my dad, and Josh, arrived at the Men's Advance . . . and as we headed in, they were just finishing playing a clip from the movie *Gladiator*. After the clip . . . was a great sermon, reminding us that we are not at home, we are exiles on Earth, and we should never try to get comfortable here, but rather we should be constantly battling evil in our everyday lives."[77]

This young man's post describes an atmosphere of spiritual warfare animated through discursive and affective dimensions. He continues,

> The [first session on the second day] started with an amazing clip from *Saving Private Ryan*, filled with explosions and bullets and blood. Pastor Mike Wilkerson then spoke on fighting the ground war. He talked about the importance of facing the reality of war, and the many things we need to keep in mind to fight as soldiers for Christ. . . . We then split into three different groups to learn about different ways to serve Mars Hill in their different mercy programs. After that . . . my dad and I went to watch *Apocalypto* in the main auditorium. The movie was great, full of gore and violence and manly stuff.[78]

War films, military missions, and boot camps were used to excite affective labor and self-sacrifice on behalf of Evangelical Empire against emergent threat on a battlefield without horizon.

VIRTUAL PROTEST OF A PORNOGRAPHIC IMAGINARY

In a post on the "themes and background" used by Driscoll to develop the William Wallace II character, Wenatchee the Hatchet, a former congregant and longtime blogger on Mars Hill, wrote, "Anyone who actually read 'Pussified Nation' could see for themselves the most damning statements seemed to be reserved for James Dobson and Promise Keepers . . . evangelical persons and groups that most people would consider anywhere between moderate to very conservative. . . . Driscoll seemed to be venting at evangelicals who had sacrificed something core he felt was necessary to authentic masculinity more than he was venting about liberals."[79] Wenatchee also shared "raw text" penned by William Wallace II, which demonstrates what was "core" to Driscoll's version of authentic masculinity:

> What the guy wants is to see a stripper, a porno, and have some phone and cyber sex. What the guy needs is a good Christian woman. The kind of woman who knows that men like unclothed and sexually aggressive women. Why? Because they are breathing. As long as a man is alive he is

ready for sex every minute of every day. Ladies, listen closely. The guy will never get the big dreams out of his head. He can either explore them with his wife, become bitter and sexually repressed, or sneak off to [the strip club] Deja Vu or log on to the net and escape in a moment of adventure . . . so it would behoove a good godly woman to learn how to strip for her husband.[80]

In "Pussified Nation," pornographic scenarios are redeemed as enacted by Christian wives rather than local strippers. Driscoll admonishes married Mars Hill women who are inevitably "uncomfortable with their bodies" to perform visual generosity in order to mitigate the future threat of their husbands' sexual infidelity online and off, providing detailed instructions through how-to examples: "Take a Polaroid and snap a few shots in various states of marital undress and bliss and sneak them into his Bible so that when the guy sits down to eat his lunch at work and read some Scripture he has reasons to praise God. . . . Or how about the occasional instant explicit message from his wife rolling across his screen giving him some reasons to expect that dessert will precede dinner that night."[81]

As he offers graphic advice on the embodiment of sexual freedom within the confines of heterosexual marriage, Driscoll uses the open source and collaborative interactivity of the unmoderated bulletin board to conjure and materialize a pornographic imaginary. In considering how the "imagination could be of the body as well as being about the body," visual cultural studies scholar Nicholas Mirzoeff uses Spinoza's conceptualization of a "network body that sees" in order to consider "the way in which empire figures its others as the embodied spectacle."[82] In Driscoll's post, pornography is simultaneously a detriment and a door to sexual and spiritual freedom. Both men and women are bullied into a paradoxical position regarding porn; its mainstream representation and industry are couched in terms of demonic temptation and capitalist exploitation. However, without compulsively desiring, visualizing, and performing "biblical" porn, congregants cannot embody authentic evangelical masculinity or femininity. In effect, biblical porn becomes a conduit for affective labor in support of Evangelical Empire. Many Christian and secular progressives blamed Mars Hill's fall on a doctrine of "male headship" that promoted a "culture of muscular Christianity" in "misogynistic and homophobic terms."[83] However, the confessions of former church leaders seeking repentance for participating in a "culture of fear"[84] and "culture of misogyny"[85] index the limitations of such explanations. If this supposed culture of muscular Christianity was airtight in its ability to dictate a "ministry that grounds itself in inequality,"[86] pastors such as Mike Anderson would not have lost their faith in the authority such a culture afforded them:

> Misogyny. There, I said it. I stood by and willingly participated in a culture of misogyny. . . . During this time I made some huge mistakes. I pressured my brilliant hard-working wife to give up her dream of law school and have a baby and be a stay-at-home mom as soon as possible. There's nothing wrong with kiddos (I love my daughter) and staying home with kids is great if you want to. What isn't great is that I allowed others to take verses from the Bible out of context and put a law on my wife and rob her of her dream. I only added pressure on her. It was wrong, and I'm terribly sorry.[87]

Even as Anderson's testimony supports critics who label Mars Hill's culture misogynistic, it signals a biopolitics of sex and affective network of control irreducible to a liberalist lexicon of inequality or binary relations of oppressor/oppressed. Rationalizations blaming muscular christianity for Mars Hill's fall without historical or cultural contextualization are limited in purview. Feminist author Susan Faludi notes that in the United States, muscular christianity emerged at the beginning of the twentieth century and was led by preachers such as Billy Sunday to protest "against an 'emasculated' church's ineffectuality in the face of industrialism's mounting ravages." However, she notes that Sunday's sermonizing also inspired "a series of working-class preachers [and] engaged more than a million Protestant men in a two-year revival campaign," including "'social action' projects" whereby "members built a Labor Temple, cleaned up local jails, and lobbied for improved garbage collection and the inspection of water and milk."[88] While his masculinist posture from the pulpit echoed Billy Sunday's railing against the "emasculated" church, Driscoll did not encourage social activism, but rather entrepreneurialism, chiding young male Christians to "man up." This paradigm shift from social justice to venture capitalism indexed Driscoll's sermonizing on biblical masculinity at the advent of the twenty-first century.

In November 2006, a group called People Against Fundamentalism announced its intention to hold a protest to stand up against "Mark the misogynist" in response to remarks Driscoll blogged concerning Ted Haggard—then megachurch pastor, president of the National Association of Evangelicals, vocal opponent of gay marriage, and consultant to the Bush administration—who was "outed" after a three-year sexual relationship with a male escort. After providing a sketch of the media frenzy over Haggard's affair, Driscoll added:

> As every pastor knows, we are always at risk from the sin in us and the sinful temptations around us. Pastoring in one of America's least churched cities to a large number of single, young people has been an eye-opening experience for me. I started the church ten years ago when I was twenty-five years of age. Thankfully, I was married to a beautiful woman. I met my lovely wife Grace when we were seventeen, married her at twenty-one, and by God's grace have been faithful to her in every way since the day we met. I have, however, seen some very overt opportunities for sin. On one occasion I actually had a young woman put a note into my shirt pocket while I was serving communion with my wife, asking me to have dinner, a massage, and sex with her. On another occasion a young woman emailed me a photo of herself topless and wanted to know if I liked her body. Thankfully, that email was intercepted by an assistant and never got to me.[89]

The threat of sexualized encounters and pornographic fantasizing without the protection of a wife and accountability of an assistant is framed as rampant. Further, Driscoll laments, "My suspicion is that as our culture becomes more sexually rebellious, things will only get worse. Therefore, as a means of encouragement, I would like to share some practical suggestions for fellow Christian leaders, especially young men."[90] The following words of "encouragement" led to the protest and were the source of much negative attention:

> Most pastors I know do not have satisfying, free, sexual conversations and liberties with their wives. At the risk of being even more widely despised than I currently am, I will lean over the plate and take one for the team on this. It is not uncommon to meet pastors' wives who really let

themselves go; they sometimes feel that because their husband is a pastor, he is therefore trapped into fidelity, which gives them cause for laziness. A wife who lets herself go and is not sexually available to her husband in the ways that the Song of Songs is so frank about is not responsible for her husband's sin, but she may not be helping him either.[91]

While Driscoll's critics and supporters debated the misogynistic character of these comments, the frequent appearance of women in this post is more telling: the woman who offered sex as she accepted communion; the woman who emailed a photo of herself topless; and "hurting single moms wanting a strong man to speak into their life, [who] would show up [at the church] to hang out and catch time with me."[92] Recurring manifestations of sexualized women vulnerable and eager to please animates a pornographic imaginary out of personal anecdote. Furthermore, Driscoll urges pastors to beware of overly intimate relationships with emotionally dependent female assistants: "I have been blessed with a trustworthy heterosexual male assistant who can travel with me, meet with me, etc., without the fear of any temptations or even false allegations since we have beautiful wives and eight children between us."[93]

In an odd affirmation of just how much buzz Mars Hill was generating at the time, angry reactions triggered by Driscoll's "practical suggestions" for young male Christian leaders nearly eclipsed coverage of Haggard's fall. On the political web page Memeorandum, described to me by a former Mars Hill member who worked in information technology as "the number one site among geeks for political news" at that time, Driscoll's post was the top trending news item among coverage from November 4–5 rather than reporting specific to the Haggard story. Additionally, directly below the link to Driscoll's blog was the *Huffington Post*'s take on his post, an article entitled "Who's to Blame for Pastor Haggard's Fall from Grace? His Fat, Lazy Wife," instead of a story on Haggard himself. The former member working in info tech also described *Memeorandum* as an "algorithm aggregation of human sentiment," which suggests that it was not Driscoll's use of inflammatory language alone that attracted attention, but also his ability to tap into and channel an aggregation of human sentiment. In fact, as the above quotes from that post demonstrate, Driscoll never directly blamed Haggard's wife for his fall from grace, nor did he call her "fat" or "lazy." What he did do, however, was commandeer the public debate and emotional narrative surrounding the Haggard scandal by sexualizing women.

In effect, Driscoll's practical suggestions had nothing to do with men who are attracted to other men and everything to do with women who do not know their place. While refusing to address any questions pertaining to Haggard's sexual identity, Driscoll trains his male audiences' gaze on women's bodies; in turn, the hypersexualized female, emotionally vulnerable and overly available, eclipses Haggard's sin. Completely ignoring the evidence that Haggard was having sex with a male escort, Driscoll transfers national attention from the fallen president of the National Association of Evangelicals to the importance of "free and frequent" sex within Christian marriage. The suggestive scenarios embedded in Driscoll's blogging on Haggard's sexual sin operate on discursive and affective registers by reinforcing the male gaze as normatively fixed on women's bodies and shaming his male audience for sinfully indulging in pornographic fantasies staged by him. Space in the gap of representation teases and titillates online users, affectively networking evangelical social subjectivity through bodily intensities of excitement and fear.

Driscoll's blog achieved several objectives (intentional or not) within and beyond the church's facilities. At Mars Hill, interest in "reforming female sexuality" stimulated a proliferation of public confessions to sexual sin by women in blogging forums and onstage performances. Testimonies to same-sex attraction, addiction to romance novels (the female version of pornography), adultery, fornication, and, most prominently, the withholding of sex by wives from their husbands, were recorded in writing or audio for public dissemination on the church website and in iTunes podcasts. In this way, women were also called to contribute affective labor in order to secure Mars Hill's empire. This self-sacrifice was not only couched in terms of submission to men's authority but also the biblical imperative to embody sexual freedom in the marital bedroom, supporting their husbands' enactments of authentic biblical masculinity while securing their spiritual salvation and marital fidelity. In effect, Mars Hill wives were bodily conscripted to provide what women's studies scholar Jane Ward identifies as "gender labor":

All genders demand work, and therefore all people both give and require gender labor. However, some genders, principally those that are masculine and especially those that intersect with other forms of power (such as wealth and whiteness), make their demands less visible and more legitimate, or deliver them with more coercive force. . . . Intimate labor, most commonly done by women, also includes offering temporary connection and authenticity, which can involve "faking" or giving someone what they want, even when the lack of "realness" is implicitly recognized by both participants.[94]

With regard to the Haggard scandal, Driscoll successfully transposed what could have been a predictable culture war debate involving the usual suspects— gay/straight, liberal/conservative, Christian/secular—into a spectacle of spiritual warfare waged against him. Once People Against Fundamentalism (PAF) announced its intention to hold a protest outside Mars Hill Ballard against "Mark the misogynist," the public conversation shifted from Haggard's sin to debates over whether it was in the interest of Christians (as many in PAF identified) to protest fellow Christians. After proclaiming fear for his family due to a barrage of death threats, the evening before the event was to be held Driscoll met with PAF leadership and apologized for his remarks, putting an end to the first of many media frenzies generated in the wake of comments he would make concerning women and sex deemed offensive by Christians and nonbelievers alike. Given they had to cancel so close to the appointed hour, PAF arrived the next day and held a banner across the street that said: "Thank You for Apologizing, Mark." I was monitoring these discussions as they unfolded online, and timed my attendance that Sunday to observe whether and how Mars Hill and PAF members interacted. Inside, the silence from the pulpit was deafening; outside, I did not linger for long. As I spoke with one (former) protestor, he pointed to a telescopic camera perched on Mars Hill's rooftop scanning us like a sniper rifle and said, "They were ready for us."

"Where is your heart?"

His office was dim, narrow, and filled with partly used bookshelves. There was a New International Version Bible on the coffee table next to the visitor's sofa. Framed family photos on his desk. He offered me a stick of gum, and I took it after turning down a coffee in the lobby. I could hear myself chew.

"Religion's always been an interest. I studied Buddhism while living in Japan, practiced meditation."

I noticed a shift. His expression clouded, and slightly suspicious eyes became sarcastic. This response drove me to explain further. After I rambled on for a minute, he had heard enough.

"There is only one Truth and that is Jesus. The question at the crossroads of history is the question that Jesus asked Paul—'Who do you think I am?'"

To answer this question for me, he read from the Bible. It was a long passage, and he spoke with little inflection, clearing his throat and coughing several times. I felt like a child being read the wrong bedtime story. By the time he finished, I was groggy but still did not know the ending.

"That's it? We don't know what happened to King Agrippa?"

"In some translations he's said to have 'almost' been persuaded, but in mine it says something else."

I was still waiting for an answer of my own.

"I can't give you permission to do research here, but I'll forward the papers to Pastor Mark."

I asked if he had more questions for me. He slowly shook his head.

"I pray that you find Jesus. I hope you drop your research and become a disciple."

He had his answer about where my heart was; a confession had been extracted.

I understood that disciples were more than "consumers" of services. From the pulpit, I often heard that Christianity was not a religion, but a lifestyle. At Mars Hill, discipleship was measured in terms of volunteer labor, but it also involved a less concrete, ambient metric of desire—submission to spiritual authority. Although Pastor Mark claimed that Mars Hill was not "legalistic" insofar as its adherence to biblical rules was concerned, distancing the church from a Fundamentalist label despite its Reformed Christian orthodoxy, spiritual authority was distributed among elders in a "first among equals" manner, with him first.

It was 2007, and Mark was preaching the *Nehemiah* sermon series, whose tagline "Building a City within a City" was visually expressed through camera angles that presented Seattle's skyline as a fortress of high walls buttressing the church's ever-extending boundaries.[1] By now, the signage over Mars Hill's entryway announcing "meaning, beauty, truth, community" within had been taken down, as "planting churches, making disciples" was adopted as a mobilizing trope. This phrase encapsulated what it meant for the church to be on mission. One young congregant who served Mars Hill for years told me that he dropped his toolbox and left for good once he saw "Membership=Discipleship" plastered in large letters on facility walls.

In her study of Moral Majority leader Jerry Falwell, anthropologist Susan Harding describes how his "sermons were jeremiads, or Protestant political sermons. Named for the Old Testament prophet Jeremiah, a jeremiad laments the moral condition of a people, foresees cataclysmic consequences, and calls for dramatic moral reform and revival."[2] She specifically refers to a jeremiad in which Falwell uses Nehemiah to fashion himself in the image of the Old Testament prophet while highlighting his political prominence and activism. She writes, "He mingled his voice with the prophetic voices of Nehemiah and Jesus and figured himself as their heir, their current fulfillment. Like Nehemiah, Falwell will *rebuild the wall. . . . the little children need help and I shall be God's instrument to deliver that help.*"[3] Harding describes this rhetorical strategy as bolstering the impression of Falwell's "efficacy as a national moral leader who was standing up, speaking out, and being counted. . . . Closing up the *breach in the wall*, he was *standing in the gap*, for God."[4]

Pastor Mark also preached as though he was the contemporary embodiment of Nehemiah and Jesus, but without the narrative devices of a jeremiad; instead, he used the book of Nehemiah verse by verse to stage his plan for Mars Hill's multigenerational legacy and global empire. Rather than pitching himself as the moral leader necessary for a lost nation, Pastor Mark cast himself in the role of Nehemiah as street fighter out to save Seattle and the world for Jesus. The last sermon in the *Nehemiah* series set the tone for supernatural and worldly battles to come; after its final iteration during the evening service in Mars Hill Ballard's sanctuary, Driscoll fired an elder despite his many years of service and friendship. Pastor Paul Petry, who provided biblical counseling for couples experiencing marriage problems and taught "Biblical Marriage and Family" classes with his wife Jonna, was the most public casualty of bylaw changes that occurred after the *Nehemiah* series drew to a close.

This violent upheaval in leadership during a period of rapid expansion intensified a sense of ongoing crisis such that conviction could be extorted, confession extracted, and repentance exploited. Petry's disciplining, and his family's subsequent shunning, was an affect-event that stoked and spread an atmosphere of spiritual warfare through which surveillance became socially simulated, rather than simply internalized. Although Driscoll endeavored to locate the false prophets of new religions firmly beyond his own pulpit, Mars Hill itself was labeled a cult once public testimony to procedures of church discipline surfaced online.

SPIRITUAL AUTHORITY AND CHURCH DISCIPLINE

On September 30, Mark preached the last sermon of the *Nehemiah* series, "Fathers and Fighting":

> I'm gonna go ahead and pray. Tonight is a great text, a guy beats up members of his church, scalps one. Ah, it really is, ah, heartwarming is what comes mind [giggling from audience] . . . and [Nehemiah] *beat* some of them [audience laughter]. I'll repeat that again [more laughter]. And beat *some* of them [more laughs]. What do we do with that? I'll tell you what I'd like to do with that [huge burst of laughter]. I'd like to follow in his example. There's a few guys right now, if I wasn't going to wind up on CNN, I would go Old Testament on 'em [audience laughs]. Even in leadership in this church [audience laughs]. Here's Nehemiah's deal. Now, Romans 13 says we need to obey the government, so you just can't walk around beating people up, tragically [long, loud laughter]. It does sim-

plify things, there's no, like, *attorneys* and *blogging*, there's just, like, I punched you in the mouth, shut up [another burst of laughter].[5]

Driscoll does not need to physically assault the nameless church leaders whom he gestures toward in langauge—the infectious laughter of his audience serves as convicting muscle on his behalf. In this threatening rebuke, Pastor Mark feeds a desire to believe not through persuasive exegesis or charismatic preaching, but violence that registers in belly laughs and gut feelings simultaneously spontaneous and orchestrated. He continues:

> I'll tell you another story, ah, there's a guy I met he's a mixed martial artist, an ultimate fighter, a good guy, loves Jesus, he was at church recently, and ah, he coaches a lot of young fighters. And so, I coach a lot of pastors, so I asked him, what do you do to a guy who just doesn't submit to spiritual authority, doesn't obey the chain of command, doesn't listen, doesn't do what he's told, just rebellious, stiff-necked, hard-hearted, and stupid. I said, "what do you do with those guys?" His answer was brilliant. He said, quote, "I break their nose" [burst of laughter from audience]. I thought wow. I mean, that's heartwarming, that is [more laughs], that makes so much *sense* to me. . . . Some men need to be confronted, some men need to be rebuked, some men *need* to be dealt with, because of that stubborn, obstinate, stiff-necked attitude. . . . [Nehemiah] fires some spiritual leaders, guys lose jobs, you're *not* a pastor here anymore, you're out of work! Furthermore [long pause], this is an incredibly important issue for our day. This is an incredibly important issue for our church.[6]

I did not know whom Mark was talking about, but someone would feel his wrath. That evening, Lead Pastor Jamie Munson sent an email to church elders announcing the immediate termination of Pastors Paul Petry and Bent Meyer. The first charge against Petry was "continual insubordination and [refusal to submit] to leadership and spiritual authority."[7] A conflation between church leadership and spiritual authority was clear and assumed. A subsequent letter to members announcing the pastors' firing began in typical fashion, with the good news of church growth.[8] It was also stated that the elders did not want "any discussion regarding this matter on the members site forums" because "speculation and gossip will only be unhelpful to the church and unkind to these men."[9] No details concerning the grounds for Petry and Meyer's termination were given, aside from the information that there were "no accusations of moral or sexual impropriety."[10] Performances of secrecy became a part of Mars Hill's DNA, such that fear, shame, and paranoia went viral.

Former Mars Hill leaders testified to a "culture of fear" which depended on systemic practices of bullying, not simply Mark's rhetoric.[11] One member described the vetting process to become a community group leader as a militarized grilling—an unscripted spiritual interrogation to discern where his heart was as a disciple:

> I met my CG [community group] leader and a campus pastor early one morning before work at a local coffee shop. Pastor X's first question was, "How is the training going so far?" I proceeded to tell him things were going okay. I went onto say that I was very humbled by the opportunity to lead a community group but that in some ways I felt inexperienced and under-prepared. The pastor stopped me and started grilling me on why I felt that way. He then informed me that I was "not living up to my true potential and everything God has called me to be." He went on "do you truly believe God calls people?" "I do," I said. "Well then you're not living up to all that God has called you to be." "Hmmm," I thought, okay I imagine that's true. The more I answered his questions, the more ammunition it seemed to provide him and the more he would grill me. I noticed he didn't really have an agenda or any questions he was reading from and that his only agenda was to confront and attack any "sinfulness" he sensed from my responses. At one point he stopped and said "I hope you don't feel like I'm attacking you . . . because we do this to all of our leaders."[12]

Scholar of American religion Jason Bivins notes, "A sense of risk and urgency is central to justificatory or identity-maintenance projects. . . . Political fear can restore order, establish allegiance and identity, or clarify the very boundaries it elsewhere seems to disturb. Political fear is always pedagogical."[13] The affect-event of Petry's firing and his family's subsequent exile from the church opened the door to a heightened sense of alarm and desire for security. This passion and desire played out through systemic forms of bullying, banishment, and social suspicion that precipitated what Bivins calls a "demonology within."[14]

Bivins uses "erotics of fear" to describe how a religion of fear is drawn to what it seeks to drive away, such as in the case of the Puritans, whose "ontological certainties were framed by an unshakeable conviction that demon Others lurked outside and within the regenerate community; in the 'savage' New World, with its woods shrouded in mystery, its dark-skinned natives, and its darker secrets."[15] At Mars Hill, this demonic assemblage included religious, racialized, and sexualized bodies within and outside of its facilities—"false" Christians, "Islam," and female sexual sinners. In addition, wives felt compelled to tell their husbands when friends confessed to feelings that could be construed as disloyal to church leadership because of an intense fear of being labeled a "gossip." In such cases, women were not only privately and publicly rebuked, silenced, and shamed, but also fired from positions on staff or left fearful and paranoid about jeopardizing their husbands' jobs in leadership and their family's status within the church. Jonna Petry describes her participation in this dynamic of surveillance before Paul was fired and her own family shunned.

> I was invited to a dinner to celebrate Grace's (Mark's wife and my friend) birthday. There were a dozen or so women in attendance and I ended up sitting next to Karen Schaeffer, who was Mark's administrative assistant—a lovely, older, godly woman whom I greatly respected. Sitting next to us was an elder's wife who was close in age and who also had quite a bit of previous ministry experience. The three of us enjoyed great conversation. . . . The next morning I heard from the elder's wife, the one Karen and I had so enjoyed—that she had shared our conversation with her husband and he felt that it showed "disloyalty" on Karen's part, was gossip, and that it needed to be brought to Mark, which he did. Karen was fired. The gist of what she shared that was branded "disloyal" was a heart of thankfulness that my husband, Paul, was being made an elder because Mark needed strong men around him who could handle and stand up to push-back. When I found out what this elder and his wife had done, I called Mark immediately in tears and asked him to forgive me for my part in that conversation. . . . After [Karen] was fired I stopped seeing

her altogether. I was afraid of what it might mean for me if I continued as her friend. It was never spoken but rather understood that to remain in contact with her would be unwise.[16]

After firing Paul as a paid elder, church leadership assessed his potential status as a volunteer lay elder by putting him on "trial," but he was not permitted to advocate for himself by addressing the accusations in person, a strategic move considering he had given up his law practice a couple years prior to devote himself to full-time ministry. The Elder's Council unanimously voted to remove him from staff entirely. Pastor James Harleman describes his decision-making process this way: "A cocktail of confusion, self-doubt, persuasive coercion and disorienting fear fueled my vote to make official the powers of leadership that were already gripping Mars Hill Church in every way except on paper."[17] Concerning motive he adds, "I didn't score high on Mars Hill's favored entrepreneurial tests or fit the personality profile, and so my discernment came into question when it came to tough love. Effectively, I was encouraged to doubt my conscience."[18] The "persuasive coercion" Harleman testifies to works on multiple registers as confusion, self-doubt, and fear steered him away from acting on his conscience.

Michel Foucault calls the "contact" between the technologies of domination and self, "governmentality."[19] These "technologies of power, which determine the conduct of individuals and submit them to certain ends or domination," operate in tandem with "technologies of self, which permit individuals to effect by their own means or with the help of others a certain number of operations on their own bodies and souls, thoughts, conduct and way of being, so as to transform themselves."[20] Harleman's confession suggests a distinct conceptualization of power is necessary for rethinking this contact between technologies of domination and self. Foucault admits, "Perhaps I've insisted too much on the technology of domination and power. I am more and more interested in the interaction between oneself and others and in the technologies of individual domination, the history of how an individual acts upon himself, in the technology of self."[21] Harleman's confession in the aftermath of Mars Hill's dissolution signals how the carnal resonance of conviction is affectively channeled through an erotics of fear that overrides conscience.

The "entrepreneurial tests" that intensified Harleman's self-doubt were among the evaluative metrics also used to lower the salaries and otherwise devalue those working in Mars Hill's Biblical Living ministry, such as Petry— those whose primary role was in the "ground war," caring for the flock. Rather than spurring self-governance or care, the contact between technologies of domination and self as described by Harleman put self-discernment and integrity into question and at risk. These entrepreneurial tests worked on a collective, affectively embodied register of individualized domination that superseded regulatory forms of governmentality—intensifying, networking, and exploiting the surplus affective value of conviction as an unruly, unpre-dictable, disaggregating instrument of biopolitics.

In a letter appealing to the elders' conscience a few weeks after his termi-nation, Paul Petry wrote:

> My greatest sins are not what I have said and done but what I have failed to say and do. I failed to speak up to confront and resist the abusive spiri-tual authority and false teaching about authority that has infected the hearts and imaginations of Pastor Mark, the Executive Elders. . . . The sins I am accused of, "disrespecting and distrusting spiritual authority and improperly handling confidential information," are they not the sins Mark and the [Executive Elder] team are guilty of because they assume some spiritual preeminence they do not have?[22]

These words did not convict the elders of the abuses in authority to which they had contributed. Even still, Paul confessed to self-doubt after send-ing the letter: "People have asked me why I remained silent these last couple of months. . . . I had a recurring daydream: that I would hear a knock at my door, it would be [Mark], and [he] would say, 'Hey buddy, I am so sorry about what happened—things really got out of hand. How about let's go grab a beer and talk?' "[23] Petry's daydream resonates with my nightmarish response to the anonymous video, when I questioned and doubted myself over Mark. Critical theorist Lauren Berlant writes, "All attachments are optimistic. . . . Cruel optimism is the condition of maintaining an attachment to a significantly problematic object."[24] If distinctly, Paul and I had become affectively attached to "Pastor Mark" against our better judgment and self-interest, showing how problematic belief is as an object of desire.

As the new bylaws passed and Petry officially resigned his church membership,[25] there was an outpouring of questions from members concerning what "spiritual authority" meant and who held it in the hierarchy of Mars Hill. In response, a thread on the members-only site, "Ask the Elders Anything," was opened from November 1–4, 2007, for seventy-two hours. Congregants' inquiries comprised forty-seven pages; the administrative response was 142. This document was titled, "Mars Hill Church: A Miracle of Jesus," and began with a cover letter that provided a narrative of Pastor Mark's personal history through which to tell the church's story. In it, Driscoll highlights a growth spurt and power grabbing by "some elders" who made his job so difficult that he had fantasies of quitting Mars Hill altogether.[26] As his letter crescendos to the present-day strife involving Petry, it mimics the vague language and beleaguered tone of its opening and reiterates a common refrain—that the council of twenty-three elders had unanimously voted that Paul was unqualified to serve as a pastor. This letter was signed "For Jesus' Fame, Pastor Mark Driscoll." Linking his name and celebrity to Jesus,' Driscoll stages the discussion concerning spiritual authority to come.

In questions bundled under the topical heading "Church Leadership," excerpts from Driscoll's book *Church Leadership* (2008) clearly state that Jesus is the highest authority and considered the head of the church, while Scripture is the "metaphorical Supreme Court by which all other things are tested."[27] Later, however, the spiritual authority of Jesus and Scripture are conflated with church leadership, "Pastors need the people in their church to obey them and respect their God-given authority."[28] Meanwhile, congregants' questions suggest confusion and suspicion: "Are we as members supposed to respect all elders equally as spiritual authority, or are some more authoritative than others?"; "I gratefully submit to pastoral leadership in the church, knowing that I am not called to be a pastor. But pastoral authority seems vastly different from 'spiritual authority,' which to me implies a priestly function that no longer exists as we are all priests with direct access to Jesus. What spiritual authority exists other than Jesus Christ? What does such authority consist of precisely? Does such authority override an individual leader's conviction?"; "Please explain your use of the term 'spiritual authority' and what this means biblically and within the context of Mars Hill."[29] Congregants' questions suggest that fear of church discipline administered without valid justification or clear rules of application amplified the affective value of conviction in tandem with paranoia, which became an ecological, rather than a pathological, matter.

In response to these questions concerning the spiritual authority of church leadership it was stated, "the elders have always operated with an understanding of a firsts among equals structure as Pastor Mark has fulfilled this role since the beginning of the church. In the last 6 months we have established a structure that includes a team of firsts among equals with multiple elders. . . . Every elder has spiritual authority which includes Jesus, The Bible, all of the Elders, church governance policy and their overseeing elder. Depending on the particular issue or decision, different authorities come into play."[30]

While Jesus is declared "senior pastor" of Mars Hill, Pastor Mark's spiritual authority in the "firsts among equals" model maps onto His.

There were also several questions about how "spiritual authority" was defined in relation to "disrespect," "lack of trust," and "submission." One member wrote, "I now have an abstract fear of 'not trusting and respecting spiritual authority,' but I'm not sure that is what God intended in that passage. Can we know what Paul did so that we might have a fear of committing the same sin?"[31] The answer was, "The biggest thing Paul did through all of this was to fail to repent of any wrongdoing, even after 23 elders voted that he was not qualified biblically as an elder."[32] In effect, conviction became a strategic relation of biopolitical control that legitimized the administration of church discipline, conscripting congregants and leaders to not only police one another, but also to discern sin and evil in their own hearts.

CHURCH OR CULT?

Driscoll addressed a group of Acts 29 pastors and church planters on October 1, 2007, the day after Petry and Meyer were fired.

> Here is what I have learned: You cast vision for your mission, and if people don't sign up, you move on. You move on. There are people that are gonna die in the wilderness, and there are people that are gonna take the hill. That's just how it is. . . . I am all about blessed subtraction. There, there is a pile of bodies behind the Mars Hill bus [chortles], and by God's grace, it'll be a mountain by the time we're done. You either get on the

bus, or you get run over by the bus. . . . Yesterday we fired two elders for the first time in the history of Mars Hill. Last night, they're off the bus, under the bus. They were off mission, so they're unemployed. I mean, this will be the defining issue as to whether or not you succeed or fail. I've read enough of the New Testament to know that occasionally Paul put somebody in the wood chipper (slight chortle, then pause), ya know?[33]

Whereas Meyer later resigned his membership from the church in good standing, Petry did not. In a letter to leaders meant to correct "exaggerated communication" from the Executive Elders, Meyer repeatedly refers to verbal and structurally violent acts: a "verbally violent rant by Mark embedded with threats" endured on the night of his termination; the "violence" of the firing process; the unwillingness of elders to confront "Mark's violence, heavy-handed use of position and demeaning characterization of others in our presence"; and several more examples of abusive administrative communication and disciplinary processes.[34] In essence, Meyer was speaking of missives and procedures such as a ruling publicly posted on the members' site by Lead Pastor Jamie Munson:

> Paul remains unrepentant, and therefore we are accepting his resignation as a member under church discipline. . . . While the treatment of an unrepentant believer may seem harsh, it is actually motivated out of love and care for the individual and the rest of the church. . . . We would discourage anyone at Mars Hill from continuing to look to Paul for spiritual leadership, counsel, instruction, or oversight in any form, formal or informal. In addition, we strongly encourage you to soberly assess your interactions with other disgruntled members as to whether they are causing further division of the church or unity in Jesus. . . . Although rejection and disassociation may seem harsh, these responses are simply a means by which the individual in question may come to an acknowledgment of their sin and repent. The idea is not that we stop caring for them, but rather that when they sin and refuse to repent we are to treat them as if they were enemies of the gospel. . . . When you put a person out of the church, you don't have him over for a meal. You don't treat him like a brother. You don't treat him as an unbeliever. You treat him like an outcast.[35]

The act of repentance intended to free Christians from sin and shame on the path to personal transformation and spiritual reconciliation with God became an instrument of population control. In turn, an ad-hoc surveillance mechanism was set in motion, inciting members to confess not only to those they sinned against but also various authorities, including husbands, pastors, and community group leaders. As fear of public shaming and shunning became an ever-present affective reality, "authentic" repentance became a biopolitical instrument wielded by no one in particular. In turn, logics of us/them could shift to accommodate myriad demonic "others" outside and within the congregation. Meanwhile, Driscoll capitalized on the firing of Paul Petry and banishment of his family to assert his own theology of spiritual warfare.

Jason Bivins discusses spiritual warfare for the Puritans of the seventeenth century as a "burgeoning fear regime [that] took shape in Cotton Mather's zeal for 'the workings of the "invisible world" '—a hidden domain populated by devils, spirit forces, witches and angels."[36] As such, spiritual warfare entailed belief "that the shadow world of spirits and demons was as real as the waking world: the devil's work was no trifling matter and, precisely because it bred such seductions and captured the imagination, required engagement and combat from the devout."[37] Bivins also notes that, as historically contextualized by the late eighteenth century, "at the center of these processes for evangelicals were contestations surrounding both demonology and the appropriate expression of religious experience. . . . The Others emerging from the evangelical imagination . . . were primarily racialized and gendered figures who manifested in fevered dreams and visions."[38] While some Evangelicals were nervous about the effects of such visions on social order, "[Jonathan] Edwards, of course, believed that not only was terror an appropriate response to the divine presence but that religious pedagogy was often most true and effective when expressed in the idiom of fear. In other words, debates about evangelical identity itself—those concerned with both the body and demonology—turned on the categories of fear, sin, and God's wrath."[39] Bivins adds that among contemporary evangelicals there is always desire and fantasy at work in the erotics of fear.[40] Fear, sin, and God's wrath are not mere categories of doctrinal engagement but affective attachments. Edwards's belief that terror was an appropriate response to the divine presence of God was not only enacted through church services at

Mars Hill, but also socially animated in congregants' everyday lives. In turn, this fear of God converged with fear of (a) man, Pastor Mark.

Presented in February 2008, *Spiritual Warfare* was a popular four-part teaching series that attracted over 128,000 views on the church's website before it was erased a couple years after its posting, at a time when long-archived audiovisual material that testified to the labor of pastors such as Petry was disappearing from the media library without comment. Although intended for an audience of Mars Hill's Biblical Living staff, who counseled congregants on patterns of past and present sin, the video's public dissemination spoke to political aims that superseded religious self-help therapy. Before his talk begins, Pastor Mark alerts those in attendance that he is "really tired" after "a rough couple of weeks," then sarcastically remarks, "You always know when you're teaching on warfare, it's gonna be great, you're gonna come in well rested, focused, no conflict, ah, that's about where I'm at."[41] A Mickey Mouse T-shirt pokes out through an unzipped sweatshirt as he prays "against the enemy and his servants and their works and effects."[42]

> The Bible talks about human beings working in concert with Satan and demons. Such false prophets lead cults; they lead new religions; they promulgate false doctrine. There are also false Christians . . . who really don't love Jesus, really don't belong to him, but they come into a church with the desire, demonic-inspired desire, to absolutely destroy. The greatest threat to any church, and this includes Mars Hill Church, is wolves *in* the flock. It's not the dark city, and the atheists, and the homosexuals, and the abortion doctors—we want them all to meet Jesus and come to repentance. But the truth is in a church like Mars Hill, it's the person who comes in and says, I love Jesus, but I don't submit to spiritual authority, I don't submit to sound doctrine, listen to me not to them, I have my own issue, my own agenda, my own ministry.[43]

According to Driscoll's theology of spiritual warfare, supernatural and worldly enemies surround and infect the church body—cults led by false prophets proliferate outside Mars Hill, while false Christians hell bent on its destruction infiltrate the congregation with an efficacy that surpasses the usual secular suspects. These insurgents are wolves that don't submit to spiritual authority.

As the church gets bigger, and it spreads, *you have to guard the gate*. I can't do it. I can't do it. I can't keep track of all of the campuses, and all of the heretics, and all of the false teachers, and all of the false leaders, and all of the people that Satan is sending in to distort the truth, lead many astray, and to be as wolves among the flock. . . . We are the fifteenth-fastest-growing church in America. As we split to multiple campuses, we have conflicts and wars on multiple fronts. We have many new Christians, we have many non-Christians, we have many people who are just coming to an understanding of the gospel. We would be the perfect place where Satan would love to sin. Would love to sin. *You have to assume that.* You have to assume that. That could get the churches in our Acts 29 Network— the churches nationally and internationally that look to us for leadership— astray. We're the fifteenth-most-influential church in America, there's a lot riding on what we do. What concerns me most is—can you flip the staff over and defend against a wolf? *You have to have that discernment*, that courage, and that ability to tell someone—you are in sin, that is false doctrine, you are not qualified to be a leader. If you do not repent, you are not welcome here. This is incredibly important, and I believe it is absolutely essential for the health and the forward progress of the church.[44]

Rather than a healing practice of deliverance through which demons are excised from sinners,[45] Driscoll commands the expelling of heretics from the church body. In this call to arms, repentance is not an antidote to sin but an ambient metric of desire used to assess submission to spiritual authority and leveraged as a weapon. Spiritual warfare is not waged in the name of individual salvation but congregational protection—it is preemptive rather than prescriptive. A relationship is rendered between imminent Satanic attack and wolves among the flock in order to ensure Mars Hill stays on mission to multiply.

In 2012, interviews with former members shunned under church discipline appeared on a popular Christian site and in the local Seattle weekly *The Stranger*. In a story posted by Christian blogger Matthew Paul Turner, a former congregant describes his first two years at Mars Hill as time spent in loving fellowship among a devoted group of believers who supported and valued him.[46] Andrew became well connected, joining a community group and volunteering for security duty. He also became engaged to an elder's daughter and then cheated on her with another woman. Within days, Andrew confessed this transgression not only to his fiancée but also his community group leader. The next month was filled with meetings during which he was asked to confess to all of his past sexual sin, after which Andrew was called a wolf and placed under church discipline. Meanwhile, there was a shift in tone and language among his friends that made him feel more like a criminal and less like a brother. He received a church discipline contract that listed his sins and what he had to do to walk in true repentance insofar as leadership was concerned:

> Andrew will not pursue or date any woman inside or outside of MH; Andrew will write out in detail his sexual and emotional attachment history with women and share it with XXX; Andrew will write out in detail the chronology of events and sexual/emotional sin with K and share it with XXX and Pastor X; Andrew will write out a list of all the people he has sinned against during this time frame, either by sexual/emotional sin, lying or deceiving, share it with XXX and develop a plan to confess sin and ask for forgiveness.[47]

This contract illustrates the prohibition-confession dynamic Foucault describes as particularly intense with regard to sexual behavior and desire, "There is a very significant difference between interdictions about sexuality and other forms of interdiction. Unlike other interdictions, sexual interdictions are constantly connected with the obligation to tell the truth about oneself."[48] He also notes, "The task of analyzing one's sexual desire is always more important than analyzing any other kind of sin. . . . sexuality is related in a strange and complex way both to verbal prohibition and to the obligation to tell the truth, of hiding what one does, and of deciphering who one is."[49] Thus, it is unsurprising that sexual sin would be a subject of intense scrutiny or used as an instrument of individual discipline and population control at Mars Hill. To be an "authentic" Christian, one had to be a disciple, which meant embodying "biblical" masculinity, femininity, and sexuality, as well as perpetually confessing and repenting of sin while submitting to church authority as/if necessary. However, even when a congregant such as Andrew left the church rather than sign a church discipline contract, the affective value of its administration and his subsequent exile had political impact. After Andrew communicated his decision to resign his membership, he was told that "Matthew 18 discipline" would be "escalated."[50] This escalation translated into a public, formal shunning decree that was posted on The City, the Mars Hill social networking site for members, complete with scripted "practical examples" to facilitate the process.

> You run into him and ask, "Andrew, how are things?" He replies, "Not so good. I don't trust the leadership and they have been heavy handed and hard on me. I feel I've prayed about leaving the church." You respond, "Andrew, I'm sorry you feel that way but you're not seeing things rightly. I agree with the elders' decision regarding you because I see how they are acting in accordance to the Scriptures. They love you and I love you. We pray the Lord would grant you repentance so we can be a family once again . . . until then, we can't pretend nothing is wrong."[51]

According to Andrew, many of his friends followed these suggestions.

A week after this story broke, "Lance" relayed a similar experience in the Seattle weekly The Stranger: he felt like a family member until sexually sinning, confessed to church leadership and submitted to "six months of counseling and spiritual probation."[52] After this period, he was fully restored to the congregation, living in a Mars Hill home with other men and paying his rent in volunteer labor. However, once a pastor ordered Lance to stop dating a woman long distance, and threatened that if he did not obey him Lance would have to move and cut off communication with congregants, Lance quit. Once again, affective attachment—desire outside the covenant of Mars Hill membership—was prohibited. It was not the threat of sexual sin that was intensely problematic, given Lance and the woman lived so far apart, but rather the prospect of losing his affective labor to the church (for example, in a move to be with her)—that was a transgression worthy of rebuke. In this sense, the prohibition-confession dynamic Foucault describes as particularly intense with regards to sexual behavior and desire, such that sexual prohibitions become closely connected to the obligation to tell the truth about oneself, holds less weight. Lance had no sexual sin to confess to, at least according to his narrative of the story. His sexual desire was not under scrutiny, his heart was. Desire became untethered from sexual activity or fantasy and the matter of conviction became a question— this biopolitics of sex concerned sensations and intensities of belief rather than sexual pleasure or sin. Rather than a fixation on Lance's sexual behavior, this order and threat from church authority was about a secrecy of the heart, a desire to believe in the spiritual authority of church leadership that continually needed to be proven in order to decipher who congregants were—wolves or sheep, true Christians or demonic insurgents—so that Mars Hill's mission would not be derailed by opposition or curtailed by distracted volunteers.

This dynamic suggests that logics of surveillance were used as a threat rather than as a means; instead of panoptic self-monitoring, spiritual authority aroused conviction by routinizing the execution of preemptive power. Writing on Foucault's concepts of governmentality and biopolitics, political theorist Maurizio Lazzarato suggests, "Power is not a unilateral relation, a totalitarian domination over individuals, such as one exercised by the *dispotif* of the Panopticon, but a strategic relation."[53] The Panopticon was designed by Jeremy Bentham in the late eighteenth century as a cost-effective antidote to the inefficient operation of institutions such as prisons, hospitals, factories, and schools. In the setting of the prison, the Panopticon was built around a central guard tower with outer windows through which a guard could monitor every inmate in their cell without being seen. This architecture promoted the sense that one was always being watched without any certainty about when or by whom, such that self-surveillance would take hold. In Foucault's terms, the effect of the Panopticon was to "induce in the inmate a state of conscious and permanent visibility that assures the automatic functioning of power."[54] However, in Lazzarato's analysis of Foucault, he reframes biopower to consider strategic relations more complex than those strictly organized through disciplinary logics of self-surveillance or biological processes of population regulation. The affective ecology of Evangelical Empire excited and networked a biopolitics of sex that was less invested in sexual prohibitions or discursive subjectification than illustrated by Foucault's history of sexuality. Despite Pastor Mark's designation as a "first" among equals, strategic relations of power are multifarious, unpredictable, and of force; thus, the gatekeepers of the church had to be various and varied in their approaches to discerning "true" from "false" Christians. In turn, technologies, moods, and demons were vital materialities that contributed to Mars Hill's affective ecology. However, in media coverage of the events surrounding the shunning of congregants, Mars Hill was labeled a cult with Driscoll figured as its autocratic, narcissistic leader, leaving no question about who held power and how it was wielded.

"Church or Cult? The Control-Freaky Ways of Mars Hill Church" ends with Lance calling Mars Hill's culture "manipulative," to which he adds, "It's how people wound up drinking the Kool-Aid."[55] Matthew Paul Turner also refers to Mars Hill's "cult-like control."[56] The online news magazine *Slate* followed suit, in a piece called "A Shunning in Seattle," whose opening paragraph identifies Driscoll's leadership style as "cultlike."[57] Scholar of American religion Sean McCloud notes, "By the late 1970s the connections between cults, brainwashing, and fraudulence had become naturalized"; however, "whether something is considered brainwashing or conversion . . . is often more a matter of personal views about the religious group in question. . . . Rather than describing an actual process, [brainwashing is] a rhetorical term that marks certain movements negatively."[58] Proclamations about Mars Hill's cultish control served to "other" the church such that its abuses were viewed as self-contained and wholly detached from "traditional" religion or "secular" institutions. While more scrutiny fell on Driscoll as a result of this negative press, such attention served to amplify his controversial appeal and the social conviction that more affective labor was required to bolster security and fortify walls in support of the church's mission.

In the cases of Andrew and Lance, resistance was not realized in their resigning membership or even in their going public with their stories. Political theorist Maurizio Lazzarato writes that Foucault is interested in "forms of subjectification and forms of life that escape [power's] control."[59] In this sense, "biopolitics is the strategic coordination of these power relations in order to extract a surplus of power from living beings."[60] In the strategic relations of power that I call a biopolitics of sex, shifting from Foucault's project of a history of sexuality, resistance is a matter of conviction rather than of conscience. Lazzarato also notes, "In his interviews Foucault criticized himself because he thought that 'like many others, he had not been clear enough and had not used the proper terms to speak of power.' He [stated,] 'Therefore it is not power, but the subject, that constitutes the general theme of my investigations.' "[61] In focusing on the subject, the affective connective tissue of social relations and bodily entanglements through which strategic relations of power move—biopolitics—gets shortchanged. Placing blame on a given religious institution or leader for abuses of spiritual authority and population control does not further understanding or foster learning concerning how dynamics of power work. Othering such cases and processes affords the opportunity for further abuses of authority in both "religious" and "secular" political domains, on a grander scale. By reframing and situating Foucault's notion of biopower in terms of an affective ecology of Evangelical Empire, I suggest that bodily sensations, pleasures, and impressions engender a continual extension of fields and forms of control—not through top-down domination or self-population regulation, but social conviction. This affective process of atmospheric attunement is not predicated on religious identity or ideologically partisan.

As these stories of shunning were reported in the media, Mars Hill representatives publicly defended the church. Pastor Jeff Bettger responded to queries from *The Stranger* regarding Lance's case:

> I personally have never known anybody at Mars Hill who would harass, blackmail, verbally abuse, or belittle ex-members. I would actually say that over the last few years Mars Hill has increasingly become more loving, kind, generous, and humble. I have been seeing this over and over from leadership at Mars Hill, and from members. We know we are not perfect, but we believe in an active God who loves us. . . . The way God is growing this Church, I don't believe anybody would even have the time, let alone the interest, to follow ex-members around. We have a difficult enough time maintaining all the work that needs to get done from week to week as well as meeting with all the people who want counsel and are hurting.[62]

In his heartfelt defense of Mars Hill, Bettger neglects to mention the shunning of the Petry family a few years prior—a forgetting that was unintentional. This oversight was not in character or a media savvy maneuver, but an expression of gut feeling. During one conversation, an elder described the church's recruitment and calibration of affective labor in terms of "aspirational hope" procured through a form of "social Darwinism."[63] As facilities multiplied, growth metrics that provided empirical evidence of God's hand fostered the drive to perform better at all times, while Driscoll publicly shamed congregants from the pulpit via anecdotes so thinly veiled insiders would know who he was speaking of. The cost of this discipleship was inadvertently testified to in an earlier, personal blog post by Bettger, a lay pastor of Member Care whose sixteen years of service to the church was for the most part unpaid:

> Yesterday at a staff meeting I heard some amazing news, but instantly became overwhelmed and worried. Why would I be prickly towards the things God is doing?
>
> Here is my logic, and excuse (justification) for my crumby attitude:
>
> #1. We do not have enough resources, including man power.
>
> #2. We are stretched thin in other areas to be able to (in my opinion at the time) effectively take hold of some of the obvious opportunities and callings God has for us.[64]

This self-doubt becomes transfigured into sin and a heart issue, as Bettger testifies to a process of conviction encouraged in the name of the Holy Spirit and church expansion:

> I began thinking we are moving too fast sacrificing the protection of the flock, by stretching everyone too thin, without enough resources to accomplish our jobs effectively. If I had things my way it would be years before any movement happened, because everything would need to be lined up perfectly and worked through with no rush or extra long hours put in.... As a Deacon at the church and one who is gifted in priestly gifts (relationships, counseling, listening) I have a tendency to push back on big level projects that will require lots of man hours. My motive is to protect the flock from burnout, bitterness against the leaders, and whatever else has played out in the past when we are overextended, and underfunded. This attitude is good when working with, and towards the things God has for us. However as soon as I care more about somebodies [sic] comfort over the obvious movement of the Holy Spirit, I become the one with bad motive, and sinful desire.[65]

Once again, sin against the church's spiritual authority is a problem of desire. This desire was conjoined to sexualized and militarized dynamics of power, but its carnal resonance as conviction was situated and amplified by precarity. Philosopher Jason Read notes that affects such as precarity have intensified in the post-Fordist, deindustrialized U.S. political economy, given the dismantling of security and stability in and at work.[66] Bettger's post demonstrates how political economy operates outside the logics of self-interest, while exploitation is "energetically, if structurally, embedded in and con-stitutive of both affective and institutional life."[67] Rather than paralyzed by conviction, Jeff is overdetermined by it.

By the time of Petry's firing, Mars Hill was firmly entrenched at the front lines of a "global church planting war," described by Driscoll in these terms: "We want every nation to know about Jesus. We want every language, every people, every tongue, every tribe to know about Jesus. That's exactly what Jesus told us to do: be his witnesses to the ends of the earth. This is why money is spent on missions. This is why organizations are started: to take the news of Jesus around the world. You see, as soon as you become a Chris-tian, you are part of a global movement."[68]

In 2008, Pastor James Harleman introduced a seminar series designed to train men in what it meant to fight in a global church planting war entitled "Praxis–Real Men."

> Real men are at war every day. . . . As Christian men we were ripped from our Father, we get reborn and we're still on the battlefield, the crappy place that all the people who don't know Jesus are, we're not in heaven and we're not at home. . . . We live in a culture that is terrified of Islam and other false religions that are killing people. They don't just use battle language to describe the spiritual war—they kill you.[69]

In this talk, shadowy threats of "Islam" and "other false religions" demark a racialized demonic menace that must be fought by evangelical men to re-claim the language of war for "right" biblical purposes. This conjuring of Islam sutures an unending global war on terror to a spiritual battle lived every day by (white, male) Christians who must reclaim the nation from those who are "killing people." Harleman utilizes Islam to convict male leaders of their duty to become "real men" by enlisting in the church plant-ing war on behalf of Mars Hill's empiric mission. Islam becomes an ambient presence of terror that agitates hate in the name of love. This discourse has affective value given that, in the words of the feminist affect theorist Sara Ahmed, "it is the emotional reading of hate that works to bind the imagined white subject and nation together. . . . The ordinary white subject is a fantasy that comes into being through the mobilization of hate, as a passionate attachment tied closely to love."[70] Situated by an unending global war on terror, terrorist assemblages are mobilized through a militarized imaginary that entangles and excites bodies, including shifty demons demarked by the signifier "Islam."

Speaking of the contemporary United States at the beginning of the twenty-first century, Jason Bivins describes a fearful sociopolitical landscape shaped by the attacks of September 11, 2001, wherein "fear chokes the very air of our culture like smog that, while it can be seen from afar, we breathe in unknowingly in deep gulps. It is no great surprise to find that American religions have been active respondents to, and participants in, our culture of fear."[71] Furthermore, he adds, the specific strategies through which Evangelicalism constructs its "others" are "driven by and responsive to a vibrant secular pop culture," especially the vivid imagery of "alterity," the "cultural construction of a usually malevolent Other that takes place in particular cultures of meaning."[72] As public confessions and testimonies by former Mars Hill leaders and members labeled its "culture" as one of "fear," they rarely discussed how this fear was couched in military language, visualized through images of combat, or networked through violent militarized imaginaries. For example, the former pastor and worship band leader Luke Abrams wrote a confession in which he sought forgiveness for "routinely sacrificing friendship at the altar of growth, taking advantage of volunteers, using their time, energy, and talent without providing commensurate shepherding and care . . . the culture of harshness and fear, the prioritization of growth over love."[73] In seeking repentance, Abrams, among others, never acknowledges the strategic use of militarized imagery and imaginaries in stoking and spreading this culture of harshness and fear. Such glaring omissions signal how effective and vital this affective priming and attunement of atmosphere was to networking the structural procedures of political economy and abuses in spiritual governance that these testimonies do mention.

Whereas Bivins highlights how the imagery, tropes, techniques, and structure of the cinematic genre of horror have been appropriated by the religion of fear, I found the affective intensities and appeal of the war film repurposed and privileged more often at Mars Hill, particularly during its men's seminars and Film and Theology Nights.[74] While the heroic narrative of these films was often a subject of discussion by Pastor James Harleman, who for many years organized monthly (then semiregular) Film and Theology Nights, his lectures also demonstrate the purposeful desire to viscerally and visually agitate and conscript social conviction through "secular" cinematic techniques and tropes. The church's use of "mainstream" war films demonstrates how conviction, as a dynamic of power that involves and exceeds evangelical identities and religious spaces, inculcates secular subjects to collective action. These "spiritual dispositions," to reiterate the words of the philosopher William Connolly, "flow below epistemic beliefs and well up into them . . . the tightening of the gut, coldness of the skin, contraction of the pupils, and hunching of the back."[75]

In examining a compelling cinematic encounter, I call attention to the ways in which a director, Kathryn Bigelow, affectively decenters narrative, plot or character development in order to convey not only the felt reality of combat during Operation Iraqi Freedom, but life itself during an ongoing global war with terror. As scholar of moving images Jennifer Barker notes, film inspires an intimate experience of connection rather than a distant experience of observation, "we share things with it: texture, spatial orientation, comportment, rhythm, and vitality."[76] In this way, "touch . . . need not be linked explicitly to a single organ such as the skin but is enacted and felt throughout the body," as a process of worlding between viewer and viewed, audience and film.[77] Thus, my "reading" of cinematic representation in Bigelow's film is not explicitly discursive but concerned with touch as ontology, a political relation of being in and of spiritual and worldly life.

Harleman's analysis of the most lauded film situated by the war on terror to date—*The Hurt Locker* (2008)—resonates with "secular" responses to its affective pull and authenticity. In Harleman's discussion of *The Hurt Locker* during a Film and Theology Night in 2010,[78] he applauds the "amazing amount of visual detail" used by director Kathryn Bigelow, crediting her and journalist-turned-screenwriter Mark Boal with capturing "authenticity in the look, feel, location, and shots."[79] Harleman emphasizes that it was the actors' "real sweat" beading on their skin in the 115-degree heat of the Jordan desert, where filming induced a "certain amount of real pain and the reality of living in this environment," including the employment of "real Iraqi refugees" as actors.[80] Such accolades were echoed by numerous film critics and critical theorists such as Steven Shaviro, who describes Bigelow's cinematography as "a perverse and powerfully stylized exercise in visual excess . . . as if subjectivity were an effect of atmosphere, or of variations in lighting . . . [of] shock patterns" in which "appearances are unstable, and must be continually reinterpreted."[81] In *The Hurt Locker*, the cameras' kinetic movements belie the notion of training the audience's attention yet exert control by constituting said attention through shrewd editing techniques. In this sense, the shock patterns produced by Bigelow's style of filmmaking vaunt the film's authenticity—the felt reality of potential threat has no need for referent given the cameras' aggressive surveillance of the actors' every movement. Even veterans who mocked the film's outdated military equipment and irreverence for protocol lauded its ability to convey the affective reality of Operation Iraqi Freedom through its visceral impact, particularly its bomb explosions.[82] Bigelow convicts her audience of the film's authenticity by voyeuristically fetishizing improvised explosive devices (IEDs), for her the "signature" of the Iraq war, and by presenting the film as an ecological rather than political project, carved out of oppressive sunlight, tight camera movements, and taut editing.[83] In this sense, her cinematic portrayal of the Iraq occupation is shaped by a shock and awe logic that resonates with U.S. military strategy during the invasion—to seize control of the environment and overload the citizenry's perceptions and understandings of events.

Throughout the film, Iraqi onlookers appear at the margins of the Explosive Ordnance Disposal (EOD) team's actions, yet their collective stare is not inarticulate; in fact, that gaze inflicts a far more intense, overt panic in soldiers Sanborn and Eldridge—"There's a lotta eyes on us, we gotta get outta here," Sanborn sternly tells Sergeant James in one scene—than do the bombs that the EOD team is there to defuse. Like the out of focus porn videos Sergeant James buys from an Iraqi boy named Beckham, or the Iraqi video cameraman on the roof who spooks Eldridge because he "looks shifty," cultural theorists who figure the Iraqis as mere bystanders "represent[ing] to the spectator the intense uncertain status of the combatant, and thus the palpable anxiety of the US soldier" are suspect.[84] Jonathan Beller argues that critical theory "must register the violence endemic to the conversion of historically dispossessed others into images and signs . . . because in being figured as bare life, multitudes, refugees, tribes, slum-dwellers, or terrorists . . . the now doubly dispossessed are materially and symbolically disappeared for politico-economic ends."[85] The ethical imperative of Beller's critique is demonstrated by the way in which Hollywood war films such as *Locker* were used in congruence with testimonies by U.S. soldiers during Mars Hill training seminars for men.

Thirty minutes into his talk at the 2008 "Praxis–Real Men" seminar, Harleman introduces a congregant and soldier named Rogers who testifies to the physical, spiritual, and moral isolation he experienced during his fifteen months in Iraq:

> There's a moral sense of isolation at war, especially being an officer and making decisions. . . . Some of my soldiers are telling me we're clear to drop a five-hundred-pound bomb on a house. They're also telling me that they're within the danger close radius, the flash radius of that, but they're pretty sure they're OK, we need to drop now—what do you do? The fact that other people are recommending that to you but it's your decision brings a weight down on your shoulders that makes you feel alone. . . . Another situation, you saw the video, that was actually a mosque we put Fox-Two missiles into, and that's a super sensitive thing, so I have to qualify it. We felt and believed that it was a military target . . . . so the snap decision is, we're receiving fire from the vicinity of the mosque, and the Imam, the religious leader of the mosque, is not letting the Iraqi soldiers in to clear it. How do we get them in? How do we stop getting fired at? Run the P.R. nightmare, do we run that risk of blowing up a mosque?[86]

In Rogers's testimony, evangelical and military grammars overlap while the preemptive exertion of excessive force becomes justifiable and routine, as certain bodies are figured worthy of protection and others as collateral damage. In *Locker*, the pervasive scrutiny of the occupier-soldiers by real Iraqi refugees portraying civilians as always-potential insurgents contributes another stifling element to the stark landscape. Framed as an element of the desert, this Iraqi stare affectively resonates with Harleman's evocation of Islam as an ever-present environmental menace—a felt reality also brought to life in Rogers's testimony:

> Insurgents don't wear uniforms. Like when you saw at the very beginning, the cigarette factory in the video clip that we started off with, when

we were leaving there we got ambushed, and we were hit with an IED from one side, and then my vehicle and another vehicle started taking fire. It was fourteen-year-old kids, like, preteen, barely teen kids, that were hiding behind a hill that we were drawing the fire from. I don't have the luxury of asking them how old they are, if they did it, where the person who did it was, so do I shoot? Who do I shoot, when they're not wearing a uniform? That instantaneous decision also contributes to that sense of moral isolation.[87]

In his book *On Suicide Bombing*, Talal Asad writes, "The military of a liberal state—unlike the terrorist—does not normally target civilians, unless it is compelled to do so, but overriding concern for its own military casualties means it must choose a strategy in which more enemy civilians die. . . . The just modern soldier incurs guilt when he kills innocent people; the terrorist does not. Or so modern theorists of just war tell us."[88] In his testimony, Rogers embodies the modern soldier's conscience and upholds the liberal state's civilizational status, while confessing to the moral isolation and spiritual exile he experienced in Iraq. His performance viscerally registers with the scenes in *Locker* in which Sergeant James interacts with Iraqi civilians: when he performs surgery on the Iraqi boy whose body has been turned into a bomb, extracting explosive cartridges like a surgeon delicately removing organs; or when he apologizes to the Iraqi father for abandoning him with a bomb encasing his body like an ungainly exoskeleton in order to survive its imminent detonation. As militarized forms of biopower compassionately endeavor to cut out cancerous tissue while keeping vital organs intact, the killing of Iraqi civilians becomes a sign of grace and the disarming of IEDs becomes a metonym for Operation Iraqi Freedom.[89]

Harleman's signature was highly visible on Mars Hill's website due to his dedicated teaching in the men's ministry, his lead role in establishing Film and Theology Nights, and his revolving positions as a pastor at various Seattle locations. In 2012, however, teaching content once prominently displayed was disappearing from the church's website without explanation. Each time a leader departed without commentary, dead links indexed their existence, encouraging viewer participation in what anthropologist Joseph Masco describes as a Cold War strategy—a "theatrical performance of secrecy" that promoted a "form of antiknowledge."[90] Harleman discusses his leaving process as a long and involved untangling of commitments that culminated in betrayal:

> After being on staff for over ten years—Executive Elders called [a friend and me] "hirelings" who were only in it for the money and "quitters" who hurt the church. With few exceptions no one reached out to us: I was effectively shunned, and my wife and I lost dear friends. While I once had teaching contributions in the Mars Hill media library second only in number to Mark Driscoll, all vestiges of my presence were erased from the church I'd participated with, from 150 people to 15,000. People from churches around the world and people inside and outside MHC who'd once been privy to my teaching or podcasts were left to assume I'd sinned or done something wrong.[91]

In 2012, the same year that Harleman resigned his membership, director Kathryn Bigelow and screenwriter Mark Boal released another collaborative effort, *Zero Dark Thirty*. In this film chronicling the hunt for Osama bin Laden, a female intelligence agent becomes another prototype of a twenty-first-century war hero who, like the EOD soldier of *The Hurt Locker*, is fundamentalist in her sense of purpose under morally conflicted circumstances. In this case, the CIA agent's unwavering pursuit of bin Laden entails her infliction of torture to ascertain information. The film opens with the graphic depiction of various techniques and implies that torture played a key role in locating the target, despite the fact that many government officials have denied this connection as well as the efficacy of torture in ascertaining valid intelligence.[92] Prior to its theatrical distribution, the movie generated Oscar buzz and received rave reviews, even from critics who found its depiction of "enhanced interrogation techniques" morally and politically questionable, including one reviewer who proclaimed it simultaneously the best movie of 2012 and an "unholy masterwork."[93] Another critic lauded the film's unflinching illustration of torture as "the intersection of ignorance and brutality . . . scenes that can make a viewer ashamed to be American, in the context of a movie whose ending scene makes viewers very, very proud to be American."[94] Although the working title of the film was *For God and Country*, its final incarnation, *Zero Dark Thirty*, is "a military term for 30 minutes after midnight . . . [that] also [refers] to the darkness and secrecy that cloaked the entire decade long mission."[95] In the title's conversion from the starkly obvious *For God and Country* to the shadowy overture of *Zero Dark Thirty*, and in the haunting erasure of elders' service and sacrifice to Mars Hill, visualizations of the secret amplify and network the affective reality of warfare. Despite evidence disproving that torture played a crucial role in locating bin Laden, Bigelow professes that her film takes an "almost a journalistic approach" to its portrayal of events, and Boal claims to use a "hybrid of the filmic and the journalistic" in his screenplay.[96] In *Zero*, the secret's brutal theatrical performance transforms antiknowledge into the only identifiable victory during an endless war on terror framed in terms of good and evil—an affect-event of moral precarity through which conviction in God and country materializes the nation form as a masculine, white, imperial, Christian body.

One attendee of a Mars Hill facility outside of Seattle writes of how Driscoll's vision casting for Evangelical Empire agitated a militarized imaginary that infected local church authorities: "Pastor Mark came down to hold what they were calling a 'vision casting' for the local church. He discussed the future of Mars Hill and how they wanted to raise up 50 leaders to lead 50 churches and they specifically wanted dozens of leaders in Mars Hill leading an army of God."[97] At the same time, congregants were told that their local pastor would no longer preach live on a regular basis; instead, Pastor Mark's sermons in Seattle would be piped in via video feed. The weekend after Driscoll's visit, the local pastor told congregants that he "needed men to step up as leaders" because "200 churches, 50 branches of Mars Hill [and] 10,000 community groups" were expected to grow from this local facility by training and engaging members through a host of Mars Hill–branded programs.[98]

In the same blog post, this anonymous attendee describes his community group as comprised of a large number of very young "singles" as well as "one couple that was outspoken, extraverted and clearly favored by our 20 something deacon."[99] The husband, like this deacon, "was young, white and Christian college educated."[100] One night, the couple shared that "they always feel the Holy Spirit telling them if they've done something wrong."[101] Later, when the men were alone, the husband "used images of warfare and torture and likened the work the Holy Spirit was doing in him to 'tearing his fingernails from his fingers by the root, one by one.'"[102] While registering his dismay that such a visceral experience would be considered a blessing—"That may be a

spirit, but not the Holy Spirit! The Holy Spirit is not akin to a torturer"—
the blogger also states, "Later that night we were informed that [this man]
had been chosen by our deacon as the next community group leader."[103]
For disciples on mission, encounters with the Holy Spirit and Satanic demons became difficult to distinguish from one another, as the carnal resonance of conviction manifested the desire to be called to such a degree of
intensity that spiritual and worldly tortures of the flesh were redeemed.

DEMONIZING WOMEN AS SEXUAL SINNERS

In his lecture on spiritual warfare, Driscoll uses anecdotal evidence and
biblical verse to justify why most of his demonic counseling work has been
with women.

> We see [Satan] first attacking Adam and Eve. What I find curious is
> that most of my demonic counseling work has been with women. Can't
> explain that, ah, Paul says that women are the weaker vessel, ah, maybe
> that's the case. He says that women are more easily deceived. I know that
> most feminists don't like those verses, ah, if they're true, then that would
> mean that women who don't like them are deceived [grins, chortles],
> which is kinda funny [audience laughter]. Ah, and what's interesting to
> me is that Satan didn't even show up and attack Adam until he was mar-
> ried. That, ah, sometimes I believe, that Satan really likes to attack fami-
> lies, Christian couples that are called for ministry. . . . In that way, you are
> sort of putting your head up, and you should really expect bullets to be
> flying, because if there really is a war, and Ephesians 6 says that we really
> are part of a war, then as soon as you wave the Jesus flag and put your
> head up, you're probably one of those people that the enemy is going to
> send a demon to shoot.[104]

As the "weaker vessel," this story goes, women are more vulnerable to demonic attack than men. In a similar vein but using a different script, he
also proposes that Christian couples serving in ministry should expect
perpetual demonic opposition and a heightened sense of spiritual warfare
in their everyday lives. This message is advantageous considering his live
audience—Mars Hill staff—but also because it reframes norms that sub-
jugate women such that they justify spiritual warfare against a sexualized
other. Not only were women instructed to submit to men's authority in

every domain—home, work, and church—but these spaces were conflated such that Driscoll's spiritual authority contaminated them all. Thus, women were not simply "demonized," or even "possessed" by demons, but were the very embodiment of demons in sexualized form. While the "demon trials" that Mars Hill women endured were not the same as Paul Petry's trial, the use of the word *trial* in both cases signals a similarly coercive administration of spiritual authority through affective tactics—namely, the bullying of Driscoll's verbally violent rants, which had emotional as well as physiological and spiritual impact.

On paper, Mars Hill's demon trials can be traced to the deliverance rituals of Third Wave Evangelicals. Driscoll published a "Spiritual Warfare Trial" guide to accompany his lecture that included a step-by-step, how-to script incorporating aspects of Third Wave practice, such as the "binding" and "naming" of the demon.[105] However, as a woman named Darlene details in testimony on the blog site *We Love Mars Hill*, the outcome of her friend's demon trial could not be couched in terms of deliverance.

> Apparently, the elders were doing demon trials on members or anyone who had oppression in their life. Mark Driscoll wrote this whole procedure on how to summon, and then put on trial the demons that are oppressing the believer. . . . I asked her why she couldn't be my friend and she said my name was brought up in a demon trial. I asked her what that meant, and she didn't answer any more questions other than "talk to your elder about it," but that she would no longer ask me for prayer, talk to me about spiritual things, etc. without giving any other reasons. . . . To this day she says she ended our friendship because of "sin." But it wasn't until that demon trial that things changed.[106]

In this instance, sin is transferred from the heart of the woman under trial onto a friend, who she cuts out of her life. Rather than reinforcing regulatory logics of self-governance and care, this technology of self "liberates" the oppressed believer by inciting self-defense and isolation so that spiritually harmful contagions cannot penetrate her porous body. Rather than individual sin and reconciliation with God, the need for securitization, ostensibly on behalf of Mars Hill's mission, is emphasized.

Scholar of American religion Sean McCloud describes Third Wave Evangelical self-help deliverance manuals as a "Gothic therapeutic," in which "the trope of haunting is used to evoke and explain the negative influence of past trauma and sin in one's present life."[107] This emphasis on habitual sin and past trauma is mimicked in the "Spiritual Inventory" section of the guide to spiritual warfare trials, but its language does not echo the tropes of self-help literature as Third Wave manuals do. McCloud identifies these idioms as "pop psychology terms and phrases," or "quizzes, grading key, self-management through quantifiable self-assessment" that in "deliverance narratives constitute a discourse about human agency that wavers between choice and imposition."[108] The spiritual inventory assessment published by Mars Hill asks those taking it to survey themselves, but not in the empowering terms of self-help. Rather than self-assessment through quantifiable measurement, a demon trial required graphic and frank confession to Mars Hill authorities. In addition, sexual sin was distinctly highlighted to a degree that rivals and in some ways exceeds even its emphasis in Third Wave texts, a difference that is clearly articulated in Driscoll's spiritual warfare lecture as he discusses the "ordinary demonic."

In his list of examples of the ordinary demonic, the first is sexual sin, which he biblically justifies with verse: "1 Corinthians 7:5, it says that a married couple that is Christian should have sexual relations frequently, they shouldn't deny one another. . . . Otherwise Satan will get in there and destroy everything. How many of you would think that a couple that doesn't have enough sex is experiencing demonic spiritual warfare?"[109] Rather than sexual sins such as adultery, fornication before marriage, or same-sex attraction, a lack of sexual frequency and freedom within marriage is primary and privileged on Driscoll's list of the ordinary demonic. He further elaborates in vivid detail how vital sex is to protecting Christian marriages against demonic infiltration, particularly when there are so many worldly, visual temptations through which husbands can betray their wives.

> What I'm talking about is the common situation, where one person in the marriage wants to be intimate more often than the other, and they're rejected, and they become bitter. Satan comes in and feeds that bitterness, baits the hook of their flesh with the temptation to the world, and all the sudden Satan puts before them images and people and opportunities to lead them astray, and to destroy everything. . . . It does give Satan

the opportunity to sleep between you and your spouse. I wanna just burn that image in your mind. . . . I tell this to couples when I meet with them, husband, wife, are you having sex enough, what's your sexual relationship like? . . . I want you to have that image, that a couple that is not having free and frequent intimacy, when they go to bed, just, just think of Satan lying in bed between the two of them . . . this demonic. This is demonic.[110]

By Driscoll's account, the withholding of sex within marriage is a demonic epidemic—one invariably attributed to the "weaker vessel." This gendered difference not only subjugated wives but also intensified their fear and paranoia. Meanwhile, Pastor Mark's desire to "burn" the image of Satan into the minds of married couples as they lie in bed demonstrates how critical visceral processes of visualization were to conjuring demonic social imaginaries such that they took on a life of their own, animating congregants' everyday lives.

Whether women submitted to these demon trials of their own volition is also in question, another factor that distinguishes them from Third Wave deliverance rituals, in which those who participate do so voluntarily. According to an account published on Matthew Paul Turner's blog and narrated by a woman named Amy, she did not ask to have any demons put on trial. She sets the scene at a Mars Hill facility, with her husband sitting next to her during a marriage counseling session: "Mark started the meeting by telling us he was convinced that I had demons, and then he went on to add that my demons were 'sexual demons.'"[111] In Amy's words, he unleashed a "fiery tirade," during which he said that all of her sins were "sex based."[112] "At one point," she stated, "he asked me which one of my husband's friends I had imagined sleeping with."[113] Then, as relayed by Turner,

> Mark stared hard at Amy and began yelling questions at her "sex demons." His fierce glare seemed to look past her as he screamed his questions at her face. He asked the demons what their names were. He asked them about sex. He asked them about Amy's past sexual sins. He asked them about Amy's current lustful thoughts. He asked them if they were planning to destroy marriages in his church. And then he asked whose marriages were they planning to destroy and how. And then, according to Amy, Mark cast the demons out.[114]

This performance resonates with, as well as importantly diverges from, Mc-Cloud's descriptions of deliverance rituals: "First, those performing the deliverance must bind the demon to free the afflicted person's mind. Satan and his demons are bound, while the individual's agency is 'loosed.' . . . The afflicted is temporarily freed . . . from demonic persuasion and must repent of the sins that invited demonization."[115] Both Driscoll's questioning of Amy with regard to others' marriages and his accusation that she was sexually fantasizing about her husband's friends signal his desire to protect the church, rather than to free her. When Turner asked Amy why her demons would be specifically "sexual," she replied,

It's always [Mark's] go-to topic. Ironically, my husband had more "demons" than one could imagine. But his demons were of no consequence and unimportant to the church. It was somehow my fault because "maybe I wasn't the godly, providing wife" I was supposed to be. That said, Mark was also aware that my husband and I had sexual troubles from day one. And regarding our sex life—because I was essentially grinning and bearing it most of the time—Mark concluded that I was a terrible wife to my husband. Even when my husband looked at porn, Mark blamed me because I wasn't doing my "wifely duty." I felt violated when sex was expected of me. I was intensely miserable and neglected throughout my marriage, but Mark deemed that irrelevant because I was the wife and my duty was to serve my husband sexually. . . . Even when I called Mark my friend, I always found it odd how he would force sexual topics into sermons and into all of our counseling sessions.[116]

As Amy testifies, Mark's ministry from and beyond the pulpit was sexualized and focused on ensuring that women performed their biblical wifely duty to sexually please their husbands, simultaneously securing their marriage and serving the church. In his lecture on spiritual warfare, Driscoll also described in graphic detail his capacity to see sexual sin in the hearts of others, which he identified as a "gift of discernment":

Some people actually see things. This may be gift of discernment. On occasion, I see things. I see things. . . . Uh [closes eyes], there was one woman I dealt with [opens eyes], she never told her husband that she had committed adultery on him early in the relationship. I said, "You know"—she's sitting there with her husband, I said, "You know, I think the root of all this, I think Satan has a foothold in your life because you've never told your husband about that really tall blonde guy that you met at the bar. And then you went back to the hotel. And you laid on your back. And you undressed yourself. And he climbed on top of you. And you had sex with him. And snuggled up with him for a while. And deep down in your heart, even though you had just met him, you desired him because secretly he is the fantasy body type." I said, "You remember that place, it was that cheap hotel with that certain colored bed spread. You did it, you had sex with the light on because you weren't ashamed and you wanted him to see you. And you wanted to see him." She was just looking at me, like [he leans back, eyes wide, an expression of awe or amazement], and I said, "You know, it was about ten years ago." [He puts his hands up and motions across his line of vision, making the sign of a horizon in front of his eyes.] I see everything. She looks at her husband. He says, "Is that true?" She says, "Yeah. He was six-two, blonde hair, blue eyes. Yeah."[117]

Rather than steady panoptic surveillance that becomes internalized, governs, and subjugates, Driscoll's cinematic capacity to "see things" in the hearts of others, particularly of a sexual nature, speaks to how a biopolitics of sex works on visceral and visual registers to agitate and circulate fear and paranoia. Violent processes of encounter realized through techniques such as demon trials, militarized imagery and imaginaries situated by the global war on terror, and visceral encounters with spirits and demons, were not only encouraged by the church's affective ecology; they were vital materialities agitating conviction as surplus affective value, even after congregants left the church. Amy's account illustrates how Driscoll's gift of discernment was imposed onto congregants such that they suffered long-term emotional and spiritual consequences. She describes being "emotionally drained" after her demon trial, which "felt like I'd experienced psychological torture. . . . The abuse I experienced [after divorcing my husband and subsequently being shunned] at Mars Hill had very damaging repercussions that lasted many, many years."[118] As conviction in the efficacy of "enhanced interrogation techniques" was affectively and narratively suggested onscreen in *Zero Dark Thirty*, Driscoll's theology of spiritual warfare legitimized the implementation of physiological terror, its bodily and spiritual experience as torture, and the bodily affects of terror and shock as pedagogical instruments to biopolitical effect. The carnal resonance of conviction, rather than render congregants unfree to act, mobilized affective labor to propagate and secure the church.

As Mars Hill perpetually multiplied its facilities, changes occurred at the Ballard location. One Sunday, I could not find the bookstore that I liked to visit before sermons. I asked a man with yellow spiky hair standing by the information desk where it had been moved, mentioning in the process my regular attendance for several weeks. "Good for you," he said, grabbing my elbow like a man leading the blind. The awkwardness I experienced as he physically directed me to a destination well within reach on my own with simple verbal instruction led me to feel condescended to at the time. However, it also struck me that he avoided touching me in any way that could be construed as affectionate. His gesture made as visible as possible that he was only helping the lost, as any disciple would.

When I received a two-sentence response from Mark via email about conducting research at the church, the paperwork that I had crafted such that he had sample interview questions, jurisdiction over where I could go and who I could speak with, and assurance that I would be sensitive to people's privacy and confidentiality while affording them say over what and how I would record information from any conversation, went unacknowledged. He said that he would not give his consent because so many people were suffering from sexual abuse at Mars Hill, and it was his duty to protect the flock.

During his sermon series on the Song of Songs, entitled *The Peasant Princess* (2008), Driscoll sermonized center stage while a background scrim of images shifted according to emotional register. During week 7, Driscoll preached on Song of Songs 6:11–7:10, verses he deemed "the most erotic, exotic, and exciting" in Scripture.[1] While lingering over an explicit line-by-line reading of an "ancient strip tease" called "Dance of Mahanaim," Pastor Mark encouraged wives to be visually generous allies—to fight with and for their husbands by providing an archive of redeemed images. Preempting critics who may have "taken a few women's studies classes in college" and would accuse him of objectifying the female body, Driscoll retorted, "Pornography turns women into parts and pieces, not image-bearers of God. . . . A husband should be captivated by his wife, that's what I'm talking about. I want the proverbial camera of his heart fixated to his wife so that his snapshots are of her."[2] His sermonizing on the everyday sins of mainstream pornography created opportunities for the proliferation of Mars Hill's own brand of biblical porn as a social imaginary, marking strategy, and biopolitical instrument. This cultural production mobilized voluntary and inadvertent affective labor in the virtual and visceral networking of sexualized discourse couched in theological terms, as interactive digital technologies and social media platforms promoted the church's influence as and through popular culture. By couching the temptation to view porn in terms of everyday spiritual warfare, Driscoll created a sense of urgency while suturing wives' sexual freedom to their husbands' visual nature. At once corporeal and global in scope, biblical porn conflated sexual freedom and biopolitical control to intensify and extend the cultural and affective value of the Mars Hill brand while arousing and circulating fear, shame, and paranoia. Wives were trained to fear that if they were not demonstrating enough sexual "freedom" in the marital bedroom to please their inherently lustful husbands, they were inviting Satan to lie between them and implicitly to blame for any infidelity. In turn, this fear amplified paranoia concerning their husbands' faithfulness, especially with regard to the single women that they encountered in their everyday lives. Wives were shamed into feeling that if they did not have sex as and when their husbands wanted, they were not fulfilling their biblical roles as women.

Throughout *Princess*, Driscoll encouraged wives to be naked without shame in the marital bedroom while graphically depicting biblically ordained fantasies for global distribution. Although wives were relegated to domestic(ated) roles according to Mars Hill's complementarian gender doctrine, women were crucial to the production of biblical porn and played a critical role as producers themselves; their sexual freedom worked on behalf of not only their marriages but also the church. First, as they sexually pleased their husbands and fostered the channeling of their affective labor into the church; second, as they publicly confessed to sexual sins that were documented in audio and in writing for the purposes of distribution, commodifying their sins in order to market the church. While Driscoll reinstated women as the proper objects of the male gaze, he articulated this objectification of their "difference" as a matter of gender equality:

> Ladies, don't judge men for being men. Don't judge your husband for being a dude. God made men and women equal but different. Your husband was made first but that doesn't mean he was the beta version of a human being and that woman was the fully matured humanity. You live in a culture that encourages you, all of us, to sort of assume that women are superior to men but they're not—the culture pressures men to sympathize, to empathize, to relate, to connect with the feminine, and that's all well and good so long as it goes both ways. . . . Women should also try to understand all that makes men men, the visual nature of men, the sexual nature of men, the aggressive nature of men.[3]

Emphasis is placed on men's visual, sexual, and aggressive nature, while women's difference is performed through bodily labor that is at once sexualized and nurturing, both assertive and caring. Driscoll's preaching on biblical sexuality reinforced strict oppositional relationships between feminism and complementarianism as he concurrently pushed the boundaries of what was permissible to preach from the pulpit. Since the 1980s, evangelical leaders have coopted feminist antipornography rhetoric, suturing supposedly normal male sexuality to the obsessive viewing of porn and lustful aggression. For example, in his contribution to U.S. Attorney General Edwin Meese's Commission on Pornography Report in 1986, Focus on the Family's founder James Dobson reiterated Robin Morgan's quote "Pornography is the theory; rape is the practice" without citation.[4] Interpretations of the Song of Songs (or Song of Solomon) are also contested, with some biblical scholars maintaining that the man and woman who metaphorically describe one another's bodies and sex acts are unmarried.[5] In addition, Songs is often read sans sexualized content, as an allegorical poem that demonstrates God's love for His people. However, among a growing number of evangelical pastors, including Driscoll, this book of the Old Testament has been increasingly preached as a how-to guide for married Christians seeking to spice up their sex lives.[6] According to *Christianity Today*, the National Association of Evangelicals has endorsed the preaching of a sex-positive theology in order to encourage healthy, stable marriages.[7] While Driscoll endeavored to put the fun back into fundamentalism, his sermons resonated with evangelical sex manuals published since the 1970s that explicitly describe the spiritual benefits of sexual pleasure shared within Christian marriage.[8]

However, as Pastor Mark paradoxically preached an antiporn doctrine using salaciously sex-focused content for online distribution, he framed Mars Hill's biblical position as more liberal than most churches—a stance that led many Evangelicals not only to criticize but also to censor him. In 2009, after Driscoll's sermonizing on the topic of sex during the *Princess* series was widely publicized in *New York Times Magazine* and on ABC's *Nightline*, the evangelical Bott Radio Network interrupted its "Family Life" program and truncated the host's interview with him once founder Dick Bott learned that he was the guest. In the *Baptist Press*, Bott said that he made the decision because of Driscoll's penchant for using vulgarity: "He interpreted Song of Songs 2:3 as referring to oral sex and then said, 'Men, I am glad to report to you that oral sex is biblical. . . . Ladies, your husbands appreciate oral sex. They do. So, serve them, love them well. . . . We have a verse. "The fruit of her husband is sweet to her taste and she delights to be beneath him." ' "[9] Bott was also offended by an anecdote Driscoll told about a wife who said that she had won her unbelieving husband to Christ by performing oral sex on him.[10]

The subjects of gender and sexuality, and the roles of testimony and confession in evangelical politics and identity formation, have been mined in religious studies scholarship, including R. Marie Griffith's *God's Daughters* (1997), Betty A. DeBerg's *Ungodly Women* (2000), Tanya Erzen's *Straight to Jesus* (2006), Amy DeRogatis's *Saving Sex* (2014), and Seth Dowland's *Family Values and the Rise of the Christian Right* (2015). While each author takes a different approach, those examinations more directly grounded in ethnographic evidence—such as Griffith's *God's Daughters* or Erzen's *Straight to Jesus*—analyze the act of confession as a performance of religious transformation and self-empowerment that fosters a sense of belonging and community. Erzen writes, "The ex-gay movement has fused a culture of self-help, with its emphasis on personal transformation and self-betterment, to evangelical Christianity, with its precepts of conversion and personal testimony, to build a global para-church movement."[11] In her study, public testimony among the men of New Hope ministry is a form of therapy that affords individuals a safe space in which to focus on experiences of pain and trauma such that transformation and healing can occur. Thus, "as a narrative strategy, these confessions are proof of religious and sexual conversion and grant the testifier power as a witness to non-Christians or those living in sin," as they "become a form of evangelism that is necessary to self-healing and to the wider dissemination of the ex-gay movement . . . function[ing] as evidence that change is possible through a relationship with Jesus."[12] In this mode, the practice of public confession to sexual sin, abuse, and other aspects of the men's private lives is linked to self-help steps and therapeutic group activities, as well as to biblical counseling, prayer, and behavioral correction based on religious proscriptions against homosexuality that are monitored and disciplined through participation in the community.

These activities and motives align with Foucault's notion of governmentality and a "participatory panopticon" through which public confession ideally functions to reinforce self-surveillance and correction, discursively constituting subjects through practices of self-care that inspire personal transformation which serves a broader political strategy.[13] However, there are distinctions to be made between the practice of public confession and its personal, religious, and political effects as described by Erzen and the methodology used at Mars Hill, the most critical being the production, mediation, and dissemination of public confessions through interactive digital technologies.

PROMOTING BIBLICAL "FREE SEX"

Pastor A. J. Hamilton blogged about the creative team's approach to the branding of *The Peasant Princess*.

> We knew that Pastor Mark would be preaching through the Song of Songs well in advance of the September launch date, but the direction he would take and the best way to support the sermon visually and conceptually were not as clear as we would have liked. Going into the time of the greatest growth potential for a church (the fall), we wanted to make sure we took full advantage of college kids starting school and summer vacations ending. Knowing that Song of Songs would be a "drawing" sermon we first began working on a sermon series branding that centered on the concept of "Free Sex." We went with this title and began working on visual concepts for about three weeks before we found out the name was changed to "Free Love" to try and tone down the in-your-face title we previously had. . . . The idea was Vegas 2050 meets Disney meets Mars Hill.[14]

To bring this "free love" theme to life, Mars Hill's production staff created an animated video introduction for the *Princess* series. The film's visuals mimicked Disney's doe-eyed characters and bright technocolors while updating this template so that its color scheme reflected the techno-infused electronic keyboards pulsating in the background—a catchy, bubble-gum pop vibe with a pronounced bass beat that encouraged head bobbing. Green and yellow birds cavorted with a pink deer bounding across a bright meadow where a chesty, grinning apple tree with well-defined pectoral muscles gyrated to the music. The video invited viewers to participate in its pastoral, family-friendly scene, offering a setting that was playfully coy. Frolicking fawns winked at the audience, signifying biblical sex as pure, lighthearted fun. The flirtatious deer were inspired by biblical imagery that, according to Pastor Mark, signified breasts—"The petting zoo is now open," he exclaimed in week 7 of the series—while the well-endowed apple tree was a metaphorical stand-in for oral sex. The illustrated characters of this animated short conjured visions of Disney characters, as Pastor Mark and his congregants fueled fantasies of Vegas 2050.

Driscoll preached in front of a glowing cross as a background screen of large tube light bulbs in neon blue, green, red, orange, and yellow oscillated like a Rorschach Lite-Brite. This LED wall, loaned by a Mars Hill member, functioned like a giant computer monitor through which images could be sent to its "brain," then filtered to individual LEDs roughly 6,500 in number.[15] The cross, pulpit, and TV frame set pieces were handmade and wired by a deacon and his wife, with each capable of displaying over 200,000 different colors.[16] As Pastor Mark sermonized, the flashing hues served to highlight the tenor of his voice and tone of his message, which hewed closer to the original theme of "free sex" than to "free love." The focus on how to embody biblical sexuality for the health of marriages as well as the church afforded the perfect platform through which to encourage congregants to openly confess and regularly repent of their sexual sin for the sake of Mars Hill's security and legacy.

In addition to its ambitious and vibrant presentation onstage, *The Peasant Princess* was a Mars Hill milestone in other ways. First, the series was video-streamed via satellite from the facility Pastor Mark typically preached live in the Seattle neighborhood of Ballard to seven of its facilities (all but one of its regional locations at that time). Rather than showing the "virtual" sermons on a one-week time delay, this afforded the opportunity to synch live and remote services such that congregants across the church's campuses could text questions in real time during question-and-answer sessions. This strategy simulated connectivity and suggested authenticity to those participating as viewers.[17]

Second, Driscoll's wife Grace joined him onstage for the first time during services. Her participation doctrinally challenged the complementarian understanding that no woman could preach from the pulpit or hold a pastoral position. However, Driscoll attributed Grace's presence onstage to his need for a female perspective, particularly with regard to queries asked by women. He also figured Grace's public counsel as biblically justified considering a husband and wife narrate the Song of Songs. As the couple sat on a couch that was rolled out after sermons, a flat screen TV projected congregants' inquiries. Once they had eliminated "stump the pastor" or off-topic hypotheticals, the production team was "left with very real, candid questions that an open microphone set-up would discourage."[18] However, Pastor Hamilton admits, "There is a false anonymity that Text Message Q&A provides. I say 'false' because each message includes the sender's number (allowing pastoral follow-up via phone), yet the ability to send a question up to the pulpit without self-identifying encourages a brazenness that makes answering 160 character questions exciting and most helpful."[19]

After sermons, queries materialized like sound-bite confessions to sexual fantasies and transgressions on screens throughout the sanctuary, confronting congregants with evidence of their sinful lusting while providing empirical proof of Pastor Mark's admonishments concerning their utter depravity. In effect, these inquiries manifested a pornographic imaginary that collectively and simultaneously figured congregants as both enslaved by, and witnesses to, sin. As they testified to the spiritual truth of Driscoll's sexualized hermeneutic, members were constituted as both subjects and objects of shame and desire through a titillating technology of surveillance. This evangelical genre of social pornography refashioned the act of confession from an institutionally endorsed mode of individual expression that publicly reveals secret sin for purposes of personal transformation into the gendered and collective affective labor of a participatory panopticon.[20]

The church's innovative use of interactive technology cultivated what Gilles Deleuze calls a "society of control," whereby power is flexible, coded, and spread out from the institutional spaces administering discipline upon individual bodies to normalize populations. In the words of digital culture and media scholar Wendy Hui Kyong Chun, "Whereas disciplinary society relied on independent variables or modes, control society thrives on inseparable variations and modulations. . . . Digital language makes control systems invisible: we no longer experience the visible yet unverifiable gaze but a network of nonvisualizable digital control."[21] In the shift from discipline to control, Chun adds, "freedom exceeds the subject. . . . Freedom differs from liberty as control differs from discipline. Liberty, like discipline, is linked to institutions and political parties, whether liberal or libertarian; freedom is not. Although freedom can work for or against institutions, it is not bound to them—it travels through unofficial networks. . . . In an odd extension of commodity fetishism, we now wish to be as free as our commodities: by freeing markets, we free ourselves."[22] In the digital networking of public confessions to sexual sins and desires, material and immaterial labor become conjoined as wives' collective sexual freedom is encouraged to market Mars Hill's "liberal" brand on the global "free" market. Through these convergences of freedom and control, women's bodies are not simply disciplined—they are trafficked. A pornographic imaginary is animated such that immaterial sex becomes an instrument of biopolitical control—embodiments of biblical sexuality *move*—exceeding disciplinary forms of self-monitoring. Chun notes, "The relationship between control and freedom in terms of fiber-optic networks is often experienced as sexuality or is mapped in terms of sexuality-paranoia."[23] By using such techniques of screening and networking to proliferate and promote its version of biblical porn as an ordained commodity, Mars Hill inspired and amplified paranoia in congregants' everyday lives, particularly among wives.

The blogger UNReformed, a former congregant from a location outside of Seattle, wrote,

> [My wife] started listening to the "Peasant Princess" series and over the course of listening to it started showing some disturbing signs of paranoia. Driscoll tells women that sex is critical to a happy marriage and unless they "put out" they are allowing Satan to sleep between them and their husbands. He directs women to pleasure their men orally, pleasure them daily and be submissive to their needs. My wife became insecure and fearful. She began having dreams about me cheating on her and began quietly checking up on me out of fear. It was as though she was worried about meeting Driscoll's expectation for her in our marriage more than my own.[24]

Mars Hill wives were convicted of their duty to embody "free sex" in order to combat demons and maintain fidelity within marriage. When they could not know whether or not their enactments of this imperative lived up to expectations, or did not feel like fulfilling their husbands' every sexual need, fear, shame and paranoia intensified. This dynamic demonstrates how biblical porn, much like its mainstream counterpart, is both slippery and sticky; its political value does not simply reside in the ideologies and norms it reconstitutes. Instead, by exciting and eliciting myriad forms of affective labor, biblical porn materialized Satan in the domestic space of the home. Wendy Chun writes, "The relation between technology and desire is highly mediated and slightly paranoid, peoples' desires too are generated by the system. . . . Control and freedom are not opposites but different sides of the same coin: just as discipline served as a grid on which liberty was established, control is the matrix that enables freedom its openness."[25] In this sense, the various technologies employed to foster "free sex" were not merely instruments, but agents themselves—bodies that inspire, enlist, and exploit gendered yet collective affective labor in the cultural production of a pornographic imaginary that is mobile, autonomous, and infectious. The way that "technical media transmits and processes 'culture,'" to borrow from the scholar of media and design Jussi Parikka, is "new materialism" in action.[26] He writes, "The basis for signal-processing, use of electronic-magnetic fields for communication, and the various non-human temporalities of vibrations and rhythmics . . . computing and networks—are based in non-solids."[27] In a version of "old materialism," a revivalist of the Second Great Awakening in the late nineteenth century, Charles Grandison Finney, used "New Measures" in evangelistic meetings that encouraged emotion and the participation of women, including the "anxious bench"—a seat at the front of the church that singled out potential converts who felt an urgency with regard to their salvation. These innovations led some ministers to call such meetings "promiscuous assemblies." In leading his own version of revival in the twenty-first century, Driscoll used and encouraged the employ of digital technologies. This social media enlisted women to contribute to the affective labor of biblical porn, marketing sin, circulating paranoia, and networking conviction as surplus affective value. A women's ministry leader at Mars Hill shared with me that during a women's retreat, the question of whether their rooms were bugged by church leadership was raised as they were getting ready to sleep.

EMBODIMENTS OF SEXUAL ENSLAVEMENT AND FREEDOM

In the first sermon of the *Princess* series, entitled "Let Him Kiss Me," Driscoll assaulted his audience with statistics on the sexual experiences of young men and women compiled by a sociology professor. In particular, he highlighted troubling figures concerning the consumption of pornography. According to his data, the porn industry generates $60 billion a year on the global market, $12 billion of which is spent by U.S. citizens. Driscoll continues to relay numbers that are intended to provoke outrage and fear, especially over the accessibility of pornography online: over 200 porn films are made in the United States every week; porn sites are 12 percent of all Internet sites; porn is 25 percent of all search-engine requests; over 40 percent of Internet users view porn; 20 percent of men admit to accessing porn at work; 13 percent of women admit to accessing porn at work; every second, $3,000 is spent on porn in America; 28,000 Internet users are viewing porn every second in America; every second, 372 Internet users in America are typing words looking for more porn; 90 percent of children between the ages of 8 and 16 have viewed porn online; the average child sees porn online for the first time at age 11; the number-one consumer of pornography is boys ages 12 to 17; and 10 percent of American adults admit to being addicted to Internet porn.[28] Such statistics served to validate paranoia concerning the rampant, compulsive viewing of online pornography, figuring its accessibility as a threat to productivity in the workplace and stability in the home. By converging salacious antiporn sermonizing with the use of interactive media technologies to publicly elicit and globally disseminate congregants' confessions to sexual sin, Mars Hill capitalized on the ways in which Internet porn has inspired depictions of electronic interchanges in and of themselves as contagious and exposed.[29]

Driscoll's teaching on biblical masculinity is shaped by a cultural milieu preoccupied by a "masculinity crisis" that has spurred industries of self-help books, *Jackass* showmen, and prescription drugs. At the time of Mars Hill's beginnings in the basement of Driscoll's Seattle home, the marketing of Viagra was pivotal in proliferating discourses on penile performance anxiety. As unemployment figures rose due to industrial outsourcing, men were encouraged to take command in the bedroom by assuaging their erections and flexing phallic power.[30] Marketing techniques and medical surveillance exerted biotechnological control over men's bodies, while the prowess of the male sexual subject became a matter of primary national concern.[31] Concurrently, porn viewership grew increasingly gender balanced and the market more varied in its depictions of sexual pleasure, as innovations in visual and new media afforded more home-entertainment options.[32] The "spending penis" of the "money shot," which had embodied "all the principles of late capitalism's pleasure-oriented consumer society: pleasure figured as an orgasm of spending," gave way to a recognition of sexual differences—a movement "from the economy of the [phallic] one to the many."[33] It was the diversification of pornographic representation, performers, and markets that Driscoll was combating by pornifying the pulpit.[34] Once male sexuality was directed into wedded bliss, sexually liberated wives could secure Mars Hill's most valued asset: entrepreneurial men who volunteered their technological skills and leadership abilities in support of the church's virtual and physical expansion. Through Pastor Mark's sexualized exegesis, the dominant phallic economy of one was socially redeemed and bodily rechanneled into evangelistic conviction, passion and pursuits that inspired the circulation of globally directed, affective political value in support of Mars Hill's empire.

Driscoll points out that sinful pornographic viewing is an issue for both men and women, but in his narrative its causes and effects differ according to gender: men are solely consumers and called "addicts" and "abusers," whereas women are "performers" and "prostitutes" oppressed by the industry.[35] He then segues into the next section of his sermon by stating that roughly one-third of the women at Mars Hill have been sexually abused. While lamenting this statistic, Pastor Mark insists that it is critical for female victims to seek biblical counseling in order to "have a fresh perspective on sex"; he also emphasizes that sex is a godly gift to be enjoyed beyond the strictures of procreation: "If it's in marriage, praise God. Have lots of pleasure. God made our bodies for pleasure."[36] While Driscoll posited porn as a source of misogyny and its industry inevitably exploitive of women, he reframed polarizing debates between antiporn and sex-positive feminists structured by an oppression/liberation binary.[37] In effect, he circumvented such dichotomies by preaching a mutually constitutive antiporn–sex positive doctrine. Sexually abused women were taught to seek biblical counseling so as to perform their blessed role as sexually available wives, offering spiritual salvation to their husbands by embodying the fantasy that sex within Christian marriage is always free and pleasurable. Driscoll succinctly summarized how crucial this "women's work" was to the future of Mars Hill's empiric mission in a statement to a room full of men aspiring to found churches affiliated with the global church planting network Acts 29. Those who attended an Acts 29 boot camp in 2007 were told that the church planter's wife has the "most important job" in a new church—"having sex with the church planter."[38]

While admonishing wives to be naked without shame for the sake of their visually lustful husbands, Driscoll railed against premarital sex and Internet porn in language that was suggestive and gloating. For example, during a sermon given on Songs 8:1–7, Driscoll repeated the biblical line spoken by Solomon's wife, "I would give you spiced wine to drink, the juice of my pomegranate," and then sarcastically remarked to his audience, "Say, where's the pomegranate? Ah, you'll get married and find it."[39] His exegesis exposed female body parts cloaked in biblical metaphor as he taunted single men with the promise and lure of locating sexual gratification within and through Christian marriage. Not only did video clips of Driscoll's frequent sermons on sexuality receive hundreds of thousands of hits on the church's website, but they also popped up in porn searches on YouTube under such titles as "Biblical Oral Sex." Additionally, while anonymously texting questions during services, congregants confessed to sexual sins and fantasies that were recorded for online distribution in "greatest hits" collections, signaling Mars Hill's entry into the business of producing its own brand of pornography as popular culture without advertising it as such.

PORN AGAIN CHRISTIAN

In addition to hosting boot camps that trained men to become masculine leaders on a spiritual battlefield, the church directly ministered to military personnel by collecting donations to ship resources to (male) soldiers around the world. One elder wrote on the *Military Mission* blog: "As a chaplain and pastor to the military community, by far the worst and most common issue I deal with is pornography. . . . One of the first and primary ways we reach into the dark world of porn and military life is through two books we send in our initial 'Troop Pack.'"[40] These materials emphasized the need for men to put down porn and take up arms for the sake of spiritual redemption and domestic security, including Driscoll's book *Porn Again Christian* (2008). First advertised as a free e-book, *Porn Again* discusses how "the act of lusting after the unclothed body of a woman is not a sin. The issue is which woman's unclothed body you are lusting after."[41] In this text still available online,[42] Driscoll assures his readers that any position is permissible between a husband and wife, punctuating his point by describing a variety of sex acts in vigorous detail.[43] While advantageously depicting Mars Hill's biblical stance on sexuality in vivid terms, Driscoll mobilizes the church's motto that sex between a husband and wife should be "free and frequent."[44]

Porn Again was initially a pamphlet, *Reforming Male Sexuality*, available at no cost in the church lobby; I picked up a copy within my first few visits to Mars Hill. The title shift, electronic format, and participatory framing of *Porn Again* mimics the appeal of an "amateur" porn site like YouPorn, whereby free and open access to seemingly authentic performances by "real people" obscures processes of mediation that proscribe desirable fantasies.[45] The reader of *Porn Again* cannot be certain whether the questions posed in it were actually asked of Driscoll by congregants or if consent was given to use such material: "I will share with you some questions that I have personally received in my pastoral counseling and the answers I have given. Some of the questions may seem too frank for many readers, but I am honored that the people in our church feel free to bring any personal question to their pastors because we would not want them to go anywhere else for answers."[46]

The question-and-answer format in this electronic publication and its depiction of free and open discussion are tactics of population control. Rather than the Internet, which in and of itself is presented by him as pornographic, Driscoll encourages Mars Hill congregants to go searching for answers pertaining to sex from church leadership. Concurrently, a virtual question-and-answer format employed for evangelistic purpose becomes a biblical twist on a new technology of sex that "requires the social body as a whole, and virtually all its individuals, to place themselves under surveillance."[47] Driscoll calibrates the doctrinal imperative for women to submit to male authorities at home and in church so that it affectively aligns with popular culture and everyday habits, such as the submission to surveillance normalized by reality television and social media. As Driscoll shares his "frank" responses to inquiries asked during pastoral counseling sessions, he confounds felt distinctions between public and private, control and freedom. By transforming confession into a process of discursive and digital openness, Driscoll redeems the pornographic imaginary conjured and networked via his e-book through "biblical" yet sexualized discourse.

For example, in the question-and-answer section entitled "Practical and Theological Reasons to Masturbate," a congregant describes a scenario in which his wife slips nude photos of herself into his briefcase so that while he is away on a business trip he can call her for phone sex and stare at her image as they mutually masturbate. The husband asks Driscoll whether this kind of erotic image, which helps to reduce temptations while he is on the road, is permissible. Driscoll replies that images of one's wife are "redeemed" and that the man need not worry but should instead "thank God for the freedom your wife enjoys with you."[48] This sense of freedom, especially as performed by wives while sexually pleasing their husbands, recurs throughout Driscoll's counsel. When asked, "Is it ok for my wife and I to masturbate ourselves if we are together and both turned on by it?," he responds in the affirmative, adding:

> Some couples have cited a number of reasons why this may be helpful. One husband and his wife do not have intercourse during her menstrual cycle and so she cares for him during that time with masturbation. Upon occasion, though, she cannot bring him to climax and so he will do so while fondling her breasts so that the two of them are still participating. Some people report that their spouse simply has no idea how to stimulate their genitals and so they stimulate their own genitals in front of their spouse to teach them what they enjoy so that their spouse could then satisfy them. Some spouses also report that during heavy petting and/or deep massage they prefer to stimulate their own genitals while their spouse stimulates other erotic zones and enjoy watching their spouse simultaneously enjoy sexual stimuli from many places on the body.[49]

With regard to having "sex according to the Bible," Driscoll assures his readers that they should not be too anxious, because "the Bible is, quite frankly, more liberated on the matter of sex than most Bible teachers."[50] He claims that in the Song of Songs many acts normally considered taboo by fundamentalists are not only condoned but encouraged, including a sexually aggressive wife, a wife who likes to perform fellatio, mutual masturbation, a wife who enjoys cunnilingus, a wife who performs a strip tease, erotic conversation, and "ongoing variety and creativity that includes new places and new positions such as making love outdoors during a warm spring day."[51]

As Mars Hill utilized interactive technologies and social networks to inspire audience participation in the production of biblical porn, practices of confession and surveillance commonly associated with self-empowerment and self-governance were transformed to capitalize on the information market. Mars Hill was an innovative leader among a group of theologically conservative yet technologically savvy churches whose pastors continue to promote their brand names through publicity stunts and sermon series that highlight a sex-positive doctrine within the confines of heterosexual Christian marriage.[52] As Driscoll criticized an evangelical establishment out of touch with popular culture to its own detriment, Mars Hill's generation and dissemination of biblical porn concurrently functioned as a proselytizing and marketing tool that circulated paranoia under auspices of sexual freedom that amplified biopolitical control.

PARANOIA AS AFFECTIVE FORCE OF HABIT

In the aftermath of the contentious blog post in which Driscoll ostensibly blamed pastors' wives for their husbands' infidelities, public discourse and interventions pertaining to women's sexuality proliferated at Mars Hill as workshops and counseling on female sexual sin visibly increased at the church.[53] For example, a workshop called "Maturity in Singleness," taught by and for women, offered strategies for retaining biblical purity before marriage. During a day-long seminar entitled "Redeeming Female Sexuality" women testified to sexual sins past and present, including same-sex attraction, promiscuity, and the denial of sex within marriage. A blog named *Reforming Femininity* appeared on Mars Hill's website as a forum for women to discuss a variety of issues, including sexual abuse and shame. Alongside a pronounced increase in the number of opportunities offered by the church for women to publicly confess to sexual sin, congregants called on one another to openly acknowledge various "feminine sins" for the salvation of the church. My experience with how this dynamic played out on the ground cannot be summarized by the content of the gender and sexuality workshops I attended, or by the conversations I had with the women I met at such events about their husbands, children, and jobs they held after marriage. Rather, it was something that I repeatedly noticed people noticing about me but which remained unspoken.

Soon after I began attending Mars Hill, it became readily apparent that my singleness mattered. I do not recall ever being asked if I was single, but it was a term often used within Mars Hill parlance, particularly when the topic concerned sexual sin—abstinence workshops on maintaining "maturity within singleness" were specifically and only designed for women. My singleness was not an aberration, and it did not classify me as an outsider in the same way that my status as a non-Christian did. The first couple of questions asked of me in the briefest of encounters were whether or not I was a Christian and how long I had been attending Mars Hill, but I was never directly asked whether I was single. Instead, it was the lack of a wedding band that branded me. I came to expect furtive downward glances to my ring finger regardless of whether I was talking with a man or woman. In a distinct manner I had never felt before, my (lack of) marital status ritually provoked an acute dis-ease.

Despite Driscoll's sermonizing on the joys of sexual freedom, sexual sin was a subject that inspired intense feelings of shame:

> Before [attending "Redeeming Female Sexuality"], there was no way that I would have said anything about sexual sin. It's so freaking uncomfortable, awkward, shameful, and gross to talk about, or even think about. Women of God, if you struggle with sexual sin, you are not alone. If you feel like you have to keep it all a secret to save face, you are not alone. If you feel like you have to deal with it yourself, you are not alone. If you have shame from your past sexual sin, you're not alone. Chances are you know more about sex and sexual practices than some of your mothers know. But something a lot of us don't know is to what extent other women share our own sexual struggles.[54]

This contributor to *Reforming Femininity* discusses sexual sin in a manner that suggests public confession is the proper, necessary response to a church-wide epidemic of suffering. Her plea that the women of Mars Hill acknowledge and share their sexual struggles with each other in order to realize that they are not alone resonates with "the traditional formula of Christian confession, [wherein] concealed sins and sicknesses must be confessed and repented, then let go."[55] In her ethnographic study of the Women's Aglow Fellowship, Marie Griffith emphasizes the transformative, healing power of public prayer. Through confessional narratives "filled with pain," Aglow women revealed secret sin and released themselves from hidden shame, which was "seen as working to thwart self-disclosure and to encourage denial of one's 'true state.'"[56] During the women's training day I attended in January 2007, "Christian Womanhood in a Feminist Culture," I also listened to confessional narratives filled with pain during which the speakers, many of them pastors' wives, began to sob as their issues with sin were revealed. However, based on conversations with several women at that event and in the intervening years since, I would not describe the outpouring of emotion I witnessed personal catharsis with the aim of self-realization, but rather as affective labor provided for the church.

Soon after my arrival at the training, I spoke with a pregnant woman in her midtwenties who shared that she began attending Mars Hill four years prior, after meeting her husband, who was already a member. During our conversation, she asked which "break-out" sessions I had signed up for; the first half of the day, we would all attend the same lectures as a group (roughly 400 women were in attendance for this free event open to nonmembers), but while registering online we were asked to choose two of four "break out" afternoon sessions that addressed specific sin issues. We could choose from "romanticism" (which entailed a sexually charged fantasy life inspired by the reading of too many romance novels and the viewing of too many Hollywood "chick flicks"); "gluttony"; "modesty"; and, "sexual sin." As we compared notes on our choices, my companion said that she did not struggle with "romanticism" or "sexual sin" but wanted to ensure that "gluttony" and "modesty" would not become problems postmarriage. She then mentioned a book she read for a Mars Hill class in which the author explained that, as she described it, "if you are out at a restaurant and your husband sees a beautiful woman, the waitress for example, even if they don't flirt or anything, he will remember her." My companion then glanced down, spied my naked ring finger, and said quietly, "Of course, I don't like thinking that way." I found myself blushing for no reason. Of the eight women I shared lunch with I was the only "single," and the only one attending the "romanticism" and "sexual sin" sessions.

In contrast to my lunchtime companions, every woman I spoke with in the "physical and spiritual adultery" session (there was a last minute change in the title) was single. The room was packed and within moments of sharing her testimony the speaker, an elder's wife, was sobbing. She cried throughout her confession to sexual sins premarriage—teenage transgressions traced back to sexual abuse suffered as a child that she had never confronted, or even recounted, until she sought biblical counseling for another seemingly unrelated issue. She also testified to experiencing physical, mental and emotional exhaustion from taking on too much work in service to the church. This compulsion to always be available to help others, she confessed, was due to the feeling that it was the only way she could finally feel worthy of being loved, especially by God. I listened as she repeatedly described herself as a "whore," both sexually and spiritually, and sensed the entire room crying. At times, the collective weeping was so overwhelming that it was difficult to hear the speaker, even though she used a microphone and I was sitting in the center of the room.

When I rejoined my lunchtime companions for the closing large group session in the sanctuary, they immediately asked in excited but hushed tones about what I had witnessed. In the few minutes it took me to find them, the emotionally raw testimony of the sexual sin session had become a buzz topic. When one of the women remarked that she was looking forward to listening to the adultery session after the audio recordings were uploaded to the Mars Hill website, I told her that I doubted what I had just heard would be publicly shared online. It was too personal, I said. My companion did not reply but simply looked at me, gently smiling. As we settled into our seats for a final prayer, it was announced that audio recordings of all the sessions would be accessible via Mars Hill's media library within a few weeks. I later discovered that the sessions were not only available as audio downloads through the church's website but also the iTunes podcast *Mars Hill Church: Everything Audio*, which included the full names of each speaker. Even as they were being taught to trust in God's grace and sovereignty, women were called on by the church and each other to habitually and publicly confess to sexual shame in the unending process of seeking repentance, challenging the misconception that they were not "equal" to men insofar as their capacity to sexually sin was concerned. By "freely" offering their sexual transgressions and sexualized bodies as signs and commodities through which to discursively and digitally promote and animate biblical porn as a social imaginary and biopolitical instrument, women's voluntary labor contributed to its viral and visceral capacity to globally network affective political and economic value.

While same-sex attraction, fornication, and lust were all sexual sins women testified to at Mars Hill, it was the withholding of sex by wives from their husbands that was most often highlighted. In a post entitled, "Not Tonight Honey, I Have a Headache," one contributor to *Reforming Femininity* wrote:

Scripture clearly states that men and women who are married are to have sex, and have it regularly (Gen. 1:28, 1 Cor. 7:5). We are not to deprive one another, and what's more, [men's and women's] bodies belong to our spouses. . . . Scripture does not command us as wives to desire our husbands sexually at all times. It is *not a sin* for a woman to lack sexual desire for her husband. The point at which it becomes a sin is when a wife is unwilling to give her husband access to her sexually. This can lead to many problems including bitterness, resentment, sexual temptation and frustration and a lack of confidence in the husband. . . . Make sex a priority, rearranging whatever is necessary in life until you have given it the proper place; remember, it's a priority in God's eyes and an entire book of the Bible is devoted to it! (Heb. 13:4) Here's the hardest part . . . *do not deny your husband* sexually.[57]

According to the doctrinal understanding articulated above, husbands and wives equally possess ownership of their spouses' bodies; but in terms of access to said bodies, wives are more prone to sexual sin than are their husbands. This anonymous contributor reiterates the biblical imperative preached by Driscoll that Christian wives prioritize sex in order to secure masculine leadership at home and in church. By performing sexual freedom in the marital bedroom, no matter what their actual sexual desires may be, wives not only make their husbands feel better about themselves but also support their fidelity in Christian marriage and service to the church. In this way, biblical porn functioned as a technology of surveillance through which women's affective labor and self-sacrifice became pornographically scrutinized for visible signs of freedom and pleasure.

BIBLICAL PORN AS A TECHNOLOGY OF SURVEILLANCE

The following discussion is excerpted from the sermon "My Dove," preached by Driscoll during week 6 of the *Princess* series.

We're all sinners. Now the question is, what do sinners do? Well, you're supposed to repent. That's the Christian's answer. Repent. All of a Christian's life is repentant. . . . I don't think most Christians even understand repentance. I believe it is widely misunderstood and it is widely ignored. Number one: it begins with conviction. Now some people misunderstand conviction as depression. . . . You are bad, did bad. So now you feel bad. That's conviction. It's a moral rudder, helps us figure out right from wrong. . . . So everyone has a conscience, and for the Christian, they also have the additional ministry of God and the Holy Spirit, who convicts us of sin. The next step is confession. Confession means you talk about it with others. Talk about it, talk about it. . . . Repentance truly begins in the mind. You think differently about sin and God and what you're doing and failing to do. You need a change of mind that comes through Scripture, and that includes Bible teaching, podcasts, lectures, community group, classes, Sunday services. . . . The beginning of repentance begins with a change of mind that leads to a change of heart. It's a change of heart that leads to a change of behavior: that's repentance.[58]

In speaking to the critical importance of conviction, confession, and repentance to Christian identity, Pastor Mark set the stage for the following week's sermon, "Dance of Mahanaim," during which he discussed the visual, aggressive, and sexual nature of men:

Men's minds involuntarily file snapshots of beautiful women, and their file is filled with images that stretch all the way back to boyhood, and show up without warning. Every time a guy sees a beautiful woman, it's a snapshot. Click. Click. Click. Click. Click. It starts when he's a little boy, and continues throughout his whole life. It's involuntary. It's how the man is made. The result is he has an ever-growing repository of pictures of beautiful women. . . . They show up, right, random shuffle, without his even being prepared or aware of it. If you're married, on your way home, ask your husband. He'll confirm it. He could be sitting in traffic, driving home from work, and all of a sudden, boop, there's the gal who sat next to him in junior high—hasn't seen her in a long time, but she's back. That file just came up. . . . Many women don't understand this, but your husbands, if you're married, are in a war every moment of every day, as images come to them or old images are archived for them, and they have to decide what to do with them.[59]

In response to this conundrum, Driscoll advised wives,

Be sympathetic to his temptations and talk openly to encourage and support him. . . . Be a visually generous wife so that he sees you as an ally on his team. . . . Lights on or off? On, right? Lot of guys: "On." Even guys who flunked out of school are going to pass this test, all right? Instead of fighting with him, fight for him, with lots of redeemed images. Let him see, and then, snapshot, snapshot, snapshot.[60]

In weeks 6 and 7 of *Princess* series, Driscoll linked the act of confession to a spiritual and worldly war in which men's visual nature affectively preconditions them to sexually sin. The barrage of images that assault men on a daily basis, archived and recalled on random shuffle, cultivates an unpredictable and uncontrollable proclivity to lust. According to Pastor Mark, wives must support their husbands by initiating open dialogue about these temptations, while ensuring that they have redeemed images to occupy their mind's eye. In effect, Driscoll primes the church's atmosphere with the felt reality of future threat in the form of feminine visual lures such that the Christian imperative to confess becomes a compulsion. This teaching was timely given that the question-and-answer sessions following sermons afforded congregants the opportunity to feel as though they could openly confess to sexual fantasies and sin in anonymity—a false promise given cell numbers were used by pastors to follow up on queries. In addition, Pastor Mark's "smokin' hot wife" (a phrase I often heard in reference to Grace) provided affective labor through both her feminine counsel and shape. A reverberation effect between the sermons and the questions that followed bolstered the legitimacy of Driscoll's spiritual authority and the authenticity of his exegesis. A pastor chose these queries behind the scenes, receiving them via email, logging them into a spreadsheet, then using software to synch them from a slide to the television onstage next to the Driscolls.[61] Thus, the questions that followed the "Dance of Mahanaim" sermon echoed its themes:

> DOWNTOWN: "What if my spouse cannot compare physically to the visual temptations of the world?"
> BALLARD: "What resources are available for men with low sex drive?"
> BELLEVUE: "Would it be sinful to videotape my wife and I being intimate?"
> BALLARD: "Should spouses confess to each other every time they sin visually or sexually?"

As these inquires demonstrate, Mars Hill's cultural production of biblical porn generated and exploited technologies of surveillance that fostered the desire to submit not only to Driscoll's spiritual authority, but also to the "work of being watched."[62] Congregants' affective labor during question-and-answer sessions was simultaneously voluntary and nonintentional; the use of cell phones and flat screens normalized and habituated the act of public confession while the service's content and performance mobilized a pornographic imaginary through which the biblical truth of Driscoll's hermeneutic and the sinful nature of his audience were affirmed. At Mars Hill, conviction and confession were processed as and through social media, not in the hope of individual healing or due to aspirations of self-empowerment, but to benefit the church's cultural influence and growing empire. Multimedia screening and digital technologies bolstered systems of monitoring that are panoptic, whereby the many are watched by the few, and synoptic, whereby the few are watched by the many—a relationship through which "surveillance [becomes] progressively more commonplace, unexceptional, and even desirable."[63] Mars Hill incorporated the seductive logics of social networks such as Facebook and cultural trends such as reality television to incite congregants' collective participation in the affective labor of visually, viscerally, and virtually embodying, networking, and simulating biblical porn.

Any visitor to the Mars Hill website was a few clicks away from "Christian Sex Q&A (Mature Content)," where a warning box announced that due to the overwhelming volume and explicit content of questions texted during the *Princess* series, the Driscolls would blog responses to certain queries. According to the MH-17 rating that appeared in a black box above these inquiries, anyone under seventeen was required to get adult permission before viewing them. Given that the church's target audience was young men who were (presumably) pornographically challenged, this play on the NC-17 film rating appeared to be a tantalizing teenage joke, rather than a serious attempt to warn readers. Under the MH-17 warning, the Driscolls blogged responses to questions such as "Can I perform anal sex on my wife?" with advice that encouraged further research online: "Do your homework, be careful if [your wife] is willing. . . . Anal sex is technically permissible, but for a host of reasons may not be beneficial. We do not endorse everything on this website, but if you want to read some commentary on the issue from Christian married women, you can go to *Christian Nymphos*."[64] Queries such as "My wife likes to masturbate me upon occasion and wants to know how to get better at it. What should she do?" or "Is it okay for me and my

wife to masturbate ourselves if we are together and both turned on by it?"
or "Is it okay for a spouse to masturbate himself or herself during the act of
lovemaking?" were also answered with candid encouragement: "Yes. The
combination [of masturbating during the act of lovemaking] may physically
heighten the degree of pleasure. For example, many wives cannot climax
from normal intercourse but can climax from stimulation of their clitoris,
which is not a point of contact during normal sexual intercourse. This can
be pleasurable for both spouses, considering that most men are visual and
this could be a display of visual generosity for him."[65]

In their responses, the Driscolls encouraged mutual masturbation as a
form of couple's therapy that encouraged those seeking their advice to reach
out and touch themselves through the church network. While flexing its
phallic power online, Mars Hill promised marital orgasms as explosive as
those procured with Viagra. Biblical porn was produced as a confessional
discourse and surveillance technology that concomitantly titillated and
monitored live and remote audiences who voluntarily subjected themselves
to invisible practices of scrutiny by plugging into the Mars Hill experience.
A holy combination of sexual tease, biblical counsel, and sex education, biblical porn proliferated as and through popular culture every time *porn* was
typed into a search engine. Thus, Driscoll's pornification of the pulpit was
achieved not simply through sexualized exegesis but entanglements of body
and technology that commodified biblical porn as a social pornography of
popular culture.

The inauguration of yet another church-affiliated website during the
Princess series further demonstrated how a desire for surveillance was cultivated at the church using innovations in media technology and tropes
of popular culture. This announcement read, "PastorMark.tv is Alive—er,
Live!"

> Pastor Mark is everywhere these days: Ireland, South Carolina, Haiti,
> Chicago. . . . Some of you dutifully track Mars Hill Church, Resurgence,
> Acts 29 channels and more to listen to his messages and read his essays—
> but that's gotten trickier recently as his content is published across more
> and more channels every year. So we gave him his own site: PastorMark.
> tv. This way, all you have to do is come to this one place to find all those
> teaching pieces. What's more, you'll also get posts from him where he'll

be speaking more personally about what's going on with him and his family.[66]

PastorMark.tv purported to offer a single portal to his teaching and an all-access pass to his ministry; as the church continued to grow, Driscoll increasingly lived in public. PastorMark.tv was concurrently "alive" and "live"—a broadcast animated by his "real time" presence in absence. Despite the megasized proportions of Mars Hill's multisite congregation, mobile communication fluency afforded the flexibility to accrue and assert affective and cultural capital through a variety of media channels. Emulating a multinational corporate enterprise, the church relied less on disciplinary models of governance than processes of screening and simulation that freed and amplified social control apart from territorial logics. As biblical porn excited and exploited digital practices of confession, it echoed and affirmed Driscoll's Calvinist-infused message that his audience was sinfully depraved and in need of frank biblical counsel on matters of sex, globally intensifying affect to political effect. Days after the week 6 sermon "My Dove," the "Mars Hill Press Room" proudly blogged:

> This week Mars Hill broke into the top three on iTunes for Religion and Spirituality downloads. What's especially encouraging is that this week's podcast was one of the hardest-hitting, straight gospel messages yet in the Peasant Princess series. Here's the sermon description that put us in the #3 spot [beneath Oprah.com's Spirit Channel and Joel Osteen's Audio Podcast]: You don't just feel bad . . . you are bad. Many of the problems come from within yourself, and you need to confess, repent, then seek restitution and reconciliation.[67]

During the women's training day, a group of us went out to lunch, driving to a nearby Baja Fresh. I was the only non-Christian and "single" in the group of eight. We located a large Formica table in the center of the cafeteria-like space, so we could all sit together after collecting our burritos on plastic trays and gathering napkins and sporks. I was the first to sit down and spiked my utensil into the flour tortilla to get in a few mouthfuls before my already lukewarm bean supreme turned cold. As soon as the cutlery perforated the skin of my meal, I stopped and stared at my food, trying to will away tiny bubbles of pinto juice and sour cream. As my companions sat, their chatter died down.

"Who wants to pray?"

I averted my eyes like an unprepared student. I always dreaded these moments in small group settings, waiting for the day that it would be my turn. For all the times that I had bowed my head, I still did not know this language. I knew my intoning of Jesus' name would sound like a put on. My heart was not in it. Also, I had never prayed in public before.

"I will," said the woman sitting across from me. As she prayed, I blushed and tried to quell the feeling that the entire room was staring. When she finished, I looked up and found her staring at me.

"Thank you," she said, looking directly into my eyes. I had no idea how to interpret this expression of gratitude and did not reply; another rush of crimson did all the talking.

On April 24, 2011, I attended a Mars Hill Easter service performed for the first and only time at Qwest Field, home to the football team the Seattle Seahawks. It struck me as ironic that I was attending a sermon center field, considering how many times I had heard Mark compare football to a religion. The same man who would proclaim that Christianity was not a religion but a lifestyle, and promised that his face would never adorn the side of a bus advertising Mars Hill, was standing onstage at the fifty-yard-line dressed in a dark suit and red tie. However, in 2007 when the church incorporated videology to win the "air war," Driscoll said that he longed "for the day that 50,000 people spill out of Safeco Field [where the Seattle Mariners play] for one church service."[1] In 2011, he would come close to having his prayers answered, although the heavens were against him.

The day was cold and rainy; hovering cloud cover cast a scene of late winter rather than early spring. The low gray sky spit large drops on those waiting in line and anyone unfortunate enough not to find seating beneath the stadium overhang. Dreary environs clashed with the canary yellow schematics of the service. A cloth scrim of sunbeams behind the stage cloyingly conjured warmth that could not be located in the chilly air or on a metal bench. I felt damp down to my bones. The choir encircled behind Driscoll wore color-coordinated robes of bright gold that matched the sunny background, whereas the large cross center stage mimicked the overcast climate and his charcoal suit. While Pastor Mark gestured emphatically to the large crowd before him and ignored the rows of empty seats behind, he made sure not to stray too far from his downstage blocking directly in front of the cross.

I knew the man preaching was Mark, but I did not recognize him from the days I had regularly attended Mars Hill Ballard. His haircut was military issue, and his neck bulged from a starched collar as he screamed at the crowd, periodically thumbing and thumping a Bible. I was unaccustomed to seeing him sport such formal attire on any occasion, even Easters past.

I never recalled seeing him in a tie. He received his biggest laugh while stating, "I will tell you this today, Mark Driscoll is a sinner. I have sinned in my past, I have sin in my present, and I have sin in my future that I have not yet gotten to, but I assure you that I will."[2] His sermon gained momentum as his hoarse voice broke, and he screwed up his face to scream in answer to the question that framed the day, "Who is Jesus?": "He *is* the dragon slayer, He *is* the sinless savior, He *is* the resurrection and the life." This husky refrain drew applause, whistles, and yelps from the audience, who egged him into pounding the Bible in his hand while intoning, "He *is* the Way, the Truth, the Life!"

After ramping up to this fiery decree, Pastor Mark wound down his sermon with an invitation to the crowd, "Friends, we are here today because we love you. We are here because Jesus loves you. We are here because *you* are in the path of the wrath of God. There is a hell, people are going there, and it lasts forever. And Jesus alone saves from sin. Jesus alone saves from death. Jesus alone saves from hell. Friends, *you* have a very important decision to make. . . . Will you give your life to Jesus? "Will you leave here as a Christian?" He continued, his voice rising: "The Bible says, repent and be baptized! *That* is what Jesus has sent me to invite you to, today!" As he prayed for the Holy Spirit to convict the lost, Pastor Mark raised his open hand to the crowd with eyes closed, blessing thousands and receiving raised arms worshipping in return. It appeared as he had professed and prophesized; Seattle was once but no longer the least churched city in America.

After this prayer, he invited those on the "baptism team" to "come on down," then exclaimed, "Friends, the reason that we baptize, is that Jesus lived, Jesus died, Jesus rose. Amen?" Amen was screamed from the crowd as the chorus behind Driscoll clapped and cheered. "When we are baptized, we are publicly professing trust in Jesus Christ. And so, if you would love to be baptized as a Christian, we would love to baptize you as a Christian. And these tubs that are set before me are not for a glorious hot tub party, they are for baptisms." People in Seahawk-green ponchos and carrying umbrellas descended from the rafters and gathered where several white tubs captured cold rainwater in front of the stage. Driscoll beckoned, directing people down the aisles from jumbo-sized flat screens. He reminded them that to be baptized is to be plunged, immersed, and brought forth from waters, reenacting the death, burial, and resurrection of Jesus for their sins. These "spontaneous" baptisms may not have been planned on by audience members, but the church was prepared to serve them, providing sweatpants, T-shirts, and changing rooms so that they did not have to get dunked in their Easter best. As hundreds waited for a chance to be submerged and transformed under a banner proclaiming "It's All About Jesus," the worship band rocked out to "Nothing but the Blood of Jesus," and a custom-made Jesus flag flew over Qwest Field, staking a claim to the city and announcing the event a success. The church later boasted that Mars Hill Easter 2011 was the largest service ever held in the Pacific Northwest; there were over 17,500 people in attendance and exactly 682 baptisms that day.[3]

I decided to walk home. It was all uphill and still wet out, but I needed to stretch my legs after shivering on the bleachers. I hoped the rain and distance would wash away an acute sense of shame that dogged me. In writing on psychologist Silvan Tomkins's analysis of shame, affect theorists Eve Kosofsky Sedgwick and Adam Frank note, "Tomkins considers shame, along with interest, surprise, 'joy, anger, fear, distress, disgust,' and, in his later writings, contempt ('dissmell'), to be the basic set of affects."[4] They further argue that Tomkins places shame at one end of what they describe as an "affect polarity" of "shame-interest," which suggests that "pulsations of cathexis around shame" enable and intensify affective entanglements.[5] The rush of shame that drove me to climb city streets with hunched shoulders and averted eyes sans umbrella was propelled by a desire to reduce further self-exposure. Sitting in Qwest Field looking down at an assembly line of baptismal tubs was disturbing.

I had witnessed a baptism during the first service I attended at Mars Hill; I knew how important they were as a public ritual for the congregation. For years, church leaders had baptized people in Seattle parks such as Gasworks and Golden Gardens, making a politically visible and spiritually indelible mark on the city's secular landscape. However, by 2011 baptisms had clearly become one of the church's key marketing tools; the assembly line of tubs at Easter was merely one manifestation. Mars Hill's digital presence was and remains irreducible to Driscoll's sermons; the preponderance of MTV-worthy baptism videos on YouTube traces how this sacrament achieved megasized production value.

One twenty-eight-minute baptism sequence from January 2011 opens with a black screen and "Jesus Paid It All" in bold white letters, the title of the video's soundtrack.[6] A snare drum and high-hat darkly illuminated in blue light set a tight $4/4$ beat, pounding and crashing before a woman's voice begins to sing lyrics that appear in white onscreen: "I hear the Savior say, Your strength indeed is small; Child of weakness, watch and pray, Find in Me your all in all." As plaintive electric guitar chords cry out in rhythm with the drums, the view shifts to three men holding hands with heads bowed, the one in the center wearing a black shirt embossed with "I Got Dunked" in white. The men talk in hushed tones on the dark stage, their faces close together and expressions difficult to read. To the refrain "Jesus paid it all" a spotlight suddenly shines on the man supported by those on either side, who cradle his head, neck, and shoulders as he falls back and fully submerges into the water of the black tub that all three share. After a brief moment underwater, he leaps up to the sound of whistles and claps from an invisible audience, hugs one of the smiling, tattooed men who held him, turns and briefly hugs the other, then steps out of the tub so the next in line can take his place. The songs change over the course of nearly thirty minutes, but the recurring pulse of drums, singing, and dunking is imitated, while the spotlight repeatedly shines onstage each time a different person is submerged. Many of the videos are set at specific Mars Hill facilities, frequently on Easter, and some have thousands of views.

One of the most popular baptism videos, with over 22,000 views as of 2017,[7] is set during Easter 2012 at the U-district location (shorthand for the neighborhood known as the University District), which reflected the church's proximity to the University of Washington campus in Seattle.[8] This video opens with the popular Mars Hill worship band Citizen performing, the drummer pounding toms with thick, heavy sticks, and the lead vocalist singing "Hallelujah." This scene shifts to follow a young family walking through the church doors, then switches back and forth from shots of the band and college-aged congregants earnestly talking with heads bowed in small groups, then smiling and laughing in line to get baptized. This baptismal pool is larger than the typical tubs, has steps and is set in the floor; its light blue cast, calm water, and rectangular shape mimics that of a custom made hot tub. The black shirts of those getting dunked read "Death, Burial" on top and "Resurrection" in bold letters below. As the singers onstage scream

"Hallelujah!" a person gets submerged in slow motion, rising from the pool with water cascading from her face, mouth wide in a cry of praise with arms raised and fists pumping. Dunking heads and grinning faces flash over and over to the uplifting soundtrack—an orgy of plural joy in the repetition of becoming.

In writing on Nietzsche's concept of eternal return, Gilles Deleuze notes that it does not imply a return of the identical or same, but rather a becoming, an affirmation in the power of "the repetition of difference."[9] In this sense, "it is not being that returns but rather returning itself is the one thing which is affirmed of diversity or multiplicity."[10] Thus, he concludes, "this is why the eternal return must be thought of as a synthesis, a synthesis of time and its dimensions, a synthesis of diversity and its reproduction, a synthesis of becoming and the being which is affirmed in becoming."[11] Deleuze considers Spinoza's theory of the body and its capacity for being affected in terms of force, noting that this power is "actualized at every moment by the bodies to which a given body is related," which is similar for Nietzsche insofar as he is concerned with "a feeling of power"—affectivity, sensibility, and sensation.[12] Thus, "all sensibility is only a becoming of forces," an "eternal joy becoming" that "includes even joy in the destroying."[13] In the slick baptism videos produced by Mars Hill, transformation is not only affectively visible; it is affectively recurring. Resurrection is not a one-time deal, but a perpetually becoming born again.

In writing on contagion theory in the age of networks, Tony Sampson takes up the notion of "virality" as it concerns "the forces of relational encounter in the social field."[14] Sampson figures virality "in an epidemiological space in which a world of things mixes with emotions, sensations, affects and moods," a "neurophysiological ecosystem boosted by the cultural amplifiers of objects and commodities . . . in which affects are significantly passed on, via suggestions made by others, more and more through networks."[15] Thus, according to Sampson, "viral love" is a contagion through which a willing engagement with faith and hope is inspired by joyful, mesmeric encounter, an investment "made by religious and political institutions of power" that requires "the raising up of new idols . . . from time to time."[16] As Driscoll turned into the celebrity pastor he once mocked, he rebranded himself from the cussing bad boy of American Neo-Calvinism into a straight-talking revivalist, camera-ready for a global audience. While concertedly marketing himself the Billy Graham of the postmodern era, Pastor Mark increasingly relied on growth statistics and blessed measurements such as baptism totals through which to prove that as high as Mars Hill had risen through God's grace, He had bigger plans.

Baptism numbers may have signaled the Holy Spirit working in and through the congregation, but did they signify actual Christian converts? According to Mars Hill's annual report in 2010, "Baptism is a one-time act— an outward witness of an inward faith in Jesus Christ alone for salvation."[17] Yet I had heard many people profess predunk that they were already Christians. The same report stated, "Public baptisms are a beautiful opportunity to communicate God's grace. The number of baptisms serves to indicate whether or not the people of the church are being led on mission. If evangelism is taking place, baptisms will follow."[18] This document also included baptism percentage breakdowns campus by campus, showing how many took place at each facility that year and what percentage of the weekly attendance this number represented. A battle over which Mars Hill location was winning the "ground war" was clearly in motion. Under this kind of incentive-pressure, how many baptisms were repeats? Were Christians moved to reaffirm their commitment to Jesus at Mars Hill because they were made to feel as though the first time was too soon or insufficient— that their Christian identity pre-Mars Hill was not "authentic" enough?

Evidence of such sentiment is narratively displayed in a 2005 document that showcases the stories of those getting baptized at Golden Gardens Park that August. Over the course of forty-seven pages, men and women (and boys and girls) ranging from the ages of nine to forty-five testify to why they are getting baptized (again). Though there was generational diversity represented, 20 year-olds predominated on the whole. Many echoed feelings of baby Christian inadequacies—an immaturity in knowing God's grace, truly committing to Jesus, or embodying life as Christian, such as in this testimony written by a twenty-one-year old named Erin: "I grew up in a Christian household, attending church every Sunday and very aware of who Jesus is. My conversion to Christianity at 5 years old, however, said more about my people-pleasing personality than my personal commitment to Jesus. My reasons for accepting Jesus at that time had more to do with making my family, friends, and church happy than recognizing truth and making a personal commitment to Jesus."[19]

Baptisms were not a *one-time act* at Mars Hill, but *ongoing desire*—a socially infectious public testament to feeling moved by the Holy Spirit. The 2011 annual report entitled "God's Work, Our Witness" bombastically announced on its cover, "Over 1,200 people baptized at Mars Hill Church," while campus-by-campus tithing percentages were inserted alongside baptism totals.[20] To enhance the affective impact of such statistics, the church released another Easter music video of MTV-quality spliced together with clips of submergence and reemergence, water cascading in slow motion from smiling young faces to deep bass lines, light symbol crashes and melodic guitar chords. This affective marketing of joy belied a detailed balance sheet of the church's 2011 assets and budget, including graphs of tithing and costs which demonstrated that from 2010 to 2011 there was a large gap in surplus income, of close to two million dollars. Like Driscoll's preaching on biblical sex, baptisms were commodified, recorded and packaged as spiritual branding for mass fundraising, networking an affective economy of shame-joy.

NO SUCH THING AS FREE PORN

In January 2012, "Porn Again: Pastor Mark and a Former Porn Star Discuss Pornography" was held at the Neptune Theater, a single-screen cinema repurposed into a performance-arts venue located a few blocks from the University of Washington campus. Details concerning this "completely free" event were disseminated on PastorMark.tv under the heading "There's No Such Thing as Free Porn."[21] Pastor Mark begins by asking his readers, "How did you find this blog post?" then presumes to already know: "Statistically, there's a 25% chance you were looking for porn. And even if you weren't searching for porn now, there's a 40% chance you looked for and viewed porn at some point this week. If you're a man between the ages of 18 and 34, the biggest demographic I speak to, that jumps to 70%. Pastors, you're not off the hook either: 33% of you admit to visiting pornographic websites."[22]

Once he establishes Internet porn's allure and accessibility, particularly to his key audience, Driscoll further advertises this primetime event as "targeted to a collegiate crowd," including a postsermon question and answer session with "a former pastor's daughter who grew up to be a porn star" from whom we will learn "the realities of the porn industry."[23] He also announces the publication of a book cowritten with his wife Grace published days prior called *Real Marriage: The Truth About Sex, Friendship, and Life Together* (2012), which includes a chapter on the addictive qualities of pornography entitled "The Porn Path," concluding his pitch with the information that "Porn Again" will also video stream via marshill.com and be replayed in March during the *Real Marriage* sermon series. During this Campaign, the first of many during which books were advertised as free but came at a cost, audiences paid for pre-sale copies of *Real Marriage* via tithes to Mars Hill. An online banner advertising the Real Marriage Campaign "pre-sale push" read, "Give $25 or More to Support Mars Hill Church and Get a *Free Copy of Real Marriage*." If a "brand," as media scholar Sarah Banet-Weiser argues, is "the series of images, themes, morals, values, feelings, and sense of authenticity conjured by the product," then the Real Marriage Campaign signaled Driscoll's gambit to augment the affective pull, monetary profit, and cultural influence of "Pastor Mark."[24] Pastor Mark the charismatic commodity accrued spiritual authority through the shame and joy circulated and intensified by affect-events such as the Easter Service at Qwest Field and the Real Marriage Campaign.

This celebrity hinged on the allure of "neuromarketing," the steering of biological and social desire by producing what digital culture scholar Tony Sampson describes as "counterfeit affective encounters with desire-events so that the flow of desire folds into and contaminates the repetitive and mostly unconscious mechanical habits of the everyday."[25] Although Pastor Mark's performance during the *Real Marriage* sermon series initially bolstered his image to economic and cultural advantage, it also produced counterfeit affective encounters that were revealed as such once proof the church surreptitiously contracted a book marketing firm to collaborate on the Real Marriage Campaign surfaced. While Driscoll appropriated neurobiological research to postulate "mirror neurons" cultivate a "porn path," the church marketed "Pastor Mark" as authentic using the neuroscience of publicity; as his image preaching from the pulpit holding a large, heavy Bible became Mars Hill's trademark, the pulsations of cathexis around shame materialized as paroxysms of joy.[26]

Tony Sampson explores "the radical relationality established between brains, bodies and sensory environments" in order to examine "the rhythmic composition of imitative encounters that position subjectivities."[27] In his analysis, capitalism targets noncognitive, affective processes, and belief is engendered by desire rather than theologically transferred to, or externally projected from, a self-contained subject. Sampson writes, "Susceptibility to the suggestions of marketers is not arrived through cognitive processes alone, but coincides, to a great extent, with noncognitive encounters associated with joy."[28] Meanwhile, "joyful encounters do not simply lead to the sharing of more joy, but also become part of an affective contagion eliciting conformity and entrainment."[29] As a social process of encounter, the affective value of joy is amplified and diffused in evangelical-capitalist enterprises such as the 2011 Mars Hill Easter service at Qwest Field. Music videos of baptisms that were liked, shared, retweeted, and upvoted also intensified emotional currents that tapped into desires for an authority figure.[30] Sampson notes, "The joyful encounter has its modern political origins in the fascisms of the late 1920s and 1930s, and in particular the Nazi propaganda machine which thoroughly grasped the purchase of appeals to pleasure as well as fear. . . . To make a population believe in fascism it was necessary to appeal directly to desires for joyful sensations as well as maintain atmospheres of absolute terror."[31] The church used a similar affective logic while advertising "free" books on "real marriage" to garner tithes and buyers' lists; while preaching on porn addiction, Pastor Mark did not employ ideological tricks but tapped into the crowd's vulnerability to joyful encounters of mass suggestion. Meanwhile, baptisms were a required segment of every Mars Hill Easter service at its various locations and often video-recorded for online dissemination. Sampson writes, "Desire for joyful sensory stimulations of this kind can be conceived of as an addiction that exceeds the commodity fetish."[32] As Pastor Mark played celebrity pastor, he was not controlling every move in this affective economy; addiction on the porn path was a social contagion.

According to Christian author Rachel Held Evans, the phenomenon of the celebrity pastor is biblical. She states that in Scripture there is "something of a 'celebrity apostle' culture in which Christians were aligning themselves with famous apostles like Paul."[33] However, she is also critical of the idolatry of celebrity pastors in contemporary U.S. Evangelicalism, wherein access to their lives and teaching via social media cultivates "reverence and awe usually reserved for Jesus or Apple products."[34] Her articulation of this relationship between Christian leaders and their followers as mediated by cultural and technological shifts is a useful appraisal of how church branding and self-promotion have become integral to evangelical purpose. However, Evans gestures at, yet fails to critique, a marketing machine that has no theological or ideological allegiance. In fact, her discussion takes a judgmental turn as she blames followers' "insecure psychology" for celebrity pastors, a tack that unhelpfully individualizes responsibility and allocates guilt instead of addressing systemic economic and cultural factors impacting the present and future of U.S. Evangelicalism.[35]

The Hartford Institute for Religion Research defines a megachurch as "any Protestant congregation with a sustained average attendance of 2,000 persons or more in its worship services."[36] While large congregations have existed throughout Christian history, megachurches have proliferated in the United States since the 1970s. Megachurches typically experience a growth spurt in less than ten years under the leadership of one pastor who, according to the conservative theology commonly used to structure leadership, is male. These men are considered charismatic and spiritually gifted as communicators.[37] Through a variety of counseling ministries, opportunities for fellowship within homes, and cultural events that inspire a sense of community, megachurches incite personal commitment among devoted members while affording new Christians or the curious a chance to maintain anonymity.[38] While these are among the general characteristics used to identify a megachurch by the Hartford Institute, it is in defining its "Protestant" character in contrast to large Catholic congregations that a more detailed description is offered: "Most [Catholic Churches] don't have strong charismatic senior ministers" or the "robust congregational identity that empowers 100s to 1000s of weekly volunteers, an identity that draws people from a very large area (sometimes an hour or more) and across parish boundaries, a multitude of programs and ministries organized and maintained by members, high levels of commitment and giving by members, seven-day-a-week activities at the church, contemporary worship, state of the art sound and projection systems."[39]

This passage indicates the vast amount of volunteer labor necessary to generate and maintain the distinctive worship experience, cultural identity, and affective economy through which a megachurch is branded, gains notoriety, and attracts new members. The very definition of a megachurch entails a marketing prerogative that is linked to the labor and sacrifice of members whose evangelical subjectivity is constituted by said labor and sacrifice.

This connection between capitalist endeavor and evangelistic spirit is furthered by the fact that "almost one half of all megachurches are independent and nondenominational . . . which gives considerable freedom to individual churches."[40] Such sovereignty affords the leaders of megachurches a great deal of spiritual and administrative authority to proclaim the "vision" or "calling" of the congregation, through which its cultural identity and public image are established.[41]

Evangelical pastor and *Christianity Today* contributor Skye Jethani wrote a response to Evans's article in which he attributed this "evangelical industrial complex" to a systemic economic force that supersedes psychological factors.[42] Jethani helpfully contextualizes his coining of this phrase by situating its language in relation to a national address by President Eisenhower in 1961, during which he warned about the effects of a military-industrial complex—a permanent arms industry that by design perpetuates warfare. Jethani draws analogies between America's militarism and a clergy celebrity class while persuasively arguing that there is a self-sustaining evangelical industrial complex manufacturing celebrity pastors.[43] In his formulation, the media industry creates and depends on megachurch pastors with thousands of congregants who will purchase their books. Thus, ministers from small or medium-sized churches are never on the main stage at conferences, while megachurch leaders who boast of best-selling author status predominate.[44] In effect, the concept of the evangelical industrial complex pokes holes in pat descriptions of megachurch leaders that suggest they are inherently charismatic and therefore deserving of their stature. What most people want to believe, but which Jethani asserts is false, is that "most godly, intelligent, and gifted leaders naturally attract large followings, so they naturally are going to have large churches, and their ideas are so great and their writing so sharp that publishers pick their book proposals, and the books strike a nerve with so many people that they naturally become best-sellers, and these leaders are therefore the obvious choice to speak at the biggest conferences."[45]

According to Jethani, none of the buzz or profit generated in the above hypothetical is due to spiritual gifts or cultural intelligence, but rather "publishers eager for a guaranteed sales win [who] offer the megachurch pastor a book deal knowing that if only a third of the pastor's own congregation buys a copy, it's still a profitable deal. The book is published on the basis of the leader's market platform, not necessarily the strength of his ideas or the book's quality."[46] Furthermore, Jethani adds, "wanting to maximize the return on their investment, the publisher will then promote the pastor at the publisher-sponsored ministry conference or other events. As a result of the pastor's own megachurch customer base and the publisher's conference platform, the book becomes a bestseller. Or if that doesn't work, sometimes sugar daddies purchase thousands of copies of the book to literally buy the pastor onto the best-seller's list where the perception of popularity results in more sales."[47] While illuminating, Jethani's discussion undersells the political effects of this economic system by calling it an "aristocracy."[48] In Evans's and Jethani's critiques of the rise of celebrity pastors, those supporting the evangelical industrial complex on the ground are either blamed or ignored. Collective sacrifice and labor is not only unrecognized but also unaccounted for, leaving the cultural, social, and spiritual costs of the evangelical industrial complex unexamined. A closer investigation into the calculated employ of an affective economy through which to enlist congregants' material and immaterial labor—both voluntary and inadvertent—in support of leaders' cultural influence and spiritual authority is necessary.

The evangelical industrial complex thrived on Driscoll's celebrity by perpetually monitoring and amplifying his controversial remarks in order to feed itself. Like the military-industrial complex, this "evangelical-capitalist resonance machine" infiltrates the logic of perception while inflecting economic interests, working simultaneously "on the visceral and refined registers of cultural identity" while requiring the self-sacrifice of all-volunteer forces to support increases in baptisms, sermon downloads, and weekly attendees.[49] While joyful encounter may appear less obvious on the porn path than in its onscreen capture in baptism music videos, there is a biopolitical relation between the affective labor of communicating, mediating, and networking joy and shame in these encounters and the sensory environments that situate them. In baptismal waters and on the porn path, desires are intensified as and through bodily and digitally mediated sensory fields.

REALITY PROGRAMMING AS PORNOGRAPHIC INDUSTRY

The video sermon "The Porn Path" is composed of alternating cutaway scenes and close-ups that bleed together through fades to black. The event opens with a reality TV tableau of Driscoll, his wife, and former porn star and pastor's daughter Crissy Moran sitting onstage surrounded by amps and mike stands against a backdrop of blood red velvet curtains. This image dissolves into Pastor Mark preaching on the spiritual and cultural sins of pornography, pacing the theater while gesturing with a leather-bound Bible dressed in groom casual—dark suit, black boots, and an open collar. His sermon begins:

> The U.S. Supreme Court can't even define pornography. They've struggled with it a long time. For the purposes of our discussion, here's what we mean—we mean movies that are explicit, photos that are explicit, websites that are explicit. In addition to the hard core forms, we are also talking about the soft core forms—some of the men's magazines that basically show as much as pornography did just a few years ago, and the same is true of the women's magazines, some of them sitting in the grocery store line, showing things that just a few generations ago would have been tucked under a shelf out of public viewing because it would have qualified as pornography, not to mention the headlines that are shouting even at children. I would go so far as to include romance novels, which encourage women to have pornographic fantasies in their mind of someone other than their husband and the same goes for men, who also are into such sinful fantasizing, and yes, it does count, sometimes pornography is in an image, sometimes it is in your imagination.[50]

Driscoll's explication of pornography is as nebulous and conflicted as he suggests legal definitions are: as pornographic representation and commerce become dangerously mundane and increasingly mainstream, porn manifests in "explicit" images and texts that are also vague and generic—just standing in the grocery store line can lead to inadvertent sin with one glance at the magazine rack. In this narrative, Driscoll does not account for diversification in terms of acts, performers, or markets; instead, he strategically highlights fearfully fluid definitions, hypervisibility, and mass commercialization as eroding cultural distinctions between the pornographic and popular.

In this way, Driscoll's antiporn doctrine is both a critique and product of what porn studies scholar Feona Attwood calls "sexualized culture," which includes "a contemporary preoccupation with sexual values, practices, and identities; the shift to more permissive sexual attitudes; the proliferation of sexualized texts."[51] Driscoll's claim—that any image, text, or fantasy that does not project, signal, or arouse sexual desire for one's spouse is sinfully pornographic—contributes to the very sexualized culture he depicts in paranoid terms. Though strict definitions of freedom and enslavement are discursively posited by him to distinguish the biblical truth of his sexualized hermeneutic from the abusive culture and crass commercialization of the mainstream porn industry, the affective labor of biblical porn advantageously obscured felt distinctions between evangelical and popular culture, animating a pornographic imaginary at once collective and embodied. Intersecting processes of cultural production and bodily mediation involved, but also eclipsed, logics of surveillance and regulatory norms, as Driscoll's neuromarketing of authenticity while preaching on the obligatory freedom of biblical sex and the addictive exploitation of the porn industry circulated shame as affective value. In this coupling of antiporn doctrine and pornographic titillation, an affective economy of shame-interest belies self-help recovery psychologizing or theories concerning the repressive hypotheses of Freud's id.[52] Instead, the networking of shame via the pornographic imaginary conjured by Driscoll's preaching on biblical sexuality amplified the affective value of his brand and the affective labor of his audience.

When Driscoll preached on the harms of pornography during the *Real Marriage* sermon series, he was reiterating a trope familiar to the initiated. Religious studies scholar Amy DeRogatis points out using the book *Real Marriage* as an example, "in the evangelical publishing industry, just like in the secular one, sex sells."[53] However, when she later observes, "Pastor Mark Driscoll and his wife Grace gave their blessing to anal sex, oral sex, and masturbation within biblical marriages. And while they undoubtedly aimed to shock . . . there is nothing new about the Driscolls,"[54] her argument is limited by its textual analysis. The Driscoll's approach to writing about sex within Christian marriage may be comparable to couples such as the LaHayes, who were penning books in a similarly graphic vein in the 1970s, but the visual and digital technologies through which the Driscolls garnered attention within and beyond evangelical audiences signal important shifts in the media industry. As Tony Sampson argues, this social media "makes for an ideal test bed, or nursery, for cultivating, triggering and potentially steering joyful emotional contagions toward some predefined consumer-driven goals."[55] Rather than capitalizing on the simple, hegemonic notion that "sex sells," the Real

Marriage Campaign exploits shame-interest to globally disseminate "free" curriculum that garners tax-free tithes.

The reality TV form and content of "The Porn Path" was aligned with Driscoll's objective to become a best-selling author by appealing to a popular self-help market. If, as religious studies scholar Kathryn Lofton argues, Oprah proffered the prosperity gospel of a spiritual capitalism by "fusing her charisma with a product's image" and "connecting the message of her show to the slogan of a new brand," then *Real Marriage* indexed Driscoll's gambit to perform and brand his image as authentic to financial and cultural gain.[56] This transformation in self-promotion was not simply a matter of refashioning his onscreen persona or repackaging his sermonizing on sex for wider distribution. Pastor Mark the charismatic commodity served as a cultural amplifier networking affective value to political and economic effect. At the outset of "The Porn Path," viewers are invited to visit PastorMark.tv in order to attain more *Real Marriage* resources without charge; then, former porn star and pastor's daughter Crissy Moran's story begins: "I grew up in Florida—Jacksonville, Florida—but when I was four years old, it was the first time I was molested by a man who lived down the street. He had three little boys and we went swimming in the pool, and he molested me. My mom and dad were together until I was about thirteen or fourteen. My dad was a preacher. He then became an alcoholic and abused my mom. And then they eventually split up."[57]

Media scholar Mark Andrejevic describes reality programming in terms of "a form of production wherein consumers are invited to sell access to their personal lives in a way not dissimilar to that in which they sell their labor power."[58] According to this logic, "the possibility of total surveillance is portrayed as power sharing: by providing information about ourselves, we supply valuable inputs to the production process and thereby help to share it."[59] Moran volunteers affective labor to the Real Marriage Campaign by sharing details of childhood trauma while growing up in a Christian household, including sexual abuse and alcohol-fueled domestic violence, submitting painful experiences as life testimony that empirically proves the porn industry is dominated by female victim-performers.

As Moran's suffering is staged for public consumption, an invitation to visit a website named iamatreasure.com flashes onscreen as an overture for audiences to monetarily contribute to her empowerment. Clicks of the keyboard link PastorMark.tv and iamatreasure.com through virtual giving online—by way of tithes that will provide access to "free" teaching materials by Pastor Mark and donations that will go toward Bibles and other "tools to freedom" for "X Girls."[60] Ovations to partake of free goods while supporting freedom from enslavement to the porn industry undersell the price of participating in a participatory branding process that affectively enlists not only money but also immaterial labor. Rather than passive consumers, viewers are contributors to processes of neuromarketing through which they become active, if inadvertent, media producers themselves, conjuring a tactile pornographic imaginary inspired by the spectacle of Moran's victimization.

THE HARMFUL TEACHING OF WIVES AS THEIR HUSBANDS' PORN STARS

During the *Real Marriage* sermon series, Driscoll preached on why God created sex in a sermon called "Can we___?" According to him, the primary reason for sex is not children but pleasure. While explaining why he and Grace use "real" inquiries from congregants in this *Real Marriage* chapter, Driscoll states, "We believe public and private ministry should be the same. The questions that we answer are questions that people ask their counselor, they ask their pastor in private; we want to take those issues public, so that people can get answers and help. And so we do not distinguish between public and private ministries."[61] In a blog post entitled "Why Do We Talk about Sex So Much in *Real Marriage*," Driscoll repeats this justification, going so far as to proclaim that "public and private ministry should be the same."[62] Andrejevic notes, "The promise deployed by reality TV is that submission to comprehensive surveillance is . . . access to the real."[63] Driscoll justifies collapsing the distinctions between private and public ministry in order to "get real" about sex within the church, which he argues is especially important given the topic is sinfully ubiquitous outside of it. Publicly scrutinizing confidential queries shared during private pastoral counseling sessions without congregants' consent becomes not only excusable but also critical to ensuring the health of marriages and the church.

During his discussion of what, according to the Bible, is sexually permissible within the confines of heterosexual marriage, Driscoll highlights the sexual freedom that should be shared between a husband and wife in order to defend against everyday pornographic temptation. He also confesses that a shroud of shame hindered sexual intimacy within his own marriage such that it affected his leadership at Mars Hill. In effect, Grace Driscoll serves as a substitute for Crissy Moran—she is both a pastor's daughter and, at least as preached by her husband, biblically obliged to embody the visual generosity of a porn star. The reader of *Real Marriage* discovers that in the early years of the Driscolls' marriage, Grace was inhibited by shame due to premarital sex with a man other than Mark, an encounter that he did not know about on their wedding day. She alludes to this secret while describing her decision-making process to participate in question-and-answer sessions on sex during the *Peasant Princess* sermon series, "I had prayed for months about whether I should join Mark onstage for this. . . . Like many, we entered marriage with a load of habits, secrets, and preconceptions that could have killed our marriage."[64] The reader discovers that the secret that could have killed the Driscolls' marriage was a sexual sin that Grace kept hidden from her husband until he saw it in a dream:

> One night, as we approached the birth of our first child, Ashley, and the launch of our church, I had a dream in which I saw some things that shook me to my core. I saw in painful detail Grace sinning sexually during a senior trip she took after high school when we had just started dating. It was so clear it was like watching a film—something I cannot really explain but the kind of revelation I sometimes receive. . . . I asked if it was true, fearing the answer. Yes, she confessed, it was. Grace started weeping and trying to apologize for lying to me, but I honestly don't remember the details of the conversation, as I was shell-shocked. Had I known about this sin, I would not have married her.[65]

This back-and-forth conversational narrative continues as the story unfolds, and Grace confesses, "I wished I hadn't ever lied. . . . He felt completely stuck; I felt total shame. . . . Where was the freedom I was supposed to feel after finally telling the truth?"[66] The freedom that is supposed to occur through confession and reconciliation appears elusive until she receives biblical counseling and a "root issue" is unearthed. Mark writes, "Grace's problem was that she was an assault victim who had never told me or anyone else of the physical, spiritual, emotional, and sexual abuse she had suffered."[67] He adds, "I grew more chauvinistic. I started to distrust women in general, including Grace. This affected my tone in preaching for a season, something I will always regret."[68] As Grace Driscoll and Crissy Moran volunteered affective labor through public testimony on behalf of the church, the collapsing of private and public ministry blurred distinctions between private and public information in the name of freedom that is never assured. In print and onstage, the Real Marriage Campaign offered access to the real through the self-conscious staging of women's testimony to sexual abuse. As Driscoll sermonizes on the sinful complicity of his audience in supporting the porn industry, contributing to the profit of corporate sponsors and exploitation of victim-performers, he also capitalizes on the seductive logics of neuromarketing that he attributes to the porn path. His sermon continues:

> And so the line between pornographic culture and pop culture is blurred if not altogether eliminated, and it's such an industry today that between $10 and $14 billion a year is spent on pornography . . . Additionally, globally, it's a phenomena often tied to the sex trade and slavery. Upwards of $90 billion a year is spent globally on porn. Some of you will say, well I don't contribute money to it, but you do, because the advertisers are the ones who pay a fee, and every time you click, you are legitimizing their existence, and participating in a culture of slavery and abuse. And there is no such thing as free porn. The people participating pay and the advertisers pay so that you can enjoy their suffering, shame, and humiliation.

The close-up of Pastor Mark preaching fades to black, then shifts to a wide-angle view of him interviewing Moran, as Grace sits silently by his side.

PASTOR MARK [LEANING TOWARD MORAN]: "So, you were sexually abused as a little girl. For women in the industry, is that common?"
MORAN: "Yeah, it's very common."
PASTOR MARK: "As far as the gals you know, friends you have, what percentage would you say have a similar experience?"
MORAN: "I would say probably all of them. It's a very common thing."[69]

This event enacts Crissy Moran's suffering and humiliation for a worldwide audience, actualizing Driscoll's adage "there's no such thing as free porn" as the collective industry of biblical porn self-fulfills his shameful prophecy. Former Mars Hill members have publicly testified to the ways in which shame circulated as Driscoll's sermonizing on biblical sex was globally marketed and affectively impacting their everyday lives.

Wendy Alsup, a former deacon and leader in women's ministry at Mars Hill, writes a blog called *Practical Theology for Women*. In July 2014 she posted on "The Harmful Teaching of Wives as Their Husbands' Porn Stars."

> Mars Hill's teaching on sex has been well exported nationally and even internationally, particularly since 2012 by way of Mark Driscoll's *Real Marriage* book. I believe addressing this might be widely helpful to the many readers of this blog who were previously exposed to this teaching at Mars Hill. . . . When I got to Mars Hill in Seattle, I valued the pleasure aspect of sex as a good gift from God to married couples . . . [but] it's clear from *Real Marriage* that, in Mark's view, sex is the key, central element to a good marriage. And this would be consistent with everything I heard while attending Mars Hill as well. . . . I felt dissonance in my heart with this teaching. I loved sex and valued pleasure in marriage, but the expectations Mark set up felt crushing—a standard I couldn't live up to. Then my pastor who taught on this subject this summer used a phrase that finally set me free—that pornography sets up a society "with crushing expectations regarding physical appearance and sexual performance." Things clicked in my head at that moment. The weight of crushing expectations that I felt as a result of Mars Hill's teaching on sex wasn't a result of what the Bible said but of the pornographic background from which they stemmed. But was this just me?! Was this just my own personal, prudish reaction?[70]

Instead of a normative sexuality based on binaries of biblical/sinful practices, Alsup describes a sense of expectation based on an ambient metric of desire. The way in which Driscoll's teaching on biblical masculinity, femininity, and sexuality promotes the networking of shame is confirmed in another woman's testimony.

> One wife, who came from a background of horrific sexual abuse . . . shared how this teaching affected her when she came to Seattle as a newly married 21 year old. . . . "I felt beaten down and further humiliated by Driscoll's view of women. Some of the things he said that have harmed

me: it's the wife's fault if the husband looks at porn if she 'lets herself go' or isn't skilled enough at sex, his obsession with talking about wives giving blow jobs and strip teases, the crass jokes, the frequent references to women being gossips."[71]

Next, Alsup turns to the story of a man who provides insight into how Driscoll's preaching on porn addiction and the embodiment of sexual freedom adversely affected his marriage.

> I was addicted to pornography for many years which was defiling to me, distorted my view of women, and ultimately defiled my wife. This is (part of) my sin. Mark's teaching in many ways supported this view of women as sexual objects by using the same "construct" of what a porn star, prostitute, or stripper does but applying it to the marriage bed. . . . The expectation that my wife believed and I readily agreed to was that she was available to me for whatever, no matter what I did, whenever, and if she wasn't *I would probably end up doing worse*. Sex was often empty and emotionally painful. So Mark's recommendation and my sinful silent agreement with the concept of your wife being your personal porn star was apt. Dead, meaningless sex.[72]

Rather than duped or brainwashed by Driscoll's teaching, his audience is convicted to be free of shame in order to enjoy biblical sex. This desire to believe in ordained sexual freedom is manipulated and exploited in the conjuring of a pornographic imaginary out of biological habit and biblical imperative. The price of biblical porn materializes in and of the flesh as the everyday matter of conviction. Meanwhile, Pastor Mark's image takes a biopolitical cast, networking affective value in support of Mars Hill's empire, mirroring rather than disrupting the abuse he pins on the porn industry.

HARDWIRED FOR BELIEF

In the next segment of "The Porn Path," Driscoll introduces "William M. Struthers, a Christian biopsychologist who is specially trained to give the physical and spiritual reasons for pornography addiction," describing his book *Wired for Intimacy* (2009) as "filling a gap in Christian circles" through "an integrated physical, psychological, and biblical perspective."[73] However, he neglects to mention its subtitle: "How Pornography Hijacks the Male

Brain." Driscoll elides the gender-specific aspect of Struthers's argument, focusing instead on his discussion of "mirror neurons" as "motor system cells that activate when you see a behavior" and "are in action when you see someone frightened and you, too, respond with fear."[74] Struthers posits that this neurological hardwiring for empathy causes men to "vicariously" participate in pornography while viewing it.[75] His discussion on this point suggests that an entanglement of body, brain, and technology is specifically promoted by "the way that a male brain is organized in being one-track, goal-oriented, and visuospatial, mak[ing] it the perfect playground for sexual fantasy" to the extent that "as a man watches a pornographic movie he can neurologically identify with the performers in the video and place himself into the HD [high-definition] signal."[76] Furthermore, Struthers frames such fantasizing as a quotidian threat, stating "it is hard to get through the day without being battered and numbed by the intrusions of pornography" because it "is everywhere."[77] Heightening the sense of danger as men actively, inadvertently, and nonconsciously enter and are infiltrated by the high-definition signal of pornographic images, Struthers describes this infectious process as "a sexual poison that becomes part of the fabric of the mind" through "repeated exposure" that results in men who become "hypnotized" and "hooked." [78] He links the biological and spiritual by postulating a porous body prone to contagion and a plastic brain habituated to sin, while considering the visceral force, visual grab, and carnal resonance of porn: "Something about pornography pulls and pushes at the male soul. . . . The minds of many men become hidden, personified adult film studios. Any women they have seen and anyone else they can imagine are their performers. As porn and fantasy take control of the mind, it becomes a dream theater that is transposed over the waking world. . . . The arousal that it produces can also have an element of fear, revulsion or a need to avoid it."[79]

Struthers's study is more than an exercise in fomenting Christian moral panic. While pornography addiction remains a disputed classification and is not included in the fifth edition of the *Diagnostic and Statistical Manual of Mental Disorders*, Struthers's discussion of the male brain's "hijacking" by porn echoes contemporary feminists like Gail Dines, author of *Pornland: How Porn Has Hijacked Our Sexuality* (2011), and recent neurological research into whether compulsive porn consumption is akin to addiction to cocaine. In the BBC documentary *Porn on the Brain* (2013), the neurophysicist Valerie Voon, of the University of Cambridge, shares evidence based on magnetic resonance imaging (MRI) scans that suggests such analogies have some merit, but also emphasizes that more studies are necessary to clearly demonstrate whether habitual porn users should be categorized as addicts.[80] Debates concerning the methodological approaches and political agendas shaping neuroscience on porn addiction continue. A reporter in *Psychology Today* used a study that employed electroencephalogram testing to examine how viewing porn affected the brain to argue "people who are [considered] problem users of porn are actually people with high libidos, not those whose brains have been warped" by it.[81] Furthermore, he noted, "fear-based arguments often invoke brain-related lingo, and throw around terms like dopamine bursts and desensitization, to describe what allegedly happens in the brains of people who watch too much porn."[82] This claim is an open critique of positions like Struthers's and the way in which the visualization of affect in the digital MRI scan is valorized as proof positive that porn addiction is real and akin to drug addiction. Such forewarnings speak to the affective value of visualization techniques in neuroscience. By adapting such discourse to suit his theology of sex while preaching on the sins of the porn industry and harms of pornographic addiction, Driscoll invites viewers to step into an HD signal that he projects. The Real Marriage Campaign incorporated social media tropes and neuromarketing techniques to capitalize on processes of affective capitalism.

Further psychological research into porn addiction at Case Western Reserve University has yielded evidence that "people who consider themselves very religious and view Internet porn even once may perceive they are addicted."[83] According to this study, Christians do not use porn any more than do non-Christians, but their moral beliefs have an impact on whether or how the practice is perceived as addictive. The threat of porn addiction has also furthered an industry of Internet safety features, a commercial enterprise already tapped by evangelical entrepreneurs. Covenant Eyes, a company that markets Internet accountability and filtering software specifically to Christian households to promote "healthy online habits," responded to the Case Western Reserve study with the kind of fearful statistics often used by Driscoll.[84] Although psychologists and neurologists presently dispute the usage of "addiction" in relation to porn, Struthers's employ of mirror neurons to make such a connection is in keeping with scholars spanning the fields of affect studies and political-communication investigating how emotions and affect can be instrumentalized for the purposes of persuasion.

For example, George Lakoff introduces his study *The Political Mind* (2008) by stating, "One of the great breakthroughs in neuroscience has been the discovery of so-called mirror neurons and the pathways that allow them to play a central role in empathy."[85] Lakoff unpacks how this brain circuitry binds body to technology via mirror neurons, using examples of interactive media from popular culture, such as reality TV, in a manner that supports Struthers's formulation concerning how pornography affects men's lives.[86] Reverberations in moral tone register between Lakoff's and Struthers's arguments as they incorporate neuroscience to examine how powers of suggestion and imitation both strategic and nonintentional adversely impact political and spiritual life. Lakoff proposes that "a misleading and destructive idea can be introduced under conditions of trauma and then repeated so often that it is forever in your synapses," in order to argue that the Bush administration used the 9/11 attacks "to impose the powerful 'war on terror' metaphor and make it stick."[87] In a similar vein, Struthers asks, "Is it any wonder why so many men can pull up clear memories of uninvited pornographic images that they were exposed to when they were young? Is it any wonder why they have been scarred in a PTSD-like fashion, unable to erase these images? And is it any wonder why men who act out in response to pornography often have these images return (both uninvited and invited) with such ease?"[88] Whereas post-traumatic stress disorder is often attributed to difficulties in processing the memory of traumatic events, in Lakoff's and Struthers's accounts a visual feedback loop draws a direct, stable correlation between traumatic image-experience and affective mediation-response.

After introducing Struthers's research in the book *Real Marriage*, Driscoll correlates it to a book written by Dr. Drew, whom he describes as:

> perhaps the most famous counselor in the world with his VH-1 reality television shows *Sober House* and *Sex Rehab* ... [and] his long-running radio show, *Loveline*. ... I (Mark) have cohosted the show with Dr. Drew, and was told I was the first pastor to do so. In what he calls "the mirror effect," Drew says that we are suffering from a culture of celebrity narcissism. ...

Narcissists want to be the center of attention, like a god, and have people worship them by paying attention to them, buying the products they promote, and emulating their behavior. Aiding them in this pursuit is everything from reality television shows, daytime talk shows, social media outlets. . . . Fans then emulate the extreme behavior of celebrities because the more they are exposed to it, the more normative or even desirable they believe it is. Simply, celebrities model, and their fans mirror.[89]

Driscoll proceeds to detail such behavior, including performances in pornographic videos that strategically go viral, in a sermon that adopts a reality TV format to promote a book that states in no uncertain terms "the biblical pattern for Christian marriage is free and frequent sex."[90] During his discussion of celebrity narcissism, Driscoll appears to be performing a self-parody. Sociologist Mike Featherstone notes that digital technologies have created new possibilities for the visualization of affect, including a "body schema" or "felt body" wherein "the body's sensor-motor capacities . . . function in a haptic manner."[91] While body *image* is commonly perceived as a public look—the impression one makes on others—body *schema* suggests a "nonvisual sense of the body, the haptic and proprioceptive feelings from the body—not just the senses of hearing, smell, and taste, but also touch and sense of body movement."[92] By this logic, body schema complicates felt distinctions between inside and outside, and real and virtual. Rather than attributable to Driscoll per se, the social conviction incited by the circulation of shame through the pornographic imaginary his preaching on the porn path conjures is a matter of "presence," which "lacks articulation and is more processual . . . a movement-image, a body in process, which can convey and receive a range of affective responses."[93] Whereas Lakoff and Struthers cleave clear distinctions between body and technology such that cause and effect are easily discerned, Pastor Mark's neuromarkets authenticity through visceral convergences and circuits of shame-joy.

CAMPAIGNING FOR *REAL MARRIAGE*

One month prior to the publication of *Real Marriage*, Driscoll encouraged an assembly of Mars Hill Community Group leaders to join a surge of support: "Over 2,000 churches have signed up to follow along with us in the sermon series and receive for free hundreds of pages of research, full marketing materials, counseling and worship guides."[94] These biblical resources were advertised as "air war and ground war strategies to help you permeate the message from the pulpit throughout each aspect of your church and ministry." They included "full *Real Marriage* branding, design, and marketing plans and materials that you can edit for your local church for such things as postcards, posters, e-vites, video commercials, social media strategy, and more," as well as "free use of Pastor Mark's sermons for the series via DVD download if you want a week off."[95]

The Real Marriage Campaign was in preparation a year before the book's release, including the efficient and profitable coordination of a legal yet ethically questionable marketing ploy that belied Mars Hill's nonprofit status unbeknownst to church members. Evidence concerning the strategies used to accrue Pastor Mark best-selling author stature would not surface until 2014, two years after the Driscolls embarked on their *Real Marriage* tour, which included speaking engagements in cities around the country and media appearances on programs such as ABC's *The View*. The paper trail of research that led to the public unveiling of Mars Hill's connection to a book marketing firm started with the Christian publication WORLD *Magazine*, which announced "unreal sales for Driscoll's *Real Marriage*." This article noted that the company ResultSource was paid "to conduct a bestseller campaign" that included not only the *New York Times*' How-To/Advice list but also the *Wall Street Journal*, *USA Today*, Barnes and Noble, Amazon, and the speaking engagements, talk show visits, and advertising opportunities that followed.[96]

While the details of this business transaction are complicated, it is clear that ResultSource received a fee of $25,000 to coordinate a nationwide network of book buyers.[97] Mars Hill paid for the purchase of at least 11,000 books, 6,000 of which were bought by individuals whose names were supplied by the church while 5,000 were bought in bulk.[98] When queried, Mars Hill representatives would not say whether these books were purchased with church funds, but the contract showed that it was important that "the make up of the 6,000 individual orders include at least 1,000 different addresses with no more than 350 per state" to circumvent metrics used to prevent authors from buying their way onto lists.[99] The varied addresses required by ResultSource were culled through the "pre-sale push" during which supporters were asked to donate $25 to Mars Hill ministries in order to receive a "free" book.[100] This campaign was the first of its kind but not the last waged on PastorMark.tv as a way of offering material to churches throughout the world.

Driscoll announced to the assembly of Mars Hill community group leaders in a video recorded talk broadcast on PastorMark.tv.

> And so January fifteenth we're going to start the "Real Marriage Campaign." That same day, we're going to open four churches in three states . . . [and] Grace and I are doing a media trip to New York for a few days. You can pray; we're trying to get on *Colbert* and the *Today Show.* . . . We have what we're calling a campaign which is about three-hundred pages of research and statistics that we've put together, as well as preaching tips, small-group tips, [and] Sunday tips for other churches, and we thought, let's invite them to go through this content and curriculum together. So far, over two thousand churches have signed up to do so, and we praise God for that. I remember still the first day the campaign director, he said, "Well, I'm praying for fifty." And the first day, I said, "Where are we at?" And he said, "Fifteen hundred." Well, prayer got answered.[101]

Research concerning how much Driscoll personally pocketed from the best-selling moniker has yielded evidence that a tax vehicle called a charitable remainder unitrust (or CRUT) named On Mission LLC was established in Colorado a year prior to *Real Marriage*'s publication, demonstrating a calculated plan to covertly manage a large income generated by "book royalties, printing, and publishing."[102] After Mars Hill Church collapsed in 2014, On Mission LLC remained viable, but not in Driscoll's name; instead, its governing person was registered as Lasting Legacy LLC.[103]

During the Real Marriage Campaign, the technologies and tropes of reality programming were employed to imitate the physiological effect of mirror neurons on the porn path. A former deacon echoed the analogy between Driscoll's preaching on porn addiction and the sense of social conviction triggered by his teaching on biblical sex when he shared with me that he considered *Real Marriage* a "gateway" to pornographic fantasizing; another male leader I spoke with called Driscoll's teaching on biblical sexuality a "theology of rape." A former elder who pastored couples by facilitating pre-marital classes told me that he resisted using *Real Marriage* in that curriculum, while a women's ministry leader shared that she was ordered to use it. This biopolitics of sex was not solely construed out of persuasion, manipulation, fear, or control, but also conviction, joy, hope, and freedom. Sedgwick and Frank note, "Without positive affect, there can be no shame: only a scene that offers you enjoyment or engages your interest can make you blush. . . . Shame, as precarious hyperreflexivity of the surface of the body, can turn one inside out—or outside in."[104] Shame-joy circulated as political and economic value in the affective labor of biblical porn, a social process of networking to which I contributed despite myself through encounters of the Body.

By the summer of 2014, evidence had surfaced online that supported several accusations against Driscoll, including the misappropriation of tithes intended as a "global fund" for churches in Ethiopia and India. Days after the protest outside Mars Hill Bellevue, I played with the microphone on my cell, checking for audio levels in a bustling roasteria while waiting for a former leader and worship band member. After he arrived, I immediately decided that there was no point in recording and put the phone away; his eyes never left it until it was in my bag. After several hours during which we discussed the effects of pornography on men and women, his fundraising to support his family while working full time at the church in a volunteer capacity, and a recently failed attempt on his part to communicate with Mark, our voices trailed off as we stared into coffee dregs. "We were duped," he said. "We all are," I replied. The open secret of the drone strikes relied on by the Obama administration in the war on terror was the first example that came to mind, and as I mentioned it, he nodded.

In straightforward terms, to be duped means to be tricked or deceived; however, such textbook definitions do not do justice to its social affects. The lexicon of betrayal that registered in averted or darting eyes during interviews undermined a one-to-one relationship between abuser and abused or hierarchical dichotomies of oppressor/victim. When I read testimonies and heard descriptions that couched these troubling feelings in terms of "spiritual abuse," they were articulated as PTSD-like symptoms such as night terrors, sobbing jags, and jumbled nerves that led to isolation, depression, insomnia, and an aversion to churchgoing.

In her book on Jerry Falwell, anthropologist Susan Harding addresses his role in the televangelist scandals of the late 1980s, including controversies surrounding Jim and Tammy Faye Bakker and the deceitful fund-raising practices of their Praise the Lord ministry (PTL). Harding notes, "Episodes of revival and religious enthusiasm in the history of American Protestant evangelicalism frequently have been occasioned . . . by scandal and controversy.

Scandals are an extreme instance of the cultural instability that is an integral and productive force in American Protestant evangelistic preaching."[1] Harding's ethnographic examination of Falwell's ministry demonstrates how evangelical preachers "narrate and act out strategic indeterminacies— gaps, excesses, anomalies, breaches—that their followers harmonize and critics intensify."[2] According to her argument, the televangelist scandals of the late 1980s did not mark an exile of conservative Protestants from the public sphere, but served to reassert their participation in the political life of the nation. She notes, "An evangelist's survival depends on his or her skill at maneuvering the gaps in a way that enables their followers to read miracles where their critics read scandals."[3] According to Harding, controversies also accrue value on a media market hungry for the "bad news" of the gospel; thus, critics within and outside Evangelicalism amplify them for the sake of profit.

However, in the twenty-first century journalists and preachers are not the only purveyors of scandal; audiences across the conservative and progressive evangelical-secular spectrum capitalize on and contribute to a social media industrial complex in which congregants and critics are not only consumers but also producers of content. The notion of "scandal" itself has a different tenor in the digital age; Mars Hill staff and members did not decide to stay or leave in the simple terms that Harding describes. Her analysis resonates with the rational choice theory frequently used to explain the drives, decisions, and political subjectivity of individuals, whereby the social and relational complexity of agency is reduced to the "free choice" of subject-consumers. In her examination, belief is a system and freedom a possession; conviction can be turned on and off. According to her argument, televangelists such as Jim Bakker elicited sacrificial giving through successfully deceptive showmanship framed in the abuser/victim terms of fiscal exploitation. However, in the affective economy socially networked via interactive media technologies and bodily processes of mediation at Mars Hill, "sacrificial giving" did not simply amount to funds.

While the Bakkers' empire collapsed as a result of scandals that they could not legally dodge, and the celebrity clout of televangelists declined after their 1980s heyday, Harding emphasizes the need to examine how the telescandals were a representational struggle similar to the Scopes Trial of 1925. In particular, she notes how one scandalized "modern" secular news anchor, Ted Koppel of ABC's *Nightline*, accused various evangelical preachers of amplifying the telescandals to turn a profit—in Falwell's case, to justify a hostile takeover of the Bakkers' PTL ministry. However, as Harding points out, "[Koppel] himself, Mr. Modern Secularity, was torn between story and spectacle."[4] In the 1980s, the distinctions and distance between media elites such as Koppel or Falwell and their audiences were vast compared to the information era in which Driscoll relied on congregants for material; participation in story and spectacle is both more overt and subtle in the affects circulated through and as social media. In this affective labor, "sacrifice" is both agentive and voluntary as well as nonintentional and involuntary. As such, this form of sacrifice undercuts the logic of rational choice theory and exceeds technologies of self. Whereas Falwell strategically cultivated a political alliance with the Republican Party through national crises he framed in terms of "moral values," Driscoll made no such gambit for political clout based on partisanship, electoral influence, or single-issue voting. However, in strategically capitalizing on scandals to elevate his celebrity for profit, cultural influence, and political pull, Driscoll was not exceptional among evangelical leaders before or after the 1980s rise of the "Christian Right."

Scholar of African American studies and religious studies Sylvester Johnson writes, "In the wake of the Second World War, the U.S. began to solidify a global constellation of military bases" in the name of defeating Communism, "enabl[ing] a fundamental shift in the theological imagination of U.S. power."[5] In particular, Johnson notes, "Jerry Falwell embodied the rising tide of political Christianity that linked the U.S. effort to become the most powerful empire to the religious grammatology of Manichaean struggle against ultimate evil. An explicitly religious tenor began to accrue in the substance and fervor of U.S. foreign policy . . . [while] the triumph of fundamentalism in the U.S. was enabled by the Cold War and specific formations of U.S. hegemony."[6] Johnson adds that in the post-9/11 era, circuits between religion and U.S. Empire have intensified; a possible terror link is a foregone conclusion whenever a mass shooting occurs and immediately couched in oppositions of good and evil. Often, this binary translates into Christian/ Muslim and American/foreigner terms commonsensically rather than logically. The "clash of civilizations"[7] foreign policy that legitimized Operation Iraqi Freedom also popularizes calls for restrictions on travelers from predominantly Islamic countries, refugee bans that target Muslims over Christians, and a Muslim registry within the United States.[8] When President George W. Bush proclaimed an "axis of evil, arming to threaten the peace of the world"[9] after the attacks on 9/11, he set the emotional tone for U.S. foreign policy at the beginning of the twenty-first century using the language of crusade.[10]

Geographer David Harvey argues that once the Republican Party and Jerry Falwell's Moral Majority created an alliance, an electoral base was born out of a distinctly Christian cultural nationalism based on "traditional" moral values inflected through sexist, racist, and homophobic rhetoric that appealed to a white working class resentful of affirmative-action policies.[11] In his analysis, Harvey writes that the effect of such discourse was to obscure and divert attention away from the harmful impact of neoliberal reforms and corporate power on this electoral base. He portrays the white working class as duped by political strategists and religious leaders who intentionally manipulate them. In turn, Harvey defines neoliberalism as "a theory of political economic practices that proposes that human well-being can best be advanced by liberating individual entrepreneurial free-doms and skills within an institutional framework characterized by strong private property rights, free markets, and free trade."[12] This passage speaks to the political and economic logics of freedom that President Bush used to justify a preemptive war on Iraq in 2003 and the rational choice theory employed by Milton Friedman to argue for the viability of an All-Volunteer Force (AVF) in the United States in the 1970s. However, this neoliberal defi-nition of freedom does not make sense during an unending war on terror in which the perpetual redeployment of soldiers is commonplace and results in many returning to the United States with traumatic brain injuries and post-traumatic stress disorder, often undiagnosed and untreated.

Driscoll's invocation of spiritual warfare in tandem with a church plant-ing war bolstered Manichean logics of good and evil framed by Christian and Muslim identities. Concurrently, his conjuring of supernatural and worldly warfare reinforced hegemonic notions of masculinity according to a system of white heteropatriarchy that supported neoliberal principles: aggressive entrepreneurialism, familial responsibility, and a willingness to sacrifice. However, combat at Mars Hill was animated through social imagi-naries and bodily affects that took hold outside of the regulatory perimeters of self-discipline, rational choice theory, or patriotic appeals. In the public confession "Hello, My Name Is Mike, and I'm a Recovering True Believer," self-professed "Minister of Propaganda" and director of Mars Hill's online ministry the Resurgence—Mike Anderson—recounts how reading Eric Hoffer's *True Believer: Thoughts on the Nature of Mass Movements* (1951) convinced him that the mission of Mars Hill had died. His story begins,

> I'm what they call a True Believer. I really like the idea of changing the world: sacrifice for the cause, singleminded drive for the "mission," a charismatic leader. As a 19-year-old I was the kind of guy that was the ideal follower for the crazies of history—the Mussolinis and the Hitlers. Fortunately for the world, the 21st-century version of this extremism isn't hyper-nationalism, it is a megachurch. There's less bloodshed than the 20th-century version, but still a lot of hurt.[13]

This testimony sounds prophetic in the aftermath of the presidential election of 2016, with the virulent rise in white nationalist discourse and openly anti-Muslim rhetoric of government officials such as Stephen Bannon, once chief strategist to the Oval Office, among others devising immigration policy within the Trump administration.[14]

Anderson's confession suggests how vital conviction is as an affective force in U.S. evangelical formations of empire as it is inflected through nationalist-theological imaginaries. Ideologically, these formations and imaginaries of empire diverge as they intersect—from globalization "flows" and "free trade" fundamentalism, to the strengthening of security and regularization of risk through the reinforcement of borders and bans on Muslim immigrants. It is the conviction in exceptionalism that is affectively seductive; its violent structural effects and spiritual affects materialize and coalesce as militarized power and processes that animate and are animated by theological imaginaries.

Anderson testifies to an affective ecology of Evangelical Empire primed through the infrastructure and atmosphere of the "air war" and "ground war," stoking and spreading conviction in the exceptionalism of Pastor Mark and Mars Hill Church: "We were trying to build a church so influential, so 'pure' that it could change the world—it could be a new reformation.... I even coauthored a book with Mark called *Campaigns* about 12 months before leaving staff. The idea behind it was to be able to rally Mars Hill and thousands of other churches behind one pulpit. I am so thankful that this never had the time to get truly implemented."[15] This dynamic of biopolitics, affect theorist Jasbir K. Puar argues, "foreground[s] floating mechanisms of continuous control, enacted through the proliferation of management devices and details."[16] In the strategy described in the e-book *Campaigns*, the air war–ground war is a mobile, marketable infrastructure with the affective capacity to rally Mars Hill and thousands of other churches behind one pulpit, Pastor Mark's.

Campaigns orchestrated biopolitical control through calculation and intervention, tweaking and modulating affect such that, in the words of Puar, "surveillance technologies activate, infect, vibrate, distribute, disseminate, disaggregate," revealing that "sensations matter as much as if not more than how things appear, look, seem, are visible, or are cognitively known."[17] In the affective ecology of Evangelical Empire promoted by *Campaigns*, "the force of mobilization takes on a different role. . . . Militarized bodies are crafted through the dissemination and diffusion of control, rather than within concentrated and isolated patches of discipline or via overt force."[18] At Mars Hill, congregants were not inspired to serve based on rationales of national or economic self-interest; instead, bodies were conscripted into duty in order to support a church so influential and pure that it could catalyze a global reformation. Language such as "air war" and "ground war" did not ideologically capitalize on wartime patriotism to accrue commitment and converts. While processes of militarization at work today in the United States were under way prior to September 11, 2001, particular tactics were set in motion by declaring a global war on terror. Anthropologist Joseph Masco writes, "The very real terrorist violence of September 2001 was quickly harnessed by U.S. officials to a conceptual project that mobilizes affects (fear, terror, anger) via imaginary processes (worry, precarity, threat) to constitute an unlimited space and time horizon for military state action."[19] *Campaigns* demonstrates how a strategy of biopolitical control was implemented in support of Driscoll's vision casting for Evangelical Empire. While the strategy of Campaigns failed to rally thousands of churches behind one pulpit, it successfully ensured that Mars Hill would rapidly decline in Pastor Mark's absence, while affording him the ability to disseminate Mars Hill sermons from a self-titled website after the church's dissolution.[20]

During Mark's six-week hiatus from the Mars Hill pulpit after the anonymous video aired, weekly attendance dwindled from approximately 13,000 to 7,000; seventeen days after he resigned from the church that he had led for eighteen years, it was announced that Mars Hill would dissolve as a corporate body on December 31, 2014. Although Driscoll attempted to shift blame for his leave-taking from himself to slanderous accusations circulating online via social media, it was Mars Hill's innovative uses of such technology that afforded him the opportunity to become what was described to me by one staff member as a "whore" for an evangelical industrial complex that both reviled and reveled in his penchant for controversy. Digital theorist Wendy Chun argues that control is persuasively leveraged and efficiently calculated due to a "blind belief in and desire for invulnerability, for this belief and desire blind us to the ways in which we too are implicated, to the ways in which technology increasingly seems to leave no outsides."[21] As she rightly points out, "Because vulnerability and a certain loss of control drives communication . . . it is by exploring the possibilities opened up by our vulnerabilities, rather than relegating this vulnerability as accidental or pornographic, that the question of democracy can be rigorously engaged."[22] Driscoll may have lost his ability to stand in the narrative gaps of the controversies that led to his scandalous retirement from Mars Hill Church, but his affective capacity to continue to attract followers testifies to the political force of conviction.

AIR WAR–GROUND WAR AS AFFECTIVE INFRASTRUCTURE

While staging ministry in terms of spiritual combat against Satan and demons, Driscoll asserted that only a coordinated strategy administered by the pulpit and diffused through small groups would protect those waging war in their everyday lives as Christian disciples.

> The Bible is clear that we live and minister in a war zone. Satan and demons are at work running people's lives, and as ministry leaders we are on the front lines to witness the casualties firsthand. Ministries doing just sermons as the primary ministry are headed in the right direction, but need to do more in terms of the ground war by promoting those sermons and using those sermons to lead the church and direct the small groups. Those ministries with strong small groups but weak corporate gatherings for preaching and teaching are also halfway there and need to think more and not less about the air war and communicating the Word of God in a way that is passionate, practical, and personal.[23]

In this introduction to the e-book *Campaigns*, he distinguishes between the "air war"—comprised of preaching and teaching—and "ground war"—entailing care and community. The air war leads the mission, has a primary visible leader, deals with the masses, is event centered, draws people to the church, and "proclaims with authority."[24] By contrast, the ground war follows the air war, has multiple and less visible leaders, deals with individuals and small groups, is relationship centered, connects people to the church, and "explains with accountability."[25] After he identifies these distinctions, Driscoll describes the value of adopting Campaigns for potential customers and remote collaborators sermonizing from church platforms around the world by narrating a sketchy thumbnail of Mars Hill's history that leaves out many important details in order to demonstrate a clear arc of success. On the heels of this story, Driscoll plugs not only his book *Real Marriage* but also a new global ministry of the church: "Starting in 2012, with the kickoff of the sermon series based on the latest book written by my wife, Grace, and me, Mars Hill Church will give away all our Campaign materials for each sermon series, free for any church to use however they desire. If you do use these materials, however, we'd ask you to consider making a donation to Mars Hill Global to help fund our efforts. You can do so by visiting marshillglobal.com."[26] This entreaty to financially support the distribution of "free" teaching content by donating to Mars Hill Global is reiterated later in the postscript of *Campaigns*. Online donations for this global ministry are repeatedly called for in a digital text announcing the global distribution of Campaign materials for churches to use in lieu of developing their own content. Churches that elected to use Campaigns resigned theological and creative control in order to adopt the preaching, visual, and digital materials necessary to channel all spiritual authority through the pulpit of Pastor Mark.

As he addresses how Campaigns connect all aspects of the church to the pulpit, Driscoll emphasizes "taking the one big idea in the pulpit and packaging it in a Campaign that permeates every aspect of your church, [so] you connect all aspects of your church to the pulpit and leverage the pulpit to move your people into mission."[27] While describing this global dissemination of biblically informed materials in concrete terms, he explains how sermons organize and pervade the intimate space of small group settings to drive and infuse the mobilization of Christian disciples on mission: "Each

Mars Hill Campaign includes Community Group curriculum that takes the previous week's sermon and applies it to the life of the people in that group. Together, the people in that Community Group are challenged by the group leader to take the learned truths of Scripture and apply them on mission at home, work, and in the broader community."[28] As Driscoll describes why Campaigns are important, he highlights their use as a technology of security that regulates risk on the scale of population.

> Campaigns guard the gate theologically. When you don't plan ahead and have a Campaign, it becomes very easy for your small groups to set their own agendas. Before you know it, they devolve into book clubs studying who knows what. This leads to division because various groups and life stage ministries are on their own missions rather than working together on mission. As your church grows, it becomes increasingly difficult for you to know what's taught in your communities and whether it's biblical or heretical. When you take the time to plan out a full Campaign that includes small group curriculum, you get to set the agenda for your small groups and you take back control of your ground war.[29]

Thus, at the same time that Campaigns promote evangelism and church expansion, they also serve as a strategy of counterinsurgency. Much like what Masco describes as an American security system which, given its inability to perfectly predict and counter threat, constitutes "nearly every domain and object of everyday life as a potential vector of attack," the affective infrastructure of the air war–ground war operates as a technology of security that creates "a nearly perfect paranoid system, but one with planetary reach."[30] Instead of a sense of protection, this infrastructure promotes excitability and agitation, as affect circulates to coordinate "subjects through felt intensities rather than reason at a mass level."[31] The affective value of this circulation registers in the testimonies of former congregants, such as those posted on the website *Mars Hill Refuge*, a "Mars Hill Survivor blog" augmented in 2012.[32] One woman writes, "It has been almost 10 months since we left our former church. I've hesitated to post our story for a number of reasons, most revolving around fear. Fear is something I struggle with greatly."[33] Soon after this introduction, however, she describes her attraction to the church in terms of acceptance and family, healing and transformation, a vibrant love.

[My husband and I] came to Mars Hill to visit and knew immediately that THIS was the church we were supposed to be at. We quickly got connected with a community group and were accepted with open arms, kids and all. I've never known such a wonderful sense of family that we've known at Mars Hill. We ate meals together, went camping together, babysat each others kids, shared our life's most intimate details. . . . It was in redemption group that I finally started to heal from my childhood issues that had held me hostage for so long. . . . Redemption group changed my life. I made amazing friends, learned how to forgive those who have hurt me, I came to LOVE Mars Hill, our local pastor, and our amazing church family. I really thought we'd be here indefinitely.[34]

In this story, intimate friendships are born out of positive experiences in community groups where weekly fellowship and the discussion of sermons fostered a network of care that provided familial support and a sense of security. Additionally, a biblical counseling ministry called Redemption Groups afforded help to this woman and her husband as she processed a troubled personal history. This process of healing was neither straightforward nor progressive, however, given Driscoll's preaching on sex: "I think the first big issue I had was hearing Mark talk of the sexually explicit 'visions' he'd had of coworkers and members of the church. . . . The idea that the leader of our church would sometimes look into someone's eyes and see abuses against them or sexual interactions they'd had truly freaked me out."[35] Later, this woman and her husband shared misgivings when the church's history was rewritten to sell its success: "There was the fund drive in December, and . . . infomercial-like sermons on Mars Hill history . . . seemed heavily edited, so many omissions, no mention of the original three founders . . . and the sudden plea for a huge amount of funds right at Christmas time seemed a bit manipulative." When she voiced this concern on the church's online social network *The City*, this woman received a phone call from a friend who suggested that she was not submitting to the leadership of Mars Hill and questioned whether she really wanted to be at the church—a viral love gone bad.[36]

Appendix C of *Campaigns* is comprised of a "Biblical Counseling Q&A with Pastor of Biblical Living Mike Wilkerson," who oversaw Redemption

Groups. In response to a question about "what would happen if leaders weren't trained to deal with some of the issues brought up in the pulpit," he responds: "People are more likely to go to friends, family or community members for help before they will seek the help of someone in an official counseling capacity. . . . So there you have the makings for a social network of counseling, where the help people receive they pass along in trusting, informal relationships. That's a huge asset to a church if the DNA of the social network is strong. If not, it's a real problem because the bad ideas go viral."[37] According to Wilkerson, an informal social network of counseling exists not only among those who support the pulpit as campus pastors or community group leaders, but also among those without any official church role or training. In effect, friends who tell friends to submit to church authority or leave the body fulfill their function in the technology of security mobilized by a social network of counseling. The spiritual authority of the pulpit was simulated through the social networking of violence-care via the affective infrastructure of the air war–ground war.

Kip, another contributor to *Mars Hill Refuge*, contemplated assuming the role of community group leader through prayer then answered the call for more leaders. After a few training sessions, he endured a pastoral "interview" conducted in the manner of bullying harassment. Kip's story illustrates the way in which Driscoll's *Fight Club* tactics and biblically infused "shock doctrine" filtered into local leadership and the training of further leaders.[38] As his testimony continues, Kip describes an email he wrote to the pastor who interviewed him and the events that ensued: "I . . . expressed a few concerns about how the interview was conducted. Because of this experience and other observations, I suspected MH believed in order to build men up, they must bully them and break them down. His reply came that he had perhaps misrepresented himself and that he wasn't simply trying to 'sin-hunt.' "[39] The pastor asked to meet again, and Kip agreed, but he was later informed that more pastors would be present for "greater accountability." Kip states, "When I tried to rescind my name from the training process and decline to meet further—I was accused of 'running' from community and my leaders who were trying to love me. So to prove that we weren't running, [my wife and I] agreed to meet [them] . . . [but] this was getting more bizarre and we began feeling more intimidated by all of this. What had I done? Hadn't

I just pointed out some concerns about their 'training' process?"[40] Kip then describes how the interrogatory style of his pastoral interview intensified rather than abated.

> Pastor Y looked at me and said . . . "God is telling me that your real issue is pride. You have a pride problem that you need to deal with. You came in here with your fists up ready to fight[,] didn't you? Well you now have a chance to respond either in pride or humility—what's it going to be?" He must have sensed that I was feeling intimidated, but with 2 pastors and my CG [community group] leader staring me down and grilling—I guess you could say I felt a little defensive. My CG leader chimed in with a laundry list of items where I had "failed" him both in the training process and outside of [it]. Pastor Y repeated the question "will you respond in pride or humility?" Pastor X was on the other side yelling "What's Jesus saying! What's Jesus saying!" I started to feel like I was suffocating or like a giant weight was crushing me. I finally broke. The tears start running and at once my wife and I and everyone else in the room was relieved that I had admitted my sin. We were convinced that my concerns were irrelevant because I was prideful. . . . Everyone patted themselves on the back and we prayed together. But from the moment we left, I felt sick to my stomach like something wrong had just happened. What happened there was anything but kind or loving. To be sure, it was the scariest most divisive most manipulative experience I have ever been through. It was more of an interrogation than anything.[41]

Kip testifies to how potential threat requires seamless monitoring by technologies of security. At Mars Hill, these biopolitical processes of control were socially networked via the affective infrastructure of the air war–ground war, regulating the population through the regularization of risk. In *Campaigns*, Driscoll also describes an overt orchestration of affective atmosphere to biopolitical effect.

AIR WAR–GROUND WAR AS AFFECTIVE ATMOSPHERE

A *Campaigns* chapter entitled "Four Principles for Planning Campaigns" instructs church leaders to "contextualize one big idea to all levels . . . to make sure you're reaching your people with a unique message that is applicable for each phase of life. . . . Ask yourself, 'How can each of our ministries amplify and complement the big idea?'"[42] Driscoll describes how to communicate and diffuse the affective capacity of "one big idea" such that it practically impacts congregants on individual, familial, and collective levels. For example, in the Real Marriage Campaign, individuals read his books with daily devotions that steered them to the Mars Hill blog and social media channels like Facebook and Twitter; married couples followed a curriculum for husbands and wives, including discussion topics and activities to work through together; community group curriculum provided questions for each week and a guide for leaders.[43] Driscoll also emphasizes how important it is to ensure that each aspect of media production evokes the proper mood: "The musicians are told the tone of the sermon in order to plan their music to match the sermon content. . . . It would be a disaster to have a tough sermon on pornography addiction followed up by a happy-clappy song to Jesus. . . . Our video team has created intro videos that tie the sermon content heard audibly to striking visual images. . . . [production material from the] bulletins to the PowerPoint slides to the posters on the walls, reiterates the sermon's message."[44] In this section of *Campaigns*, there is a clear strategy in place to pedagogically and aesthetically brand each sermon such that it affectively registers in congregants' everyday lives and is globally diffused throughout the church body.

By strategically assuring that the big idea communicated from the pulpit is imitated and amplified, not only through verbal suggestion or onstage performance but also the various commodities, technologies, emotions, and sensations marketed through and mobilized by each Campaign, Mars Hill calibrates the affective space of encounter to steer conviction. Tony Sampson notes that the point of this contemporary form of biopower "is to mesmerize the consumer (and voter) to such an extent that her susceptible porousness to the invention of others, received mostly unawares, becomes an escalating point of vulnerability."[45] This networking of control, according to Sampson, "occurs at the intersection point between conscious volition and involuntary, mechanical habit. It is at these vulnerable intersections that the mostly unconscious desire to imitate the suggestions of others is appropriated by social invention."[46] In appendix B of *Campaigns*, Worship Director Jonathan Dunn explains how music is coordinated to imitate the message and tone emanating from the pulpit, encouraging social invention during moments of vulnerability in worship.

> At the worship direction level, when preparing for a Sunday service we first consider the trajectory or goal for that week. For example, if the week's Scripture passage leads us to joy, there needs to be a cohesive plan to properly lead the congregation to joy. . . . Pastor Mark goes over the vision for the week and how we can achieve our goals. At the end of the meeting, we will usually have a rough outline of what the songs are going to be for Sunday. Then that information gets flushed out to the individual bandleaders to capture the emotional vibe for that week.[47]

Joel Brown, the worship pastor at Mars Hill Ballard, adds, "We want to be unified with the preaching pastor on the overall emotional trajectory of the service. . . . Music has, more than any other art form, tremendous emotional capacity. . . . After the sermon we play four songs that are in response to the message. After the congregants' hearts have been tenderized by the message, it's crucial that the music leads people to the proper response."[48] This joyful encounter of social invention was atmospherically primed by worship music as an instrument of biopolitical control, affording congregants the freedom to raise their arms in worship or not, so long as their hearts were tenderized.

Reflecting on "affective atmosphere," geographer Ben Anderson notes that the concept signals a transpersonal dimension to affective life, a generative ambiguity in distinctions between presence-absence or subject-object that affords openings to rethink the formation of subjectivity.[49] He adds, "Atmospheres are . . . always in the process of emerging and transforming. They are always being taken up and reworked in lived experience—becoming part of feelings and emotions that may themselves become elements within other atmospheres."[50] The affective capacity of atmosphere to globally rally assemblages of militarized bodies, mobilizing them on a transsubjective register, gives it an important role in Campaigns. Anderson writes, "We can say that atmospheres are generated by bodies—of multiple types—affecting one another as some form of 'envelopment' is produced. Atmospheres do not float free from the bodies that come together and apart to compose situations. Affective qualities emanate from the assembling of the human bodies, discursive bodies, nonhuman bodies, and all the other bodies that make up everyday situations."[51] In Campaigns, media technologies and invisible demons are agents rather than tools, constituting affective atmospheres with and through congregants.

Mars Hill Global received its own visual branding and promotional advertising before sermons. To the accompaniment of stridently somber, liltingly uplifting organ music, congregants in-house and online watched a video of Lead Pastor Sutton Turner, head of the church's financial organization. Wearing khaki safari pants, he stands, Bible in hand, in front of a hut whose location is unclear: "Howdy, Mars Hill Church and our extended family of Mars Hill Global. Pastor Sutton Turner here, and I'm really, really thankful that you have decided to join us for our global services today."[52] The visual punctuation to these welcoming words provides evidence of Mars Hill's global scope. The picture shifts from Turner to a panoramic view of a field of homes as seen from a cliff. As the camera pans over this landscape, Turner says: "Our global services are broadcast all over the world, based on your time zone." At the end of this sentence, the scene cuts to the Mars Hill Bellevue stage lit up in royal blue, with the big idea of the sermon hovering over Pastor Mark on a large screen as he preaches. Turner continues, "So that you can see, all of what Jesus . . . ." [the camera shifts again to a view of a man raising his arms in praise, in what looks to be a smaller, humbler congregation (presumably) in Africa], "at our local church." Then we are back at Mars Hill Bellevue, where worship pastor and Christian rock celebrity Dustin Kensrue leads the congregation in song, an amped acoustic guitar around his neck.

As Turner continues, "Let me first say, you should be part of a local church," we see in close-up an open Bible in the lap of an African congregant in a pew. Mars Hill Bellevue congregants worship as sun streams in through large windows, reflecting off the camera lens. "Fellowship and community is super important," Turner intones as we again see him standing in front of the hut. "So you should give to your local church. Above and beyond that, we want you to be a part of the extended family of Mars Hill Global. Jesus is doing some crazy awesome things"—the picture shifts to friends hugging in a schoolyard in Africa—"at Mars Hill, and we want you to be a part of that"—we see an African child laughing, then a circle of African men arm-in-arm with heads bowed—"with your prayers and your gifts"—the camera settles back on Turner—"above and beyond your offering to Mars

Hill Global. So, welcome to the services, and thank you for joining us." The screen goes black, and "Support the Mission" appears in white above "marshill.com/global." During this commercial, we never learn where Turner is standing, let alone what churches Mars Hill Global supports or how. After the one-minute advertisement, the sermon would proceed. Following its broadcast on May 25, 2014, Driscoll preached on wolves during a period when financial and administrative scandals long brewing had become widely publicized. In addition to the ResultSource debacle, there was also another fiscal controversy stemming from documents leaked by someone within "central" (leadership) concerning where the money from the "global" fund actually went.

In July 2014, in response to inquiries concerning expenditures, the Mars Hill Global "Frequently Asked Questions" web page provided a sketch of spending which showed that the global fund budget was not so global in terms of its distribution. During the fiscal period from 2009–2014, over $10 million was given to Mars Hill Church by "the Mars Hill global family."[53] That money was "spent on church planting in the US, India and Ethiopia."[54] Donations "helped to plant churches in Bellevue, WA; Everett, WA; Tacoma, WA; Phoenix, AZ; and soon Spokane, WA, as well as helped translate materials, distribute Bibles, fund evangelists in Ethiopia, church planters in India, and so much more."[55]

An even more telling indictment surfaced in a confidential Executive Elders memo leaked to an evangelical contributor on the religion blogging site Patheos.

> The vision and activities connected to the Global Fund must focus on reaching the worldwide church. As a person sits in front of their computer in Qatar, London, Cape Town or Sydney, he does not care about Mars Hill church planting in Everett [Washington]. As an international citizen, however, he cares greatly about global evangelism, global missions, global causes for Jesus, global church planting, etc. Though the sentiment is rare among Americans, people abroad feel a sense of belonging and kinship with the global community.[56]

Under "benefits," the deceptiveness of this affective strategy was fiscally quantified: "For a relatively low cost (e.g. $10k/month), supporting a few missionaries and benevolence projects would serve to deflect criticism, increase goodwill, and create opportunities to influence and learn from other ministries. Many small churches who may consider joining Mars Hill hesitate because they do not believe we support 'missions.' The Global Fund would serve as a simple, easy way to deflect such criticism and help lead change in these congregations."[57] Mars Hill's own mission came under question due to financial scandals surrounding the global fund, as well as reports of systemic bullying and micromanagement that resulted in PTSD-like symptoms which contagiously spread among former Mars Hill staff and congregants.

SPIRITUAL ABUSE AND TESTIMONIES TO TRAUMA

In 2013, when Pastor of Biblical Living Mike Wilkerson was asked to mediate conflict between former staff and the Executive Elders, those he spoke with testified to PTSD-like symptoms resulting from a sense of betrayal.

> I found it difficult to gain the cooperation of the complainants, those former staff members who had expressed grievances. Their emotional affect in phone conversations was marked by what I would regard as extreme fear. They were reluctant to cooperate with the conciliation process we had offered them [due to a] lack of trust that Mars Hill was adequately equipped to address the problems; Belief that other leaders are complicit in the reinforcing of the problems; Self-descriptors of symptoms that indicate emotional depletion, despair, and terror, such as feeling like a "corpse" after engaging in phone calls related to the conflict, feeling "alone," or panicking when seeing the caller ID indicating a call from me, possibly about Mars Hill conflict; Unwillingness to report grievances because of perceived past failures to see reports successful.[58]

Wilkerson also notes that Executive Elders had recently acknowledged a "culture of fear" at the church and dramatic staff turnover rates, adding, "These indicators appear strongly correlated with the phenomenon of workplace bullying."[59] His discussion is framed by biblical verse and secular scholarship, including research from an edited volume entitled *Bullying and Harassment in the Workplace: Developments in Theory, Research, and Practice* (2011).[60] Highlighting certain points relevant to his investigation, including empirical evidence and interview material gathered in conversations with former staff, Wilkerson discovers many intersections between his discoveries and academic conclusions concerning the effects of workplace bullying. From the outset of his report, he frequently reiterates that while bullying may be associated with dramatic threat, it is often highly covert and indirect.[61] To have such widespread, severe, and lingering affects and effects, bullying must be imitative, inventive, and systemic—a social, embodied process that is structurally embedded, rather than individually perpetrated or perceived.

In a section on the organizational factors that enable bullying, Wilkerson includes authoritarian leadership, lack of accountability for perpetrating violence, tacit complicity throughout the management system, and drift into uniformity and conformity.[62] He also devotes a prominent section of his study to the psychological and health effects of workplace bullying, including PTSD-like symptoms: strong emotional reactions such as fear, anxiety, helplessness, depression, and shock; a change in the individual's perceptions of their work environment and life in general to one of threat, danger, insecurity, and self-questioning; and pervasive emotional, psychosomatic, and psychiatric problems.[63] The research Wilkerson cites is driven by psychological models that concern the traumatic effects of bullying on individual victims, and that describe PTSD as a reaction to one or more events that have threatened the physical integrity of the self or others. Thus, the symptoms which surface entail a persistent reexperiencing of a given traumatic event in memories, flashbacks, or nightmares; avoidance of reminders of the stressors and emotional numbing; and persistent physical arousal.[64]

In the aftermath of her family's exile from the church, Jonna Petry experienced PTSD-like symptoms, which she attributes to spiritual abuse.

> Words do not adequately describe the shock, horror, betrayal, and rejection [our family] felt. The weight of the loss was excruciating . . . I was emotionally and spiritually devastated. I was often tormented by fear. I had nightmares and imagination of someone trying to physically harm Paul, me, and the children. If Mark had had ecclesiastical power to burn Paul at the stake I believe he would have. I literally slept in the fetal position for months. I stayed in bed a lot, bringing the children in bed with me to do their schoolwork. I became severely depressed and could hardly bring myself to leave the house except when absolutely necessary. I cried nearly every day for well over a year thinking I must soon cry it out, right? But, the sorrow was bottomless. My faith was gravely shaken.

How could a loving God allow this? Later it became clear that I had typical symptoms of Post Traumatic Stress Disorder and Depression and that these reactions were common in someone who has experienced spiritual abuse.[65]

In *The Evil Hours*, a "biography" of post-traumatic stress disorder, former marine and journalist David J. Morris notes that as it is understood today, PTSD is a "heterogeneous disease, a junk drawer of disconnected symptoms which include the numbing of emotions, hypervigilance, and a variety of intrusive manifestations, such as nightmares and hallucinations."[66] Noting that PTSD is increasingly monitored, testified to, and marketed via neuroscience, social media, and popular culture, Morris concludes, "As a cultural meme, PTSD is everywhere now. . . . We live now in an aftermath culture."[67] He muses, "Is there something about the War on Terror . . . that has made us all a little nuts? Is there something about the larger war against Islamic extremism that has made [Americans] fear the outside world?"[68] Such questions beg for an analysis of PTSD as a symptom of history, rather than as a pathology of the psyche or a trigger on the brain.

As a cultural meme, PTSD signals desire that lacks a particular object and affective networking that is socially inventive and imitative. It is not only the predominance of unruly PTSD-like symptoms, but also the proliferation of public testimonies to their causes, affects, and effects—performed bodily and narratively—that suggests a social desire to "vow to tell . . . as material evidence for truth."[69] The term *PTSD* is a vernacular in our historical moment, while testimony is a privileged mode of transmission and education, a cultural witnessing of and to ourselves.[70] Morris describes trauma as "a transfer of energies: like a bullet, it enters the body, with a surplus of power, eager to transmit it to whatever flesh it finds, doing its work then exiting, leaving the troubled body behind . . . looking for another body to complicate."[71] In bodily and narratively bearing witness to the social suffering signaled by PTSD's contagiousness, social justice is politically reimagined and affectively reconfigured. Studying the causes and effects of PTSD incurred during military combat, psychologist Jonathan Shay claims that its physiological changes of the nervous system index "moral injury" resulting from a breach of "social trust in the expectation that power will be used in accordance with 'what's right.' "[72] This definition resonates with what Jonna Petry calls "spiritual abuse," which "occurs when someone uses their power within a framework of spiritual belief or practice to satisfy their own needs at the expense of others. It is a breach of sacred trust."[73] These overlapping definitions of moral injury and spiritual abuse figure power as an object wielded by someone or a body other than the sufferer-victim; trust, be it "social" or "sacred," is broken by an outside authority.

However, as affect theorist Lauren Berlant points out, such accounts of trauma reinforce a limited perspective, rendering "the historical present as the scene of an exception that has just shattered some ongoing, uneventful ordinary life that was supposed just to keep going on and with respects to which people felt solid and confident."[74] She adds, "Trauma theory conventionally focuses on exceptional shock and data loss in the memory and experience of catastrophe, implicitly suggesting that subjects ordinarily archive the intensities neatly and efficiently with an eye toward easy access."[75] Although the literature that Wilkerson references is couched in such terms with relation to symptoms—the reexperiencing of a given traumatic event in memories, flashbacks, or nightmares—these "symptoms" were embedded in Mars Hill's infrastructure and airborne in its atmosphere, "an assemblage of contagions."[76] The affects of spiritual abuse are not the effects of dominion theology, cult-like authority, or complementarian gender doctrine, but rather a collective, embodied affective labor that is recurring, regenerative, and imitative—serial shocks of social invention rather than an individual pathology or historical present with a particular cause or origin.

According to Berlant, optimism is the structure of attachment, even when attachments "do not *feel* all optimistic."[77] This optimistic attachment takes form in "knotty tethering to objects, scenes, and modes of life."[78] Cruel optimism materialized in sensations that emotionally and physically overwhelmed Petry, signaling trauma that is not hers. The affects that continue to infectiously and unpredictably surface as PTSD-like symptoms among former Mars Hill staff, as well as in the embodied narratives of soldiers returning from battle, testify to surplus affective value that is not possessed by any given person. In his confession, Mike Anderson states, "We used to call this church and its influence a 'movement.' The movement was everything to me—this was literally the hand of God moving across the world to make it 'better.'"[79] He references Hitler and hypernationalism alongside growth metrics, the rhetoric of exceptionalism, and marketability that blurs divisions between evangelical and popular culture. His individual biography and bearing witness to history in the present are mutually constituted by his conviction in the mission of a megachurch, whereby aspirations to empire become purified—a sign of God's hand literally moving across the world to make it better. Later, after he describes the feelings of distrust in leadership that motivated him to leave the church, Anderson's story echoes Jonna Petry's: "It took a long time after leaving for my conscience to come back, and I began to get perspective. It started out as PTSD-like symptoms—I had a doctor ask me point-blank, without knowing my story, if I was experiencing PTSD (there are dozens and dozens of former leaders like me that report the same thing—I've even seen people joke publicly about "MHPTSD" and everyone knows exactly what it means). Next came the guilt. What have I done?"[80]

The sense of self-doubt indexed in Anderson's question and the social betrayal signaled by his PTSD-like symptoms after resigning membership demonstrate the importance of examining cruel optimism in the study of religion and power—within and outside of contexts and situations that are explicitly "religious," such as a church. Religious studies scholar Donovan Schaefer writes, "Cruel optimism . . . makes sense of the moments when religion resolutely exceeds what passes for rational self-interest . . . complex structures of feeling that cut against . . . the sovereign self's own assessment of its best course of action."[81] Anderson denigrates his single-minded adoption of "religion," which he does not define in doctrinal terms of belief, but later in this post as he proclaims, "I had spent about a decade listening to every word Mark Driscoll preached. I was in. I made a decade of decisions based on his conviction and not my own. That's my fault. Is it???"[82]

This conflicted feeling of conviction resounds with the cruel optimism experienced, Schaefer writes, "when the nonsovereignty of the self blazes through."[83] Philosopher Jason Read discusses how Spinoza's "anthropology of desire" affords a critique of capitalist power at the level of economy and social relations that is also attuned to the affective dimensions of narrative and political imagination.[84] Spinoza's conceptualization of the "conatus," or "the striving underlying every existence," is an opportunity to reconsider political economy beyond rationales of self-interest, and testimony without an intentional subject, by suggesting that desire is distinctly singular yet constitutes "man's very essence" given that "the direction and orientation of this striving is shaped by affects and the history of encounters."[85] In Anderson's testimony to the addiction of true belief, references to change, sacrifice, and drive suggest a desire for transformation that worked against his self-interest in lieu of "the cause." This cause is mobilized through convergences of spiritual and worldly warfare and conviction in formations of Evangelical-U.S. Empire conjured by a theological-nationalist imaginary of exceptionalism.

In August 2014, I was standing with protestors outside of Mars Hill Church, again. By now, Pastor Mark was preaching in a high-end strip mall in the Seattle suburb of Bellevue, in a beige big box cathedral next to an equally nondescript Barnes and Noble. I approached the group of people standing with signs next to the parking lot, none of whom I knew, and chose one of my own from the stack resting against a low brick wall.

What distinguished this gathering of protestors from the first in 2006, other than its larger size of several dozen, was its predominant composition of former Mars Hill staff and members. There were also photojournalists and news vans, a few reporters and researchers passing out business cards for interviews. On the local TV news that night, I caught a glimpse of myself standing next to a woman with whom I would quickly become close. A week later I visited the house where she lived with her husband in a northern Seattle suburb for an early lunch and wound up staying long past dinner. I shared cigars with a group of men in their backyard one Thanksgiving.

Placards marked with the word *misogyny* signaled overlap in talking points, but there were several others filled with new phrases, fresh questions about the Global Fund, and names familiar yet expunged from church annals, such as Paul Petry's. Each protestor's sign raised important challenges and necessary queries, but it was not the sum of their parts that brought anyone there. The overriding resolve of the protest was to see Driscoll removed from leadership, so that the church could become healthy again. No one spoke of hate, but out of concern for the future of Mars Hill, its current members, Mark, and his family.

I spent time with a woman in her late twenties that came without her husband. Their marriage, she willingly shared, had been rocky for years due to tensions over living out the gender and sexuality doctrine of the church. The couple no longer lived in Seattle, a distance from their entanglements with Mars Hill that felt healthy. They happened to be visiting, so she had decided to come to the protest, but her discomfort was apparent. She was visibly shaken, fidgeting and distracted, as though constantly looking over her shoulder. She never grabbed a sign. I later learned that a biblical marriage counseling session she and her husband had with Mark turned into a demon trial performed in the violent manner that I had read about online.

During our conversation, those tasked with providing hospitality on behalf of the church passed by with pink boxes of sticky glazed donuts turning gooey in the midday sun. Church greeters soon followed, offering us welcome packets containing, we were told, a free book by Pastor Mark. After we declined these gifts, the volunteers moved up the line. I don't want this to happen again, my companion intoned wistfully, staring at their backs.

On October 14, 2014, Driscoll submitted his resignation from the roles of Executive Elder and preaching pastor at Mars Hill Church. At that time, the Board of Overseers (BOO), which comprised four men, had just finished evaluating a series of charges against him. A document signed by twenty-one former Mars Hill pastors leaked in August 2014 provides a snapshot of these accusations: Pastor Mark used threats and verbal assaults against those he considered threatening; slandered leaders within and outside of the church; and displayed domineering arrogance in staff meetings, including statements to the effect of "You're not the brand, I'm the brand!"[1]

In 2013, the Board of Advisors and Accountability (BOAA) included Mars Hill's Executive Elders—Mark Driscoll, Dave Bruskas, and Sutton Turner—as well as Paul Tripp, the face and president of a parachurch organization that bears his name, and James McDonald, lead pastor of Harvest Bible Chapter, a multisited megachurch of roughly 12,000 serving the Chicagoland area, and longtime partner in crime of Driscoll's.[2] In 2014, when Tripp resigned from the BOAA, he announced that Mars Hill was "without a doubt, the most abusive, coercive ministry culture I've ever been involved with,"[3] although he had been a guest speaker and paid consultant on the church's payroll while supporting the development of community and redemption ministries. Despite his harsh assessment of Mars Hill, the church stated, "Dr. Tripp graciously submitted his resignation from the BOAA in early June so that he can more extensively serve our church as a consultant. We are excited to continue this work with him, and are thankful for his continued support of Mars Hill Church."[4]

Meanwhile, at the time of his own resignation, McDonald issued this statement.

I want to make clear this change is not because I am unhappy with Mark's response to board accountability. . . . I have found him to be exemplary in his current readiness to live under the BOAA oversight. I am not resigning because I doubt Mark's sincerity in any way. I believe in Mark Driscoll and his heart to leverage difficult lessons in service to Christ and his church in the years ahead. I am excited to continue to support that trajectory as Mark's friend, as I focus my efforts on Harvest Bible Fellowship.[5]

In August 2014, a group of seven elders, plus one member of what became known as the Board of Overseers (BOO) after Tripp and McDonald left, were charged with conducting an investigation concerning Driscoll's qualifications as a pastor. They compiled "1,000 hours of research," including interviews with "more than 50 people" and "200 pages of information" with "Pastor Mark's support and cooperation."[6] Two men on the BOO were local Seattle members of Mars Hill (Matt Rogers and Jon Phelps); the other two men lived outside of Washington State and were not directly affiliated with the church.[7] The BOO was charged with evaluating the evidence compiled during the review process. After deliberation, the members declared Pastor Mark "guilty of arrogance, responding to conflict with a quick temper and harsh speech, and leading the staff and elders in a domineering manner," which were issues that he needed to address in his life but that did disqualify him from pastoral ministry.[8] Furthermore, the BOO found that Driscoll did nothing immoral or illegal, adding that he had "publicly confessed and apologized for a number of the charges against him, some of which occurred as long as 14 years ago."[9] The BOO concluded by stating, "We commend Mark for acting upon the vision God gave him to start Mars Hill Church and for his ministry of faithfully teaching the Word of God for the past 18 years," emphasizing that he was not asked to resign and that they were surprised to receive his letter.[10] In said letter, Driscoll reiterated many of the points highlighted in the BOO's decision then added, "Recent months have proven unhealthy for our family—even physically unsafe at times—and we believe the time has now come for the elders to choose new pastoral leadership for Mars Hill."[11]

The response to Driscoll's resignation among supporters and critics within and outside of the church was swift and emotional. Former Mars Hill member Zach Malm responded, "[The Mars Hill crisis] was all so avoid-able, but the arrogance that led to it all is clear."[12] Specifically, Malm pointed to Driscoll's resignation letter as evidence of this arrogance: "He spends so much time informing the reader that he was cleared of all charges, frames his sin as in the past, and basically says he's leaving only because he's a hus-band and father, and this is best for his family."[13] Malm added that he had been reconnecting with old Mars Hill friends, some of whom were driven away from Christianity altogether—one in particular "described himself as feeling 'allergic to Scripture.' "[14] Malm also alluded to broken friendships due to strife during and over the church's fall.

The most poignant remarks regarding Pastor Mark's resignation were written before his letter was even conceived, predating it by several months. In July 2014, after the anonymous video aired, former leader of women's ministry Wendy Alsup published a post on her blog, *Practical Theology for Women*, entitled "Godly Sorrow Leads to Repentance."[15] Alsup begins by quoting Dietrich Bonhoeffer's *The Cost of Discipleship* (1959): "Cheap grace is the preaching of forgiveness without requiring repentance."[16] She then argues that by publicly posting a video in which he generally apologizes for wrongdoings without acknowledging the specific details or names of those with grievances, Pastor Mark's apology exemplifies what the Apostle Paul calls "worldly sorrow." In turn, Alsup explains the difference between godly sorrow and worldly sorrow: "When faced with confrontation or other natu-ral consequences of your sin, you can mourn your sin in a way that leads you to confess to God, change your direction, and repair with those you have hurt. And that response allows you to get up and go forward without regret. . . . Godly sorrow producing repentance is beautiful."[17] She then con-trasts this transformation with worldly sorrow, which demonstrates "grief and lament in response to the consequences of one's sin that does not understand and appropriate Christ's payment for it." She notes, "Any hope of 'forgiveness' without clear, specific repentance is exactly what Bonhoef-fer labels cheap grace."[18] As Alsup summed up the distinction between Godly sorrow and worldly sorrow with the word *repentance*, she wrote of social transformation: "True repentance always starts with a specific nam-ing of your sin, and it always includes a change in your ways."[19]

When Mark announced his decision to step down from the pulpit for six weeks as the charges against him were investigated, his statement included a chorus of sentences that began and ended with "I'm very sorry," but that never specified his sin or those he sinned against: "I want to say to my Mars Hill family, past and present, I'm very sorry . . . I'm very sorry for the times I've been angry, short or insensitive. I'm very sorry for anything I've done to distract from our mission by inviting criticism, controversy or negative media attention."[20] Although he said, "I have begun meeting with a professional team of mature Christians who provide wise counsel to help further my personal development and maturity before God and men," he never mentioned repenting.[21]

In fact, just days after his resignation from Mars Hill, Mark would take the stage at a different church led by one of the mature Christians providing him wise counsel. On October 20, 2014, Driscoll spoke briefly at Gateway Church in suburban Dallas/Fort Worth, Texas, at the invitation of Pastor Robert Morris. Originally, Driscoll was meant to give a formal address at a conference hosted by Gateway, but he requested to be present simply as an attendee. Nevertheless, Morris urged him to say a few words: "We could crucify him, but since someone's already been crucified for him. . . . It's very sad that in the church, we're the only army that shoots at our wounded. And I'd like you to stop it."[22]

Microphone once again in hand, Mark shared that he was praying for Jesus to reveal "blind spots" where he could grow. Rekindling the sarcastic timing that he had perfected from the Mars Hill pulpit he added, "There are a lot of things I could say that would make me feel better. I don't know if it would make me look better, but I don't think it would make Jesus look better."[23] He then asked the audience to pray for his family and confessed, "I've cried a lot lately. It's been a rough season for the family," summarizing this period with details of vandalism perpetrated against his home, death threats, and hovering helicopters that led his eight-year-old son to don a military jacket and load his Airsoft rifle in an effort to protect the family: "He didn't have any concept of media coverage. He thought it was bad guys coming to kill his family."[24]

As he left the stage, Pastor Mark received a standing ovation for a performance that epitomized the lie of worldly sorrow. He was clearly not walking the path of true repentance; even I, a nonbeliever, could see that. The homepage of his new church plant, the Trinity Church in Scottsdale, Arizona, continues to advertise *Real Marriage* (2012) as he sermonizes yet another series through its pages as of February 2017; meanwhile, his pastoral biography makes no mention of his previous ministry at Mars Hill Church.[25]

THE POLITICAL LIMITATIONS OF LOVE AND THE ETHICAL
POSSIBILITIES OF VULNERABILITY

Godly sorrow was at work among those who were willing to speak with me from the years of 2014–2016, some of whom I did not seek out but who wrote to me after reading my research online. During this period, many former leaders publicly confessed to their sins and invited others to reach out to them so that they could specifically and privately repent to them. As I spoke with these men, their desire to redeem the positions that they held at Mars Hill in pastoral care, marketing, and information technology was apparent. Even as this godly sorrow was an ongoing process that involved self-doubt and social suffering, it was becoming without regret, a vulnerability of encounter.

Love has been theorized as an affect of political mobilization and resistance in ways that vulnerability has not. In an interview-dialogue with Michael Hardt and Lauren Berlant entitled "On the Risk of a New Relationality," they discuss love as a political concept.[26] Both Hardt and Berlant theorize love as a nonsovereign social-subjective formation, a collective becoming-different that can inform alternative social imaginaries.[27] While Hardt sees love as an ontologically constitutive, generative force, for Berlant love disorganizes our lives such that we move beyond ourselves and invest in social change.[28] Hardt states, "Love makes central the role of affect in the political sphere," confounding the notion of interest in lieu of collective, sustained transformation.[29] In turn, Berlant speaks of love as "one of the few places where people actually admit they want to become different. . . . So it's like change without trauma, but it's not change without instability . . . because it's entering into relationality."[30]

In a critique of Hardt and Negri's politics of love, and by extension Berlant's formulation as well, affect theorist Melissa Gregg writes of skepticism concerning love's capacity to inspire social relations and networks of "radical experiment."[31] Hardt and Negri distinguish between the "corruption" of love in its "identitarian" form, which asserts love of the same, as in patriotism and fascism; and its "unification" form, which promotes the notion of two as one, such as in marriage. Gregg writes, "Hardt and Negri's turn to love is part of a wider movement to disassociate love from the conventions of middle class propriety, where property and intimacy are linked together in a mutually beneficial pact."[32] She adds, "It is this limited imagination of love—our reluctance to explore its 'wild syncretism' (Berlant 2001, 448)— that Hardt and Negri appear to lament."[33] Thus, Gregg concludes, "Love is the only repetitive-compulsive behavior that society openly celebrates."[34] It is this celebration that Gregg rightly finds suspicious. In her critique, "radical" love elides material concerns as it locates revolutionary hope in the multitude of the poor, leaving matters of geography and class inequality, as well as forms of exclusion necessary for participation in neoliberal economies, forgotten and unrecognized.

Love did not sustain Mars Hill after Pastor Mark's resignation in 2014; love did not "Trump" hate as many hoped during the 2016 Election. The backlash against "political correctness" and threat of "radical Islam" that precipitated Driscoll's rise as a celebrity pastor foretold Donald Trump's presidency and the love shown him by "alt-right" leaders such as white nationalist Richard Spencer and trolling "provocateur" Milo Yiannopolous, whose Neo-Nazi performances and hateful speech have provoked physical violence.[35] The love demonstrated by Trump's followers became the ringing endorsement for prejudicial policies and inflammatory discourse pushed by his administration within weeks of his inauguration. These executive orders included an immigration freeze and refugee ban that blatantly discriminated against Muslims while privileging Christians,[36] and a vow to "destroy" a law restricting political speech by tax-exempt churches.[37] In 2017, radical love is not revolutionary in the way that Hardt and Berlant theorized; it is about "Making America Great Again" through exclusion, abandonment, ad hominem, intimidation, bullying, and the intensification of the affective reality of future threat. In August 2014, we protested against these very practices and testified to their collective harm a stone's throw from Mars Hill.

White evangelicals turned out for Trump in a show of support that many attributed to predictable trends in Republican partisanship and "pro-life" stances, "values voters" in the mold of Jerry Falwell's Moral Majority. However, in the months before the election, evangelical pundits and leaders questioned and debated whether this partisan voting block would or should support Trump's candidacy. Most across the conservative and progressive spectrum assumed his campaign could not withstand his racially discriminatory stump speeches, calls for a Muslim registry, and sexualized verbal attacks against women caught on tape, among many other prejudicial public remarks and tweets. I never doubted the likelihood of his victory.

On the night of the election, the vote count went as I imagined, not *despite* but *due to* the controversies generated by Trump during his campaign. When Focus on the Family founder James Dobson called Trump a "baby Christian," it was laughable.[38] When white evangelical leaders stopped claiming or defending Trump and said that they were rallying behind him because of perceived threats to their security and identity, that resonated.[39] Exit polls showed that over 80 percent of white evangelicals voted for Trump in 2016, but I know of former Mars Hill members (who are also "pro-life") who did not, citing his aggressive stance on refugees and misogynistic tendencies among their reasons; of those that did, it was their boasting in victory that made me sick to my stomach.

This examination suggests that there is freedom in vulnerability. The sense of vulnerability of which I speak intersects with, yet is distinct from, what Judith Butler theorizes as a vulnerability in resistance.[40] By her logic, resistance figures vulnerable bodies exposed in solidarity; to protest as a public assembly is to be vulnerable. In vulnerability, people find ways to resist institutions and reveal how disproportionate force is used against the vulnerable. Butler's concept is twofold given subjects of precarity are vulnerable not only to neoliberal systems but also to the symbolic systems that structure how they act and identify with others and themselves.[41] Thus, resistance is a matter of uniting in vulnerability; social mobilization requires vulnerability with/in each other.

The protest outside of Mars Hill in 2014 was the kind of public assembly in resistance to institutional power that Butler describes, and in this sense it was a success. My participation also inspired conversations and relationships cultivated out of mutual vulnerability and embodied solidarity across differences of identity and worldview in ways that I never imagined possible and value to this day. However, Butler's analysis of vulnerability in resistance is too neat and tidy in its construction; social subjectivity is unnecessarily twofold or dialectical. In Butler, relation is a twinning rather than a becoming, and singularity is a sentence to be lived out rather than a bodily process. For her, the subject is always-already subjugated, even as it engages in strategies of resistance; sociality is based on this subjugation rather than freedom.

Rather than mapping Hardt's or Berlant's conceptualization of love onto what I am calling vulnerability *of encounter* rather than *in resistance*, I will say that the shift from "resistance" to "encounter" and from "love" to "vulnerability" affords an analysis of social subjectivity that begins from a place of freedom rather than of subjugation, and the nonsovereign rather than the agentive. In vulnerable encounter, one does not *try* to empathize or sympathize with "the other" through words, gestures, or "self" transformation. This social relation is not based on identity, ideology, or public assembly, but rather assemblages of human and nonhuman bodies always-already vulnerable, precarious, and at risk.

Rethinking biopower is generative for analyzing dynamics of freedom and vulnerability that do not depend on dialectics of domination-resistance. Mario Lazzarato notes, "Foucault interrogates power beginning with the 'freedom' and the 'capacity for transformation' that every 'exercise of power' implies."[42] Rather than theorizing resistance from the position of the institutionally or symbolically subjugated, Foucault conceives of resistance as "creation that calls every organization that is transcendental, and every regulatory mechanism that is extraneous . . . radically into question."[43] Thus, freedom is the resistance of *forces*, rather than of *subjects*. Lazzarato asks, in the language of Foucault, "How are we to liberate this new conception of power, one based upon the potential, difference and autonomy of forces, from the model of 'universal domination?' How are we to call forth a 'freedom' and a force that is not merely one of domination and resistance?"[44] This freedom is not won or possessed, and unnecessarily feels all that free.

When asked about the relation between resistance and creation, Foucault replied: "Resistance was conceptualized only in terms of negation. Nevertheless . . . resistance is not solely a negation but a creative process. To create and recreate, to transform the situation, to participate actively in the process, that is to resist."[45] Freedom is not located in the act of protest as such, but the social innovation of vulnerable encounter—the ethical action of worlding ongoing as I type.

Notes

INTRODUCTION

1 This transcription was done in July 2014, when the video was available on the now defunct Mars Hill Church website. However, evidence of the video's distribution and content are available at Alex Murashko, "Mark Driscoll Admits He Should Have 'Acted with More Love and Pastoral Affection' during Leadership Changes at Mars Hill, "*Christian Post*, July 23, 2014, http://www.christianpost.com/news /mark-driscoll-admits-he-should-have-acted-with-more-love-and-pastoral -affection-during-leadership-changes-at-mars-hill-123712; and at "Mark Driscoll - Mars Hill Seattle and the 'Pinocchio' Syndrome (They're Anonymous)," YouTube video, posted by "alphapa," July 31, 2014, https://www.youtube.com/watch?v=ds GDCd1iLls.

2 Driscoll, "Anonymous."

3 Driscoll, "Anonymous."

4 To clarify, I was raised a Catholic—baptized, took communion, and confirmed in our local parish. To do so, I attended Confraternity of Christian Doctrine (CCD) classes until I was thirteen. My participation was for my parents, not for myself, and as soon as I was confirmed I no longer attended church except for the occasional Christmas or Easter service with family. Throughout my teens and twenties, I vacillated on the agnostic-atheist spectrum, finding spiritual sustenance in books such as Dostoevsky's *The Brothers Karamazov*, Kafka's *The Trial*, and everything by Albert Camus. My most rigorous education in any religious tradition before attending Mars Hill was in Buddhism, with an emphasis on its Mahayana branch, as a student at Sophia University in Tokyo, Japan. I participated in various forms of meditation while living in Japan for four years. Since returning to the United States, I continue to go on ten-day long Vipassana meditation retreats, during which students are not permitted to speak, read, or write and spend the majority of their days sitting, focusing on breath and sensation. I currently do not identify with any religious tradition, or as an atheist or agnostic.

5 Driscoll, "Anonymous."

6 Gilles Deleuze and Felix Guattari, *Anti-Oedipus: Capitalism and Schizophrenia* (Minneapolis: University of Minnesota, 1983), 200.

7 Brian Massumi, *Politics of Affect* (Cambridge, UK: Polity, 2015), ix.

8 Massumi, *Politics of Affect*, vii, ix.

9 Massumi, *Politics of Affect*, 5, 19.

10 William E. Connolly, *Neuropolitics* (Minneapolis: University of Minnesota Press, 2002), 8.

11 Massumi, *Politics of Affect*, 8.

12 Mark Driscoll, "Spiritual Warfare: Who, What, and Why," July 2014, http://marshill.com/2014/07/24/spiritual-warfare-who-what-and-why.

13 Susan Harding, *The Book of Jerry Falwell: Fundamentalist Politics and Language* (Princeton: Princeton University Press, 2000), 35.

14 Harding, *The Book of Jerry Falwell*, 35.

15 Harding, *The Book of Jerry Falwell*, 59. The pastor to whom Harding refers is Reverend Melvin H. Campbell of Jordan Baptist Church in Lynchburg, Virginia.

16 William E. Connolly, *Capitalism and Christianity, American Style* (Durham: Duke University Press, 2008), 65.

17 My use of *worlding* deliberately distinguishes this study from one invested in the notion of the "public sphere," "the public," or "publics," as formulated by theorists such as Jürgen Habermas. Habermas distinguishes between a public sphere, which in the eighteenth century was "coextensive with public authority" such as the state, and a "private sphere" of civil society and social labor (*The Structural Transformation of the Public Sphere: An Inquiry into a Category of Bourgeois Society* [Cambridge: Massachusetts Institute of Technology Press, 1989]). In Habermas's theorization, the "'authentic' public sphere" spans these so-called public and private realms such that it becomes conceptually distinct from the state and a site of the production and circulation of discourse that may be critical of such a governing or ruling body. I do not engage in discussions of participatory democracy or the ideological forms of political action in such a manner, nor is my focus on rhetoric or discourse. My investments concern bodily processes of *worlding* rather than of *worldview*. This distinction becomes clearer as I discuss my formulation of "affective ecology," insofar as it does not presume a preexisting social entity (comprising only humans)—a "public" known as "the social," "the political," "political action," or "civil society." Michael Warner demonstrates how even a culturally and historically contextualized examination of "publics" abstracts and reifies social processes into social entities, worlds with prescribed ideological and political boundaries that agentive subjects may transgress, but that nevertheless exist on their own terms: "Much of the texture of modern social life lies in the invisible presence of these publics that flit around us like large, corporate ghosts. Most of the people around us belong to our world not directly, as kin or comrades or in any other relation to which we could give a name, but as strangers. How is it that we nevertheless recognize them as members of our world?" (*Publics and Counterpublics* [New York: Zone, 2002], 7). My

examination does not presume "a world," "our world," or "their world," distinct, abstract worlds to which we do or do not belong; rather than recognition, I purposively focus on bodily and social processes of world*ing*—a verb that is both intentional and non-intentional, that does not reside in preexisting ideological worldviews or publics.

18 Kathleen Stewart, "Precarity's Forms," *Cultural Anthropology* 27, no. 3 (2012): 518.

19 There was evidence of Driscoll's usage of this term here: https://www.youtube.com /watch?v=J8sNVDyW-ws; there is also evidence found in Molly Worthington, "Who Would Jesus Smack Down?" *New York Times*, January 11, 2009, http://www .nytimes.com/2009/01/11/magazine/11punk-t.html.

20 Don Hinkle, "Bott Network Blocks Pastor Mark, Replaces Segment Mid-Show," *Baptist Press*, June 17, 2009, http://www.bpnews.net/30700/bott-radio-blocks -driscoll-replaces-segment-midshowStation.

21 Mark Driscoll, "The Porn Path," *Real Marriage*, 2012, http://markdriscoll.org /sermons/the-porn-path/.

22 Mark Driscoll, *Porn Again Christian*, 2008, http://campusministryunited.com /Documents/Porn_Again_Christian.pdf.

23 Driscoll, *Porn Again*.

24 Mark Driscoll, "Dance of Mahanaim," *Peasant Princess* series, MarsHill.com, 2008, available at "20081109 Dance of Mahanaim Vodcast - Peasant Princess," YouTube video, posted by "Mike Thibault," May 7, 2015, https://www.youtube.com/watch ?v=zZo6ck9dDTw.

25 Mark Driscoll, "The Porn Path," *Real Marriage*, 2012, http://markdriscoll.org/sermons /the-porn-path/26. Driscoll, "The Porn Path"; Driscoll, "Dance of Mahanaim."

26 Driscoll, "The Porn Path"; Driscoll, "Dance of Mahanaim."

27 My use of "social imaginary" draws from anthropologist Arjun Appadurai's formulation in *Modernity at Large* (1996, 31): "the imagination has become an organized field of social practices, a form of work (in the sense of both labor and culturally organized practice), and a form of negotiation between sites of agency (individuals) and globally defined fields of possibility." However, in my examination "social imaginary" signals the conflation of visual, virtual and visceral processes that are ongoing and unruly, troubling distinctions between subject/object, self/other and local/global, while calling the agentive individual and intentionality of the subject into question. I analyze "social imaginary" in terms of collective bodily affects rather than individual participants or strictly agentive subjects, thus subjectivity is understood as always already social, not as an entity but as emerging process.

28 Michael Hardt and Antonio Negri, *Empire* (Cambridge: Harvard University Press, 2000), 293.

29 Susanna Paasonen, *Carnal Resonance: Affect and Online Pornography* (Cambridge: Massachusetts Institute of Technology Press, 2011), 16.

30 Paasonen, *Carnal Resonance*, 16.

31 Paasonen, *Carnal Resonance*, 16.

32 Stephen Maddison, "Beyond the Entrepreneurial Voyeur? Sex, Porn and Cultural Politics," *New Formations*, nos. 80–81 (winter 2013): 103, doi:10.3898/NewF.80/81.06.2013.

33 Maddison, "Beyond the Entrepreneurial Voyeur?," 103.

34 Maddison, "Beyond the Entrepreneurial Voyeur?," 107.

35 Maddison, "Beyond the Entrepreneurial Voyeur?," 107.

36 Michel Foucault, *The History of Sexuality, Volume One: An Introduction*, trans. Robert Hurley (New York: Vintage, 1978), 77.

37 Wendy Brown, *Politics Out of History* (Princeton: Princeton University Press, 2001), 92.

38 Mike Anderson, "Hello, My Name Is Mike, and I'm a Recovering True Believer," *Mike Anderson* (blog), 2013, http://mikeyanderson.com/hello-name-mike-im-recovering-true-believer.

39 Jennifer Wicke writes that social pornography "is the name for the pornographic fantasies the society collectively engenders and then mass culturally disseminates, usually in the case of anti-pornography," in "Through a Gaze Darkly: Pornography's Academic Market," *More Dirty Looks: Gender, Pornography, and Power*, ed. Pamela Church Gibson, 176–187 (London: British Film Institute, 2004), 184. I expand on this concept while examining the affective labor of producing such a genre of evangelical social pornography in the context of Mars Hill and the communication, marketing, mediation and embodiment of what I call "biblical porn."

40 Foucault, *The History of Sexuality*, 139.

41 Foucault, *The History of Sexuality*, 139–43.

42 Foucault, *The History of Sexuality*, 152.

43 Jabir K. Puar, *Terrorist Assemblages: Homonationalism in Queer Times* (Durham: Duke University Press, 2007), 154.

44 Jasbir K. Puar, "I Would Rather Be a Cyborg than a Goddess," EIPCP, January 2011, http://eipcp.net/transversal/0811/puar/en.

45 Jason Read, "The Order and Connection of Ideology Is the Same as the Order and Connection of Exploitation: Or, Towards a Bestiary of the Capitalist Imagination," *Philosophy Today* 59, no. 2 (spring 2015), 175–89, doi:10.5840/philtoday201522059.

46 I develop a theory of affective ecology instead of relying on formulations of "public" (and "counterpublic"), in order to demonstrate how an embodied yet social sense of conviction goes viral in ways both calculated and uncontrollable.

47 The primary mission of the church, and one of the key slogans branding its teaching material, was "Planting Churches, Making Disciples." I discuss the meaning and process of this aim—how churches were planted and disciples were made—in chapters 1 and 2.

48 Foucault, *The History of Sexuality*, 106.

49 Foucault, *The History of Sexuality*, 152–53.

50 Jane Bennett writes of vital materialities as, "a subsistent world of nonhuman vitality. To 'render manifest' is both to receive and to participate in the shape given to that which is received. What is manifest arrives through humans but not entirely because of them . . . This sense of a strange and incomplete commonality with the out-side may induce vital materialities to treat nonhumans—animals, plants, earth, even artifacts and commodities—more carefully, more strategically, more ecologically." *Vibrant Matter: A Political Ecology of Things* (Durham, NC: Duke University Press, 2010), 17–18. It is this sense of a strange and incomplete commonality with the out-side that I wish to analyze in the development of my concept "affective ecology."

51 Massumi, *Politics of Affect*, 31.

52 Massumi, *Politics of Affect*, 33.

53 Feona Attwood, "Sexed Up: Theorizing the Sexualization of Culture," *Sexualities* 9, no. 1 (2006): 78.

54 Skye Jethani, "The Evangelical Industrial Complex and the Rise of Celebrity Pastors," *Christianity Today*, February 20, 2012, http://www.christianitytoday.com /le/2012/february-online-only/evangelical-industrial-complex-rise-of-celebrity -pastors.html.

55 Linda Williams, *Hard Core: Power, Pleasure, and the "Frenzy of the Visible"* (Berkeley: University of California Press, 1989), x.

56 Tony Sampson, *Virality: Contagion Theory in the Age of Networks* (Minneapolis: University of Minnesota Press, 2012), 5.

57 Wendy Hui Kyong Chun, *Control and Freedom: Power and Paranoia in the Age of Fiber Optics* (Cambridge: Massachusetts Institute of Technology Press, 2006), viii.

58 Chun, *Control and Freedom*, 82.

59 The requirement to receive Pastor Mark's permission to speak to individual church leaders and members is another reason why I do not engage in discussion of "the public." While the IRB was fine with my visiting public events open to nonmembers—which any visitor to an evangelical megachurch knows are plentiful, given the incentive to proselytize and convert nonbelievers—the concept of the public does not do justice to the sensation of being in such spaces. It also struck me as ironic that I could formally "talk" to individuals only with the consent of a pastor whose authority was clearly inflected through investments in heteropatriarchy and therefore reluctant to relinquish such control to a feminist anthropologist in the academy doing research on the politics of marriage. I found myself limited by institutional conditions presumed "ethical" that were in fact detrimental to ethical action. The IRB seemed more invested in protecting the liability of the University of Washington than in protecting the subjects of

my study, let alone my own integrity as researcher. I learned about the ethical dimensions of ethnographic fieldwork *despite* the regulatory practices of the IRB, not because of them.

60 Warren Cole Smith, "Unreal Sales for Driscoll's *Real Marriage*," *World Magazine*, March 5, 2014, https://world.wng.org/2014/03/unreal_sales_for_driscolls_real_marriage.

61 Dave Kraft et al., "Statement of Formal Charges and Issues—Mark Driscoll," Patheos.com, http://wp.production.patheos.com/blogs/warrenthrockmorton/files/2014/08/FormalCharges-Driscoll-814.pdf.

62 See Repentant Pastor (blog), http://repentantpastor.com/.

63 Rather than suddenly recognizing that I belonged to this "public" in any abstract sense, I felt compelled to bodily stand with the protestors rather than at a distance from them. I felt that I belonged, but not because we shared a worldview or common cause, but because we were already in social relation. I am thankful that "We Are Not Anonymous" existed as a public *Facebook* page, but I never joined the group as a member because I did not feel it was my place to do so. That distinguishes how my feeling, and my examination, is different from what is described in terms of "the public" or "a public." Having said that, I would offer that "We Are Not Anonymous" did constitute a "counterpublic" in the terms that Michael Warner describes (2002), intentionally against, or counter to, the discourse of Mars Hill surrounding the protestors and issues under protest that challenged Mark's qualifications to pastor.

64 Lisa Blackman, *Immaterial Bodies: Affect, Embodiment, Mediation* (London: Sage, 2012), ix.

65 Blackman, *Immaterial Bodies*, 1.

66 Blackman, *Immaterial Bodies*, 22.

67 William Mazzarella, "Affect: What Is It Good For?," in *Enchantments of Modernity: Empire, Nation, Globalization*, ed. Saurbh Dube (New York: Routledge, 2009), 91.

68 Mazzarella, "Affect," 93.

69 Kevin Lewis O'Neill, "Beyond Broken: Affective Spaces and the Study of Religion," *Journal of the American Academy of Religion* 81, no. 4 (2013): 1095.

70 Sara Ahmed, "Affective Economies," *Social Text* 79, no. 4 (2004): 117.

71 Ahmed, "Affective Economies," 119.

72 Ahmed, "Affective Economies," 119.

73 Kathleen Stewart, *Ordinary Affects* (Durham: Duke University Press, 2007); Joseph Masco, *The Theater of Operations: National Security Affect from the Cold War to the War on Terror* (Durham: Duke University Press, 2014).

74 Stewart, *Ordinary Affects*, 1.

75 Donovan O. Schaefer, *Religious Affects: Animality, Evolution, and Power* (Durham: Duke University Press, 2015).

76 Ann Pellegrini, "Signaling through the Flames: Hell House Performance and Structures of Religious Feeling," *American Quarterly* 59, no. 3 (2007): 911–35.

77 Harding, *The Book of Jerry Falwell*, 58.

78 Harding, *The Book of Jerry Falwell*, 59.

79 Harding, *The Book of Jerry Falwell*, 59.

80 Joel Robbins, "What Is a Christian? Towards an Anthropology of Christianity," *Religion* 33 (2003): 193.

81 Peter Benson and Kevin Lewis O'Neill, "Facing Risk: Levians, Ethnography, Ethics," *Anthropology of Consciousness* 18, no. 2 (2007): 27.

82 Benson and O'Neill, "Facing Risk," 31.

83 Interview by author, April 2016.

84 Email by author, July 2014.

85 Puar, "I Would Rather be a Cyborg than a Goddess."

86 Puar, "I Would Rather be a Cyborg than a Goddess."

87 *Mars Hill Visitor's Guide*, 2005.

88 *This Is Mars Hill* (2010).

89 *This Is Mars Hill*.

90 Robert Webber, "Introduction," in *Listening to the Beliefs of Emerging Churches: Five Perspectives*, ed. Robert Webber (Grand Rapids: Zondervan, 2007), 15. Also see Janet Tu, "Pastor Mark Packs 'Em In," *Seattle Times*, November 28, 2003, http://community.seattletimes.nwsource.com/archive/?date=20031128&slug=pacific-preacher30. For recent anthropological scholarship on emerging churches, including national affiliates of Acts 26, see James Bielo's ethnographic account in *Emerging Evangelicals: Faith, Modernity, and the Desire for Authenticity* (New York: New York University Press, 2010).

91 *Mars Hill Visitor's Guide*.

92 *Mars Hill Visitor's Guide*.

93 *Mars Hill Visitor's Guide*.

94 *Mars Hill Visitor's Guide*.

95 James Wellman, "The Churching of the Pacific Northwest: The Rise of Sectarian Entrepreneurs," in *Religion and Public Life in the Pacific Northwest: The None Zone*, ed. Patricia O' Connell Killen and Mark Silk (Walnut Creek, CA: AltaMira, 2004), 80.

96 "The Church Report's 50 Most Influential Churches for 2006," Reclaiming the 7 Mountains of Culture, July 11, 2006, http://www.7culturalmountains.org/apps/articles/default.asp?articleid=39901&columnid=4338.

97 *Mars Hill Visitor's Guide*.

98 Mark Driscoll, "Is Jesus the Only God?" *Vintage Jesus* series, MarsHill.com, 2006.

99 Tu, "Pastor Mark Packs 'Em In."

100 Tu, "Pastor Mark Packs 'Em In."

101 Tu, "Pastor Mark Packs 'Em In."

102 Driscoll, "Is Jesus the Only God?"

103 Christian Smith, *The Bible Made Impossible: Why Biblicism Is Not a Truly Evangelical Reading of Scripture* (Grand Rapids, MI: Brazos, 2012), 63–64.

104 Mark Driscoll, *Confessions of a Reformission Reverend: Hard Lessons from an Emerging Missional Church* (Grand Rapids: Zondervan, 2006).

105 Collin Hansen, "Young, Restless, Reformed," *Christianity Today*, September 22, 2006, http://www.christianitytoday.com/ct/2006/september/42.32.html; Worthington, "Who Would Jesus Smack Down?"

106 Webber, "Introduction."

107 Mark Driscoll, "Devout Biblicism and the Emerging Church," *Listening to the Beliefs of the Emerging Church: Five Perspectives*, ed. Robert Webber (Grand Rapids, MI: Zondervan, 2007), 21.

108 Driscoll, *Confessions of a Reformission Reverend*, 98.

109 Mark Driscoll, *The Flight from God*, speech delivered at the Leadership Network Conference, 1997, audiocassette.

110 Driscoll, *The Flight from God*.

111 Driscoll, *The Flight from God*.

112 Wenatchee the Hatchet, "Spiritual Abuse and Emotional Abuse—Cycles of Provocation and Escalation," *Wenatchee the Hatchet* (blog), November 9, 2012, http://wenatcheethehatchet.blogspot.com/2012/11/spiritual-abuse-and-emotional-abuse.html.

113 Wenatchee the Hatchet, "Spiritual Abuse and Emotional Abuse."

114 Driscoll, *Confessions*, 97.

115 Driscoll, *Confessions of a Reformission Reverend*, 96.

116 Driscoll, *Confessions of a Reformission Reverend*, 96.

117 Mark Driscoll, *Genesis* (2005).

118 Driscoll, *Genesis*.

119 Driscoll, *Confessions of a Reformission Reverend*, 22.

120 Mark Driscoll, "Brian McLaren on the Homosexual Question 3: A Rant by Mark Driscoll," *Christianity Today*, January 2006, http://www.christianitytoday.com/le/2006/january-online-only/brian-mclaren-on-homosexual-question-3-prologue-and-rant.html.

121 Kraft et al. "Statement of Formal Charges and Issues—Mark Driscoll."

122 Stoyan Zaimov, "Mark Driscoll Rebuked for 'Judging' Obama's Faith with Controversial Twitter Post," *Christian Post*, January 22, 2013, http://www.christianpost.com/news/mark-driscoll-rebuked-for-judging-obamas-faith-with-controversial-twitter-post-88675/.

123 Zaimov, "Mark Driscoll Rebuked for 'Judging' Obama's Faith with Controversial Twitter Post."

124 Warren Cole Smith and Sophia Lee, "Changing Course?" *WORLD*, August 9, 2014, https://world.wng.org/2014/07/changing_course.

125 Smith and Lee, "Changing Course?"

126 Smith and Lee, "Changing Course?"

127 Smith and Lee, "Changing Course?"

128 Smith and Lee, "Changing Course?"

129 Rob Asghar, "Mars Hill: Cautionary Tale from the Enron of American Churches," *Forbes*, September 16, 2014, http://www.forbes.com/sites/robasghar/2014/09 /16/mars-hill-cautionary-tales-from-the-enron-of-american-churches /#7f62f3306f85.

130 Kate Shellnutt and Morgan Lee, "Mark Driscoll Resigns from Mars Hill," *Christianity Today*, October 15, 2014, http://www.christianitytoday.com/ct/channel /utilities/print.html?type=article&id=125142.

131 Wendy Alsup, "The Harmful Teaching of Wives as Their Husbands' Porn Stars," *Practical Theology for Women* (blog), July 28, 2014, http://www.theologyforwomen .org/2014/07/the-harmful-teaching-of-wives-as-their-husbands-porn-stars.html.

132 Jethani, "The Evangelical Industrial Complex."

133 *Mars Hill Membership Covenant* (2007).

1 | AROUSING EMPIRE

1 Mark Driscoll, "How Human Was Jesus?," *Vintage Jesus* series, MarsHill.com, October 2006. While I was in attendance for this sermon, there is currently evidence of it at https://www.youtube.com/watch?v=kLCMloIvIX8.

2 Driscoll "How Human Was Jesus?"

3 Driscoll, "How Human Was Jesus?"

4 Driscoll, "How Human Was Jesus?"

5 Driscoll, "How Human Was Jesus?"

6 Driscoll, "How Human Was Jesus?"

7 Driscoll, "How Human Was Jesus?"

8 Nathan Finn, "Why Does a Church Need a Security Team?," MarsHill.com, May 2011, previously accessible at http://marshill.com/2011/05/05/why-does -a-church-need-a-security-team.

9 Brian Massumi, "The Future Birth of the Affective Threat: The Political Ontology of Threat," in *The Affect Theory Reader*, edited by Melissa Gregg and Gregory J. Seigworth (Durham: Duke University Press, 2010), 53.

10 Finn, "Why Does a Church Need a Security Team?"

11 Sean McCloud, *American Possessions: Fighting Demons in the Contemporary United States* (New York: Oxford University Press, 2015), 51.

12 Taylor Svendsen, "Fear, Abuse at Mars Hill," *Falcon*, February 8, 2012 http:// www.thefalcononline.com/2012/02/fear-abuse-at-mars-hill/.

13 Mark Driscoll, "Spiritual Warfare: Who, What, and Why," MarsHill.com, July 2014, formerly available at http://marshill.com/2014/07/24/spiritual-warfare -who-what-and-why.

14 Kathleen Stewart, "Atmospheric Attunements," *Rubric* 1 (2010): 4.

15 Sara Ahmed, "Affective Economies," *Social Text* 79, no. 4 (2004): 117.

16 Jasbir Puar, *Terrorist Assemblages: Homonationalism in Queer Times*. Durham: Duke University Press, 2007.

17 Puar, *Terrorist Assemblages*, 174.

18 Mark Driscoll, "Air War and Ground War," *Nehemiah* series, MarsHill.com, October 2007.

19 Driscoll, "Air War and Ground War."

20 Driscoll, "Air War and Ground War."

21 Driscoll, "Air War and Ground War."

22 Stewart, "Atmospheric Attunements," 5.

23 Jonna Petry, "My Story," *Joyful Exiles* (blog), March 2012, https://joyfulexiles .files.wordpress.com/2012/03/jonna-mhc-story-29.pdf.

24 Driscoll, "Air War and Ground War."

25 Driscoll, "Air War and Ground War."

26 Brian Massumi, *Politics of Affect* (Cambridge, UK: Polity, 2015), 29.

27 Puar, *Terrorist Assemblages*, 184.

28 Interview by author, January 2015.

29 Mark Driscoll, *Confessions of a Reformission Reverend: Hard Lessons from an Emerging Missional Church* (Grand Rapids, MI: Zondervan, 2006), 129.

30 Michael S. Kimmel, "Masculinity as Homophobia: Fear, Shame and Silence in the Construction of Gender Identity," *The Gender of Desire: Essays on Male Sexuality* (Albany: State University of New York Press, 2005), 25, 40.

31 Mark Driscoll, "Pussified Nation," Midrash, December 5, 2000, available at Matthew Paul Turner, "Mark Driscoll's Pussified Nation," MatthewPaulTurner .com, July 29 2014, http://matthewpaulturner.com/2014/07/29/mark-driscolls -pussified-nation/.

32 Interview by author, January 2015.

33 Judith Butler, *Bodies That Matter: On the Discursive Limits of "Sex"* (New York: Routledge, 1993), 125.

34 Zach Malm, "Ask Mark Anything," *We Love Mars Hill* (blog), 2014, http:// welovemarshill.com/post/87313536668/zach-malm.

35 Malm, "Ask Mark Anything."

36 Driscoll, "Pussified Nation."

37 Thomas Csordas, "Malediction, Exorcism, Evil," *Immanent Frame* (blog), November 17, 2014, http://blogs.ssrc.org/tif/2014/11/17/malediction-exorcism-and -evil/?disp=print.

38 Driscoll, "Pussified Nation."

39 Interview by author, October 2014.

40 *Mars Hill Multisite Campus Plan*, pamphlet, 2006.

41 *Mars Hill Multisite Campus Plan.*

42 Mark Driscoll, "Videology," 2008. This video has been scrubbed from the Internet, but evidence of its existence can be found here: http://leadnet.org/driscoll _explains_why_use_video_sermons/.

43 Driscoll, "Videology."

44 Driscoll, "Pussified Nation."

45 Driscoll, *Confessions of a Reformission Reverend*, 130.

46 Henry A. Giroux, "Private Satisfactions and Public Disorders: *Fight Club*, Patriarchy, and the Politics of Masculine Violence," *JAC* 21, no. 1 (2001): 1–31.

47 Driscoll, *Confessions of a Reformission Reverend*, 131–32.

48 Interview by author, December 2014.

49 Clifford Geertz, *The Interpretation of Cultures* (New York: Basic, 1973), 440.

50 Donovan Schaefer, *Religious Affects: Animality, Evolution, and Power* (Durham, NC: Duke University Press, 2015), 67.

51 David S. Gutterman, *Prophetic Politics: Christian Social Movements and American Democracy* (Ithaca: Cornell University Press, 2005), 52.

52 Mark Driscoll, *Proverbs* series, MarsHill.com, 2001.

53 Alexander Strauch, *Men and Women, Equal Yet Different* (Colorado Springs: Lewis and Roth, 1999).

54 Talal Asad, *Formations of the Secular: Christianity, Islam, Modernity* (Stanford: Stanford University Press, 2003), 14.

55 Susan Jeffords, *The Remasculinization of America: Gender and the Vietnam War* (Bloomington: Indiana University Press, 1989).

56 Gutterman, *Prophetic Politics*, 95.

57 Gutterman, *Prophetic Politics*, 96.

58 Gutterman, *Prophetic Politics*, 95.

59 Gutterman, *Prophetic Politics*, 9.

60 Susan Faludi, *Stiffed: The Betrayal of the American Man* (New York: Harper's, 2000), 214.

61 Matt Grant, "Mengineering 101," 2007.

62 Barbara Cruikshank, *The Will to Empower: Democratic Citizens and Other Subjects*, Ithaca: Cornell University Press, 1999.

63 Mark Driscoll, *A Good Soldier: A Conversation with Pastor Mark Driscoll*, available at "A Good Soldier," YouTube video, posted by Resurgence, April 28, 2007, https://www.youtube.com/watch?v=JIrIKbCz3n4.

64 Mark Driscoll, "The Ox," lecture delivered at an Acts 29 boot camp, 2008.

65 James Harleman, "Reborn on the Battlefield," lecture delivered at the Men's Advance 2007: Reborn on the Battlefield conference.

66 Al Lobaina, "Biography of a Christian Soldier, Part One," *Military Missions* (blog), 2008, formerly available at http://www.theresurgence.com/.

67 Lobaina, "Biography of a Christian Soldier."

68 Deborah Cowen, "Fighting For 'Freedom': The End of Conscription in the United States and the Neoliberal Project of Citizenship," *Citizenship Studies* 10 (2) 2006: 167–183.

69 Giroux, "Private Satisfactions and Public Disorders," 6. See also Deborah Cowen, "Fighting for 'Freedom': The End of Conscription in the United States and the Neoliberal Project of Citizenship," *Citizenship Studies* 10, no. 2 (2006): 167–83.

70 Hanna Rosin, "The End of Men," *The Atlantic,* July 2010, https://www.theatlantic .com/magazine/archive/2010/07/the-end-of-men/308135/.

71 Lobaina, "Biography of a Christian Soldier."

72 Cowen, "Fighting for 'Freedom.'"

73 Driscoll, *A Good Soldier.*

74 Driscoll, *A Good Soldier.*

75 Steven Shaviro, *Cinematic Body.* Minneapolis: University of Minnesota Press, 1993.

76 Schaefer, *Religious Affects,* 81.

77 Sam Gregory, "Cultural Learnings of Mars Hill's Men's Advance," *Proxy,* 2007.

78 Gregory, "Cultural Learnings of Mars Hill's Men's Advance."

79 Wenatchee the Hatchet, "So William Wallace II Was a 'Character' but Where Did Driscoll Get the Themes and Background for the Character?," *Wenatchee the Hatchet* (blog), September 23, 2014, http://wenatcheethehatchet.blogspot.com /2014/09/so-william-wallace-ii-was-character-but.html.

80 Wenatchee the Hatchet, "William Wallace II."

81 Wenatchee the Hatchet, "William Wallace II."

82 Nicholas Mirzoeff, "Invisible Empire: Visual Culture, Embodied Spectacle and Abu Ghraib," *Radical History Review* 95 (spring 2006): 37.

83 Hollis Phelps, "Blame Muscular Christianity for Driscoll Fiasco," ReligionDispatches.org, August 25, 2014, http://religiondispatches.org/blame-muscular -christianity-for-driscoll-fiasco/.

84 Luke Abrams, "Vote With Your Nickels and Your Noses," March 2014, http:// www.patheos.com/blogs/warrenthrockmorton/2014/03/25/former-mars-hill -church-worship-leader-luke-abrams-to-current-members-vote-with-your -numbers-and-noses/.

85 Mike Anderson, "Hello, My Name is Mike, I'm a Recovering True Believer," 2013, http://mikeyanderson.com/hello-name-mike-im-recovering-true-believer.

86 Phelps, "Blame Muscular Christianity."

87 Anderson, "True Believer."

88 Faludi, *Stiffed,* 257.

89 Mark Driscoll, "Evangelical Leader Quits amid Allegations of Gay Sex and Drug Abuse," Resurgence, November 3, 2006, http://theresurgence.com/md_blog _2006-11-03_evangelical_leader_quits/.

90 Driscoll, "Evangelical Leader Quits."
91 Driscoll, "Evangelical Leader Quits."
92 Driscoll, "Evangelical Leader Quits."
93 Driscoll, "Evangelical Leader Quits."
94 Jane Ward, "Gender Labor: Transmen, Femmes, and the Collective Work of Transgression," *Sexualities* 13 (2010): 238–39.

2 | UNDER CONVICTION

1 Less than a decade later, in 2016, the idiom of a fortress would become a vitriolic campaign slogan for the Republican presidential nominee, Donald J. Trump, and a rallying cry for his followers. Trump pledged that Mexico would pay for a wall at the US border and that Muslim migration to the United States would be severely curtailed, if not prohibited.

2 Susan Harding, *The Book of Jerry Falwell: Fundamentalist Politics and Practice* (Princeton: Princeton University Press, 2000), 161.

3 Harding, *The Book of Jerry Falwell*, 162.

4 Harding, *The Book of Jerry Falwell*, 162.

5 Mark Driscoll, "Fathers and Fighting," *Nehemiah* series, MarsHill.com, September 30, 2007, transcribed from the now defunct Mars Hill site, but audio evidence is available at *Joyful Exiles* (blog), https://joyfulexiles.files.wordpress .com/2012/03/driscoll-09–30–2007-sermon-clips.mp3.

6 Driscoll, "Fathers and Fighting."

7 Jamie Munson, "Termination of Employment of Paul Petry and Bent Meyer," *Joyful Exiles* (blog), October 1, 2007, https://joyfulexiles.files.wordpress.com /2012/03/10–01–2007-email-from-jmunson.pdf.

8 Jamie Munson, "Important Message from the Lead Pastor," *Joyful Exiles* (blog), October 2, 2007, https://joyfulexiles.files.wordpress.com/2012/03/10–02–2007 -important-message-from-the-lead-pastor.pdf.

9 Munson, "Important Message from the Lead Pastor."

10 Munson, "Important Message from the Lead Pastor."

11 Jason Bivins, *Religion of Fear: The Politics of Horror in Conservative Evangelicalism* (New York: Oxford University Press, 2008), 26.

12 Kip, "Kip's Story," *Mars Hill Refuge* (blog), March 19, 2012, http://marshillrefuge .blogspot.com/2012/03/kips-story.html.

13 Bivins, *Religion of Fear*, 27.

14 Bivins, *Religion of Fear*, 17.

15 Bivins, *Religion of Fear*, 30.

16 Jonna Petry, "My Story," *Joyful Exiles* (blog), March 19, 2012, https://joyfulexiles .com/2012/03/19/my-story-by-jonna-petry/.

17 James Harleman, "James Harleman's Confession," Repentant Pastor (blog), January 31, 2015, http://repentantpastor.com/confessions/james-harlemans-confession/.

18 Harleman, "James Harleman's Confession."

19 Michel Foucault, *Technologies of the Self: A Seminar with Michel Foucault*, edited by Luther H. Martin, Huck Gutman, and Patrick H. Hutton (Cambridge: University of Massachusetts Press, 2008).

20 Michel Foucault, "Technologies of Self," in *Technologies of the Self: A Seminar with Michel Foucault*, ed. Luther H. Martin, Huck Gutman, and Patrick H. Hutton (Cambridge: University of Massachusetts Press, 2008), 18.

21 Foucault, "Technologies of Self," 19.

22 Paul Petry, "Letter to the Elders," *Joyful Exiles* (blog), October 25, 2007, p. 2, https://joyfulexiles.files.wordpress.com/2012/03/draft-confession-request-for-redress-to-the-elders-of-mars-hill-church.pdf.

23 Paul Petry, "Letter to Mark Driscoll," *Joyful Exiles* (blog), January 26, 2008, https://joyfulexiles.files.wordpress.com/2012/03/01-26-2008-ltr-mark-driscoll.pdf.

24 Lauren Berlant, *Cruel Optimism* (Durham: Duke University Press, 2011), 23–24.

25 Paul Petry, "Email Resigning Mars Hill Church Membership," *Joyful Exiles*, November 2, 2007, https://joyfulexiles.files.wordpress.com/2012/03/withdraw-as-members-11-02-2007.pdf.

26 Mars Hill Elders, "Response to Members' Questions," *Joyful Exiles* (blog), November 4, 2007, https://joyfulexiles.files.wordpress.com/2012/03/elders-response-to-questions-11-9-07.pdf.

27 Mars Hill Elders, "Response to Members' Questions."

28 Mars Hill Elders, "Response to Members' Questions."

29 Mars Hill Elders, "Response to Members' Questions."

30 Mars Hill Elders, "Response to Members' Questions."

31 Mars Hill Elders, "Response to Members' Questions."

32 Mars Hill Elders, "Response to Members' Questions."

33 Mark Driscoll, untitled audio recording, *Joyful Exiles* (blog), October 1, 2007, https://joyfulexiles.files.wordpress.com/2012/06/preaching-paul_edits1.mp3.

34 Bent Meyer, "Correcting Exaggerated Communication," *Joyful Exiles* (blog), November 11, 2008, https://joyfulexiles.files.wordpress.com/2012/03/bent-meyer-letter-to-the-mh-elders-01-11-2008.pdf.

35 Jamie Munson, "Update on Paul Petry," *Joyful Exiles* (blog), December 5, 2007, https://joyfulexiles.files.wordpress.com/2012/03/elders-mh-website-jamie-munson-update-on-paul-petry-forum-12-05-071.pdf.

36 Bivins, *Religion of Fear*, 30.

37 Bivins, *Religion of Fear*, 30–31.

38 Bivins, *Religion of Fear*, 31.

39 Bivins, *Religion of Fear*, 31.

40 Bivins, *Religion of Fear*, 35.

41 Mark Driscoll, "Introduction," *Spiritual Warfare* series, MarsHill.com, February 2008, formerly available at http://marshill.com/media/spiritual-warfare/introduction-to-spiritual-warfare. This lecture was transcribed from videos downloaded from the now defunct Mars Hill media library.

42 Driscoll, "Introduction."

43 Driscoll, "Introduction."

44 Driscoll, "Introduction."

45 Sean McCloud, *American Possessions* (New York: Oxford University Press, 2015), 51.

46 Matthew Paul Turner, "Mark Driscoll's Church Discipline Contract: Looking for True Repentance at Mars Hill Church? Sign on the Dotted Line," *Matthew Paul Turner* (blog), January 24, 2012, http://matthewpaulturner.com/2012/01/24/jesus-needs-new-prmark-driscolls-church-discipline-contract-looking-for-true-repentance-at-mars-hill-church-sign-on-the-dotted-line/.

47 Turner, "Mark Driscoll's Church Discipline Contract."

48 Foucault, "Technologies of Self," 16.

49 Foucault, "Technologies of Self," 16.

50 Turner, "Church Discipline Contract."

51 Matthew Paul Turner, "Mark Driscoll's 'Gospel Shame': The Truth about Discipline, Excommunication, and Cult-like Control at Mars Hill," *Matthew Paul Turner* (blog), January 24, 2012, http://matthewpaulturner.com/2012/01/24/jesus-needs-new-prmark-driscolls-gospel-shame-the-truth-about-discipline-excommunication-and-cult-like-control-at-mars-hill/.

52 Brendan Kiley, "Church or Cult? The Control-Freaky Ways of Mars Hill Church," *The Stranger*, February 2012, http://www.thestranger.com/seattle/church-or-cult/Content?oid=12172001.

53 Maurizio Lazzarato, "From Biopower to Biopolitics," *Warwick Journal of Philosophy* 13 (2002): 106.

54 Michel Foucault, *Discipline and Punish: The Birth of the Prison*, trans. Alan Sheridan (New York: Vintage, 1977), 7.

55 Kiley, "Church or Cult?"

56 Turner, "Mark Driscoll's 'Gospel Shame.'"

57 Ruth Graham, "A Shunning in Seattle," *Slate*, February 10, 2012, http://www.slate.com/articles/life/faithbased/2012/02/mars_hill_pastor_mark_driscoll_faces_backlash_over_church_discipline_case_.html.

58 Sean McCloud, *Making the American Religious Fringe* (Chapel Hill: University of North Carolina Press, 2004), 129.

59 Lazzarato, "From Biopower to Biopolitics," 99.

60 Lazzarato, "From Biopower to Biopolitics," 104.

61 Lazzarato, "From Biopower to Biopolitics," 108.

62 Kiley, "Church or Cult?"

63 Interview by author, October 2014.

64 Jeff Bettger, "A Sling and a Stone," Locust and Honey, June 28, 2011, http://www
    .locustnhoney.com/?p=318.

65 Bettger, "A Sling and a Stone."

66 Jason Read, "The Order and Connection of Ideology Is the Same as the Order
    and Connection of Exploitation: Or, Towards a Bestiary of the Capitalist Imagi-
    nation," Philosophy Today 59, no. 2 (2015): 179.

67 Read, "The Order and Connection of Ideology," 179.

68 Mark Driscoll, "Live Your Life in Light of Eternity," MarsHill.com, 2011, http://
    marshill.com/2011/08/23/live-your-life-in-light-of-eternity.

69 James Harleman, "The War," MarsHill.com, http://marshill.com/media/real-
    men/the-war.

70 Sara Ahmed, "Affective Economies," Social Text 79, no. 4 (2004): 118.

71 Bivins, Religion of Fear, 25.

72 Bivins, Religion of Fear, 33.

73 Luke Abrams, "Vote with Your Nickels and Your Noses," March 2014, http://
    www.patheos.com/blogs/warrenthrockmorton/2014/03/25/former-mars-hill
    -church-worship-leader-luke-abrams-to-current-members-vote-with-your
    -numbers-and-noses/.

74 Bivins, Religion of Fear, 35.

75 William E. Connolly, Capitalism and Christianity, American Style (Durham:
    Duke University Press, 2008), 65.

76 Jennifer Barker, The Tactile Eye: Touch and the Cinematic Experience (Berkeley:
    University of California Press, 2009), 2.

77 Barker, The Tactile Eye, 2.

78 James Harleman, "The Hurt Locker," 2010, now available here: http://mp3skull
    .com/mp3/pastor_james_harleman.html.

79 Harleman, "The Hurt Locker."

80 Harleman, "The Hurt Locker."

81 Steven Shaviro, "Kathryn Bigelow," The Pinocchio Theory (blog), March 8, 2010,
    http://www.shaviro.com/Blog/?p=862.

82 Matt Ford, "Real Hurt Lockers in Iraq: Life Is No Movie," San Diego Union Tri-
    bune, March 8, 2010, http://www.sandiegouniontribune.com/sdut-real-hurt
    -lockers-in-iraq-life-is-no-movie-2010mar08-story.html.

83 Jennie Yabroff, "Kathryn Bigelow: Road Warrior," Daily Beast, June 18, 2009,
    http://www.thedailybeast.com/newsweek/2009/06/18/kathryn-bigelow-road
    -warrior.html.

84 David Denny, "On the Politics of Enjoyment: A Reading of The Hurt Locker,"
    Theory and Event 14, no. 1 (2011), doi:10.1353/tae.2011.0009.

85 Jonathan Beller, "Wagers Within the Image: Rise of Visuality, Transformation of Labour, Aesthetic Regimes," *Culture Machine* 13 (2012), http://www.culture machine.net.

86 Rogers, "The War," Mars Hill, transcribed from audio formerly available at http://marshill.com/media/real-men/the-war.

87 Rogers, "The War."

88 Talal Asad, *On Suicide Bombing* (New York: Columbia University Press, 2007), 37–38.

89 Nicholas Mirzoeff notes (2009), "In the counterinsurgency manual, military intervention is understood as militarized bio-power: the preservation of life, determined by foreign policy interests. Counterinsurgency now actively imagines itself as a medical practice: 'With good intelligence, counterinsurgents are like surgeons cutting out cancerous tissue while keeping other vital organs intact' " (U.S. Dept. of the Army 1–126).

90 Joseph Masco, " 'Sensitive but Unclassified': Secrecy and the Counterterrorist State," *Public Culture* 22 (2010): 441.

91 Harleman, "James Harleman's Confession."

92 Alex Van Tunzelmann, "*Zero Dark Thirty*'s Torture Scenes Are Controversial and Historically Dubious," *Guardian*, January 25, 2013, https://www.theguardian.com/film/filmblog/2013/jan/25/zero-dark-thirty-reel-history.

93 David Edelstein, " 'Hurt Locker': American Bomb Squad in Baghdad," NPR.org, June 26, 2009, http://www.npr.org/templates/story/story.php?storyId=1059 64997.

94 Spenser Ackerman, "Two Cheers for *Zero Dark Thirty*'s Torture Scenes," *Wired*, December 10, 2012, https://www.wired.com/2012/12/zero-dark-thirty/.

95 Anthony Breznican, "New Documents Explain Pentagon, CIA Cooperation on *Zero Dark Thirty*," *Entertainment Weekly*, August 28, 2012, http://www.ew.com/article/2012/08/28/zero-dark-thirty-documents.

96 Dexter Filkins, "Bin Laden, the Movie," *New Yorker*, December 17, 2012, http://www.newyorker.com/magazine/2012/12/17/bin-laden-the-movie; Mark Harris, "Inside the Making of *Zero Dark Thirty*," *Vulture*, December 9, 2012, http://www.vulture.com/2012/12/mark-boal-kathryn-bigelow-on-zero-dark-thirty.html.

97 UNReformed, "My Experience Inside the Cult of Mars Hill–Part 1," *UNReformed* (blog), January 24, 2012, http://twocleareyes.blogspot.co.id/2012/01/mars-hill-altar-of-doctrine-and-occult.html.

98 UNReformed, "My Experience Inside the Cult of Mars Hill–Part 1."

99 UNReformed, "My Experience Inside the Cult of Mars Hill–Part 1."

100 UNReformed, "My Experience Inside the Cult of Mars Hill–Part 1."

101 UNReformed, "My Experience Inside the Cult of Mars Hill–Part 1."

102 UNReformed, "My Experience Inside the Cult of Mars Hill–Part 1."

103 UNReformed, "My Experience Inside the Cult of Mars Hill–Part 1."

104 Driscoll, "Introduction."

105 McCloud, *American Possessions*, 66–67.

106 Darlene Lopez, untitled post, *We Love Mars Hill* (blog), 2014, http://welove marshill.com/post/89675576093/darlene-lopez.

107 McCloud, *American Possessions*, 66–67.

108 McCloud, *American Possessions*, 66–67.

109 Mark Driscoll, "The Devil," *Spiritual Warfare* series, MarsHill.com, February 2008.

110 Driscoll, "The Devil."

111 Matthew Paul Turner, "Exorcism at Mars Hill: One Woman's Story of Sex, Demons, and Mark Driscoll," *Matthew Paul Turner* (blog), June 20, 2012, http://matthewpaulturner.com/2012/06/20/jesus-needs-new-prexorcism-at-mars-hill-one-womans-story/.

112 Turner, "Exorcism at Mars Hill."

113 Turner, "Exorcism at Mars Hill."

114 Turner, "Exorcism at Mars Hill."

115 McCloud, *American Possessions*, 88.

116 Turner, "Exorcism at Mars Hill."

117 Mark Driscoll, "Christus Victor," *Spiritual Warfare* series, MarsHill.com, February 2008.

118 Turner, "Exorcism at Mars Hill."

3 | PORN AGAIN CHRISTIAN?

1 Mark Driscoll, "Dance of Mahanaim," *Peasant Princess* series, MarsHill.com, 2008, available at "20081109 Dance of Mahanaim Vodcast - Peasant Princess," YouTube video, posted by "Mike Thibault," May 7, 2015, https://www.youtube.com/watch?v=zZo6ck9dDTw.

2 Driscoll, "Dance of Mahanaim."

3 Driscoll, "Dance of Mahanaim."

4 Linda Williams, *Hard Core: Power, Pleasure, and the "Frenzy of the Visible"* (Berkeley: University of California Press, 1989), 78.

5 Jennifer Wright Knust, *Unprotected Texts: The Bible's Surprising Contradictions about Sex and Desire* (New York: HarperOne, 2011).

6 Dagmar Herzog, *Sex in Crisis: The New Sexual Revolution and the Future of American Politics* (Philadelphia: Basic, 2008).

7 Adelle M. Banks, "Evangelicals Push 'Theology of Sex,' Abortion Reduction," *National Catholic Reporter*, May 21, 2010, https://www.ncronline.org/news/politics/evangelicals-push-theology-sex-abortion-reduction.

8 Amy DeRogatis, *Saving Sex: Sexuality and Salvation in American Evangelicalism* (New York: Oxford University Press, 2014).

9   Don Hinkle, "Bott Radio Blocks Driscoll, Replaces Segment Mid-show," *Baptist Press*, June 17, 2009, http://www.bpnews.net/30700/bott-radio-blocks-driscoll-replaces-segment-midshow.

10 Hinkle, "Bott Radio Blocks Driscoll."

11 Tanya Erzen, *Straight to Jesus: Sexual and Christian Conversion in the Ex-Gay Movement* (Berkeley: University of California Press, 2006), 20.

12 Erzen, *Straight to Jesus*, 13.

13 Mark Andrejevic, *Reality TV: The Work of Being Watched* (Lanham, MD: Rowman and Littlefield, 2004).

14 A. J. Hamilton, "Making the *Peasant Princess*: Insights into a Mars Hill Sermon Series, Part 1," *Mars Hill Blog*, 2008.

15 Hamilton, "Making the *Peasant Princess*," part 1.

16 Hamilton, "Making the *Peasant Princess*," part 1.

17 Andrejevic, *Reality TV*.

18 Hamilton, "Making the *Peasant Princess*," part 1.

19 Hamilton, "Making the *Peasant Princess*," part 1.

20 Jennifer Wicke, "Through a Gaze Darkly: Pornography's Academic Market," in *More Dirty Looks: Gender, Pornography, and Power*, ed. Pamela Church Gibson, 176–87 (London: British Film Institute, 2004), 184.

21 Wendy Hui Kyong Chun, *Control and Freedom: Power and Paranoia in the Age of Fiber Optics* (Cambridge: Massachusetts Institute of Technology Press, 2006), 8–9.

22 Chun, *Control and Freedom*, 10.

23 Chun, *Control and Freedom*, 11.

24 UNReformed, "My Experience Inside the Cult of Mars Hill–Part 1," *UNReformed* (blog), January 24, 2012, http://twocleareyes.blogspot.com/2012/01/mars-hill-altar-of-doctrine-and-occult.html.

25 Chun, *Control and Freedom*, 71.

26 Jussi Parikka, "New Materialism as Media Theory: Medianatures and Dirty Matter," Communication and Critical/Cultural Studies 9, no. 1 (March 2012): 95.

27 Parikka, "New Materialism as Media Theory," 96.

28 Mark Driscoll, "Let Him Kiss Me," *Peasant Princess* series, MarsHill.com, 2008.

29 Chun, *Control and Freedom*.

30 Susan Bordo, *The Male Body: A New Look at Men in Private and Public* (New York: Farrar, Strauss, Giroux, 1999).

31 Melika Loe, "The Viagra Blues: Embracing or Resisting the Viagra Body," in *Medicalized Masculinities*, ed. Dana Rosenfeld and Christopher A. Faircloth (Philadelphia: Temple University Press, 2006), 21–44.

32 Jennifer Juffer, "There's No Place Like Home: Further Developments on the Domestic Front," in *More Dirty Looks: Gender, Pornography, and Power*, ed. Pamela Church Gibson (London: British Film Institute, 2004), 45–58.

33 Williams, *Hard Core*, 114.

34 In "Sound Doctrine; Sound Words," a talk delivered at a leadership conference in 2009 and subsequently uploaded to YouTube, the evangelical blogger and executive director of Grace to You radio programming Phil Johnson coined the phrase "pornification of the pulpit" to describe "the tendency of so many pastors lately to employ things like profanity, cruel and obscene words, vile subject matter, carnal topics, graphic sexual imagery, erotic language, filthy jokes." While Johnson's belief in the inerrancy of Scripture theologically aligns him with Driscoll on paper, their rift signals a culture war among Evangelicals. As Phil Johnson states, the justification usually offered for pornification of the pulpit "is that coarse language and sexual themes are the tools of contextualization—it's a way to make us sound more relevant. Lots of voices in the church are insistent that this is absolutely essential if you want to reach certain segments of our culture. . . . *New York Times Magazine* recently did a feature article on Mark Driscoll in which this was a major theme—'Who Would Jesus Smack Down?' was the title of the article, and here's the lead sentence: 'Mark Driscoll's sermons are mostly too racy to post on an evangelical, family-friendly website.' . . . And so this is a subject that almost everyone, including the *New York Times* is already talking nonstop about, and yet it seems to me that people in the evangelical world are not thinking very biblically about it. What language, and what kind of subject matter are suitable for the public, suitable for the pulpit in a public worship service?" http://www.youtube.com/watch?v=8EFXP04ke20.

35 Driscoll, "Let Him Kiss Me."

36 Driscoll, "Let Him Kiss Me."

37 Lisa Duggan, "Censorship in the Name of Feminism (1984)," in *Sex: Sexual Dissent and Political Culture*, ed. Lisa Duggan and Nan Hunter (New York: Routledge, 1995), 40; Juffer, "There's No Place Like Home."

38 Mark Driscoll, "The Ox," lecture delivered at an Acts 29 boot camp, 2008.

39 Mark Driscoll, "Do Not Awaken Love," *Peasant Princess* series, MarsHill.com, 2008.

40 Steven Mulkey, "Mars Hill Military Mission: Victory over Porn through the Gospel," *Military Missions* (blog), 2009, once available on the now defunct Mars Hill website.

41 Mark Driscoll, *Porn-Again Christian*, 2008, http://campusministryunited.com/Documents/Porn_Again_Christian.pdf.

42 Driscoll, *Porn Again.*

43 Driscoll, *Porn Again Christian.*

44 Driscoll, *Porn Again Christian.*

45 Niels Van Doorn, "Digital Spaces, Material Traces: How Matter Comes to Matter in Online Performances of Gender, Sexuality and Embodiment," *Media, Culture and Society* 33 (2011): 531–47.

46 Driscoll, *Porn Again Christian*.

47 Chun, *Control and Freedom*, 11.

48 Driscoll, *Porn Again Christian*.

49 Driscoll, *Porn Again Christian*.

50 Driscoll, *Porn Again Christian*.

51 Driscoll, *Porn Again Christian*.

52 For example, see XXXchurch.com; Anugrah Kumar, "'Sexperiment': Pastor, Wife to Spend 24 Hours in Bed on Church Roof," *Christian Post*, January 7, 2012, http://www.christianpost.com/news/pastor-wife-to-spend-24-hours-in-bed -on-church-roof-to-teach-sex-lessons-66640/.

53 Mark Driscoll, "Evangelical Leader Quits amid Allegations of Gay Sex and Drug Abuse," Resurgence, November 3, 2006, http://theresurgence.com/md_blog _2006–11–03_evangelical_leader_quits/.

54 Anonymous, *Reforming Femininity* (blog), MarsHill.com, 2007.

55 Marie E. Griffith, *God's Daughters: Evangelical Women and the Power of Submission* (Berkeley: University of California Press, 1997), 120.

56 Griffith, *God's Daughters*, 113.

57 Anonymous, *Reforming Femininity*.

58 Mark Driscoll, "My Dove," *Peasant Princess* series, MarsHill.com, 2008.

59 Driscoll, "Dance of Mahanaim."

60 Driscoll, "Dance of Mahanaim."

61 A. J. Hamilton, "Making the *Peasant Princess*: Insights into a Mars Hill Sermon Series, Part 2," *Mars Hill Blog*, 2008.

62 Andrejevic, *Reality TV*.

63 Richard V. Ericson and Kevin D. Haggerty, eds., *The New Politics of Surveillance and Visibility* (Toronto: University of Toronto Press, 2006), 51.

64 Grace Driscoll and Mark Driscoll, "Christian Sex Q&A (Mature Content)," Mars Hill.com, http://marshill.com/categories/christian-sex-qa-mature-content, 2008.

65 Driscoll and Driscoll, "Christian Sex Q&A."

66 Driscoll and Driscoll, "Christian Sex Q&A."

67 Mars Hill Press Room, "Climbing the Charts for Jesus," *Mars Hill Blog*, 2008, once available on the Mars Hill website.

4 | THE PORN PATH

1 Mark Driscoll, *Videology*, 2007.

2 Mark Driscoll, Easter service, 2011. Footage of this service, including not only Pastor Mark's sermon but also the baptisms, is available on *YouTube*: https:// www.youtube.com/results?search_query=mars+hill+easter+2011.

3 Mark Driscoll, "Raising the Jesus Flag: Easter at Qwest," Mars Hill Church Archive, December 4, 2011, http://marshill.se/marshill/media/gods-work-our -witness/gods-work-our-witness/raising-the-jesus-flag-easter-at-qwest.

4   Eve Kosofsky Sedgwick and Adam Frank, "Shame in the Cybernetic Fold: Reading Silvan Tompkins," *Critical Inquiry* 21, no. 2 (1995): 500.

5   Sedgwick and Frank, "Shame in the Cybernetic Fold," 500.

6   https://www.youtube.com/watch?v=kMdtN73cuws&t=167s.

7   https://www.youtube.com/watch?v=ZXk1g5q8yjM.

8   https://www.youtube.com/watch?v=ZXk1g5q8yjM.

9   Gilles Deleuze, *Nietzsche and Philosophy*, trans. Hugh Tomlinson (New York: Columbia University Press, 1962), 46.

10 Deleuze, *Nietzsche and Philosophy*, 48.

11 Deleuze, *Nietzsche and Philosophy*, 48.

12 Deleuze, *Nietzsche and Philosophy*, 62.

13 Deleuze, *Nietzsche and Philosophy*, 63, 70.

14 Tony Sampson, *Virality: Contagion Theory in the Age of Networks* (Minneapolis: University of Minnesota Press, 2012), 4.

15 Sampson, *Virality*, 4–5.

16 Sampson, *Virality*, 143.

17 *This Is Mars Hill*, 2010.

18 *This Is Mars Hill*.

19 Erin Adams, contribution to Mars Hill Church, *Golden Garden Baptisms: Believers Tell Their Story* (Seattle: Mars Hill Church, 2005).

20 Mars Hill Church, *God's Work, Our Witness*, Mars Hill Church Annual Report, (Seattle: Mars Hill Church, 2011).

21 Mark Driscoll, "There's No Such Thing as Free Porn," PastorMark.tv, January 2012, http://pastormark.tv/2012/01/10/theres-no-such-thing-as-free-porn.

22 Driscoll, "There's No Such Thing as Free Porn."

23 Driscoll, "There's No Such Thing as Free Porn."

24 Sara Banet-Weiser, *Authentic: The Politics of Ambivalence in a Brand Culture* (New York: New York University Press, 2012), 4.

25 Sampson, *Virality*, 12.

26 Dave Kraft et al., "Statement of Formal Charges and Issues—Mark Driscoll," Patheos, http://wp.production.patheos.com/blogs/warrenthrockmorton/files/2014/08/FormalCharges-Driscoll-814.pdf.

27 Tony Sampson, "Various Joyful Encounters with the Dystopias of Affective Capitalism," in "Affective Capitalism," special issue of *Ephemera* 16, no. 4 (November 2016): 54.

28 Sampson, "Various Joyful Encounters," 56.

29 Sampson, "Various Joyful Encounters," 56.

30 Sampson, "Various Joyful Encounters," 57.

31 Sampson, "Various Joyful Encounters," 60.

32 Sampson, "Various Joyful Encounters," 64.

33 Rachel Held Evans, "When Jesus Meets TMZ: Why Celebrity Culture Is Over-taking Our Pulpits," *Relevant*, February 9, 2012, http://www.relevantmagazine.com/god/church/features/28236-when-jesus-meets-tmz.

34 Evans, "When Jesus Meets TMZ."

35 Evans, "When Jesus Meets TMZ."

36 Hartford Institute, "Megachurch Definition," http://hirr.hartsem.edu/megachurch/definition.html.

37 Hartford Institute, "Megachurch Definition."

38 Hartford Institute, "Megachurch Definition."

39 Hartford Institute, "Megachurch Definition."

40 Hartford Institute, "Megachurch Definition."

41 Hartford Institute, "Megachurch Definition."

42 Jethani, "The Evangelical Industrial Complex," 1.

43 Jethani, "The Evangelical Industrial Complex," 1.

44 Jethani, "The Evangelical Industrial Complex," 1.

45 Jethani, "The Evangelical Industrial Complex," 1.

46 Jethani, "The Evangelical Industrial Complex," 1.

47 Jethani, "The Evangelical Industrial Complex," 1.

48 Skye Jethani, "Part 2: The Evangelical Industrial Complex and Rise of Celebrity Pastors," *Christianity Today*, February 2012, http://www.christianitytoday.com/le/2012/february-online-only/part-2-evangelical-industrial-complex-rise-of-celebrity.html.

49 William Connolly, *Capitalism and Christianity, American Style* (Durham: Duke University Press, 2008), xii.

50 Mark Driscoll, "The Porn Path," *Real Marriage* series, Mark Driscoll Ministries, 2012, http://markdriscoll.org/sermons/the-porn-path/.

51 Feona Attwood, "Sexed Up: Theorizing the Sexualization of Culture," *Sexualities* 9, no. 1 (2006): 77.

52 Sedgwick and Frank, "Shame in the Cybernetic Fold," 504.

53 Amy DeRogatis, *Saving Sex: Sexuality and Salvation in American Evangelicalism* (New York: Oxford University Press, 2014), 42.

54 DeRogatis, *Saving Sex*, 42.

55 Sampson, "Various Joyful Encounters," 56.

56 Kathryn Lofton, *Oprah: The Gospel of an Icon* (Berkeley: University of California Press, 2011), 23.

57 Driscoll, "The Porn Path."

58 Andrejevic, *Reality TV*, 7.

59 Andrejevic, *Reality TV*, 6.

60 http://iamatreasure.com/#sthash.FW9P3BiA.Usktuotc.dpbs.

61 Mark Driscoll, "Can We?," *Real Marriage* series, Mark Driscoll Ministries, 2012, http://markdriscoll.org/sermons/can-we-_____/.

62 Mark Driscoll, "Why Do We Talk About Sex So Much in Real Marriage?" (blog post), MarsHill.com, 2012, http://marshill.com/2012/03/18/why-do-we-talk-about-sex-so-much-in-real-marriage.

63 Andrejevic, *Reality TV*, 3.

64 Mark Driscoll and Grace Driscoll, *Real Marriage: The Truth About Sex, Friendship, and Life Together* (Nashville: Thomas Nelson, 2012), 4.

65 Driscoll and Driscoll, *Real Marriage*, 11–12.

66 Driscoll and Driscoll, *Real Marriage*, 12.

67 Driscoll and Driscoll, *Real Marriage*, 16.

68 Driscoll and Driscoll, *Real Marriage*, 13.

69 Driscoll, "The Porn Path."

70 Wendy Alsup, "The Harmful Teaching of Wives as Their Husbands' Porn Stars," *Practical Theology for Women* (blog), July 18, 2014, http://www.theologyforwomen.org/2014/07/the-harmful-teaching-of-wives-as-their.html.

71 Alsup, "The Harmful Teaching of Wives as Their Husbands' Porn Stars."

72 Alsup, "The Harmful Teaching of Wives as Their Husbands' Porn Stars."

73 Driscoll, "The Porn Path."

74 Driscoll, "The Porn Path."

75 William Struthers, *Wired for Intimacy: How Pornography Hijacks the Male Brain* (Downers Grove: InterVarsity, 2009), 96.

76 Struthers, *Wired*, 96.

77 Struthers, *Wired*, 13.

78 Struthers, *Wired* 13.

79 Struthers, *Wired*, 45–46.

80 https://www.theguardian.com/science/head-quarters/2013/sep/30/neuroscience-psychology.

81 David J. Ley, "Your Brain on Porn—It's Not Addictive," *Psychology Today*, July 25, 2013, https://www.psychologytoday.com/blog/women-who-stray/201307/your-brain-porn-its-not-addictive.

82 Ley, "Your Brain on Porn."

83 Susan Griffith, "Strong Religious Beliefs May Drive Self-Perception of Being Addicted to Online Pornography," *Think*, February 12, 2014, http://blog.case.edu/think/2014/02/12/strong_religious_beliefs_may_drive_selfperception_of_being_addicted_to_online_pornography.

84 Luke Gilkerson, "Do Christians Overhype Porn Addiction?," Covenant Eyes, April 28, 2014, http://www.covenanteyes.com/2014/04/28/christians-overhype-porn-addiction/.

85 George Lakoff, *The Political Mind: A Cognitive Scientist's Guide to Your Brain and Its Politics* (New York: Penguin, 2009), xiiv.

86 Lakoff, *The Political Mind*, 39.

87 Lakoff, *The Political Mind*, 125.

88 Struthers, *Wired for Intimacy*, 103.

89 Driscoll and Driscoll, *Real Marriage*, 146.

90 Driscoll and Driscoll, *Real Marriage*, 161.

91 Mike Featherstone, "Body, Image and Affect in Consumer Culture," *Body and Society* 16 (2010): 194.

92 Featherstone, "Body, Image and Affect in Consumer Culture," 194.

93 Featherstone, "Body, Image and Affect in Consumer Culture," 199.

94 Mark Driscoll, "Campaigns," PastorMark.tv, http://pastormark.tv/campaigns /real-marriage (link no longer active).

95 Driscoll, "Campaigns."

96 Warren Cole Smith, "Unreal Sales for Driscoll's Real Marriage," WORLD Maga-zine, March 2014, https://world.wng.org/2014/03/unreal_sales_for_driscolls _real_marriage.

97 Smith, "Unreal Sales for Driscoll's Real Marriage."

98 Smith, "Unreal Sales for Driscoll's Real Marriage."

99 Smith, "Unreal Sales for Driscoll's Real Marriage."

100 Mark Driscoll, "Inside Look at Real Marriage," PastorMark.tv, December 7, 2011, http://pastormark.tv/2011/12/07/inside-look-at-real-marriage (link no longer active).

101 Driscoll, "Inside Look at Real Marriage."

102 James Duncan, "How Mark Driscoll Pockets the Money He Gives to Mars Hill," *Pajama Pages* (blog), March 16, 2014, http://www.pajamapages.com/how-mark -driscoll-pockets-the-money-he-gives-to-mars-hill/.

103 "Corporations Division—Registration Data Search: Lasting Legacy LLC," Washington Secretary of State website, https://www.sos.wa.gov/corps/search _detail.aspx?ubi=603199549.

104 Sedgwick and Frank, "Shame in the Cybernetic Fold," 518.

5 | CAMPAIGNING FOR EMPIRE

1 Susan Harding, *The Book of Jerry Falwell* (Princeton: Princeton University Press, 2000), 249.

2 Harding, *The Book of Jerry Falwell*, 249.

3 Harding, *The Book of Jerry Falwell*, 249.

4 Harding, *The Book of Jerry Falwell*, 256.

5 Sylvester A. Johnson, "Religion and US Empire," *Religion in American History* (blog), October 17, 2013, http://usreligion.blogspot.com/2013/10/religion-and -us-empire.html.

6 Johnson, "Religion and US Empire."

7 Contemporarily, this hypothesis that religious and cultural identity would be the primary source of conflict in the post-Cold War era can be traced to an

article entitled, "The Roots of Muslim Rage" published in 1990 in *The Atlantic* by British American Historian and scholar of "oriental studies," Bernard Lewis. In this essay, Lewis states, "Islam has brought comfort and peace of mind to countless millions of men and women. It has given dignity and meaning to drab and impoverished lives. It has taught people of different races to live in brotherhood and people of different creeds to live side by side in reasonable tolerance. It inspired a great civilization in which others besides Muslims lived creative and useful lives and which, by its achievement, enriched the whole world. But Islam, like other religions, has also known periods when it inspired in some of its followers a mood of hatred and violence. It is our misfortune that part, though by no means all or even most, of the Muslim world is now going through such a period, and that much, though again not all, of that hatred is directed against us ... At times this hatred goes beyond hostility to specific interests or actions or policies or even countries and becomes a rejection of Western civilization as such, not only what it does but what it is, and the principles and values that it practices and professes. These are indeed seen as innately evil, and those who promote or accept them as the 'enemies of God.'" https://www.theatlantic.com/magazine/archive/1990/09/the-roots-of -muslim-rage/304643/. However, the "clash of civilizations" did not become a theory taken up as foreign policy until its articulation in a 1992 lecture by political scientist Samuel Huntington at the American Enterprise Institute, later published as an essay entitled "Clash of Civilizations?" in *Foreign Affairs* (1993). In this article, Huntington argues, "The fundamental source of conflict in this new world will not be primarily ideological or primarily economic. The great divisions among humankind and the dominating source of conflict will be cultural ... the principal conflicts of global politics will occur between nations and groups of different civilizations. The clash of civilizations will dominate global politics. The fault lines between civilizations will be the battle lines of the future." https://www.foreignaffairs.com/articles/united -states/1993–06–01/clash-civilizations. In his argument, Huntington divides "Chinese," "Westerners," and "Arabs" into distinct "civilizations." Furthermore, he maintains, given processes of economic modernization and social change are weakening the nation-state as a source of identity, "fundamentalist" religions are flourishing as a form of cultural identification. Thus, Huntington concludes, "as people define their identity in ethnic and religious terms, they are likely to see an 'us' versus 'them' relation existing between themselves and people of different ethnicity or religion." As such, the "clash of civilizations" occurs at the "microlevel, as adjacent groups along the fault lines between civilizations struggle, often violently, over the control of territory and each other," as well as "at the macro-level," whereby "states from different civilizations compete for relative military and economic power ... and competitively promote their particular political and religious values." In this "clash," military interaction between Western and Islamic states will not decline, Huntington asserts, but become more virulent. Huntington's thesis has been strongly critiqued by cultural theorist and scholar of Middle Eastern studies Edward Said, among others, for its dogmatic approach to defining discrete, static "civilizations" that are hierarchically racialized and do not account for the dynamic interactions and interdependence between and among different cultures within various nation states.

8   These were talking points during Donald Trump's 2016 Presidential campaign that would become policy initiatives during the early stages of his administration.

9   "Bush State of the Union address," CNN, January 29, 2002, http://edition.cnn.com /2002/ALLPOLITICS/01/29/bush.speech.txt/.

10   "Bush State of the Union address," CNN, January 29, 2002, http://edition.cnn.com /2002/ALLPOLITICS/01/29/bush.speech.txt/; Peter Ford, "Europe Cringes at 'Crusade' against Terrorists," *Christian Science Monitor*, September 19, 2001, http: //www.csmonitor.com/2001/0919/p12s2-woeu.html.

11   David Harvey, *A Brief History of Neoliberalism* (New York: Oxford University Press, 2005), 49.

12   Harvey, *A Brief History of Neoliberalism*, 2.

13   Mike Anderson, "Hello, My Name Is Mike, and I'm a Recovering True Believer," 2013, *Mike Anderson* (blog), http://mikeyanderson.com/hello-name-mike-im -recovering-true-believer.

14   According to *USA Today*, Stephen Bannon, the former chief strategist to the White House, has called Islam "the most radical" religion in the world and professed that the United States is engaged in a "civilizational struggle" that will entail further military action in the Middle East. Steve Rally and Brad Heath, "Steve Bannon's Own Words Show Sharp Break on Security Issues," *USA Today*, January 31, 2017, http://www.usatoday.com/story/news/2017/01/31/bannon -odds-islam-china-decades-us-foreign-policy-doctrine/97292068/.

15   Anderson, "Hello, My Name Is Mike."

16   Jasbir Puar, *Terrorist Assemblages: Homonationalism in Queer Times* (Durham: Duke University Press, 2007), 115.

17   Puar, *Terrorist Assemblages*, 129.

18   Puar, *Terrorist Assemblages*, 156.

19   Joseph Masco, *The Theater of Operations: National Security Affect from the Cold War to the War on Terror* (Durham: Duke University Press, 2014), 1, 7.

20   See Mark Driscoll Ministries, https://markdriscoll.org/.

21   Wendy Hui Kyong Chun, *Control and Freedom: Power and Paranoia in the Age of Fiber Optics* (Cambridge: Massachusetts Institute of Technology Press, 2006), 30.

22   Chun, *Control and Freedom*, 76.

23 Mark Driscoll, *Campaigns*. http://dna.ncfchurch.org.za/wp-content/uploads /2012/07/campaigns_e-book.pdf, 6.

24 Driscoll, *Campaigns*, 6

25 Driscoll, *Campaigns*, 6.

26 Driscoll, *Campaigns*, 7.

27 Driscoll, *Campaigns*, 13.

28 Driscoll, *Campaigns*, 13.

29 Driscoll, *Campaigns*, 18.

30 Masco, *The Theater of Operations*, 20.

31 Masco, *The Theater of Operations*, 20.

32 This story was previously published with the woman's name attached at "More Stories," *Mars Hill Refuge* (blog), http://marshillrefuge.blogspot.com/p/more -stories.html. For unspecified reasons, it has been removed from the site. I have used it here as Anonymous, "My Story," without identifying details, so as to protect her identity.

33 Anonymous, "My Story."

34 Anonymous, "My Story."

35 Anonymous, "My Story."

36 Anonymous, "My Story."

37 Mike Wilkerson, Appendix C "Biblical Counseling Q&A with Pastor Mike Wilkerson," *Campaigns*, http://dna.ncfchurch.org.za/wp-content/uploads/2012 /07/campaigns_e-book.pdf, 48.

38 Naomi Kline uses the phrase "shock doctrine" in the title of her book examining Milton Friedman's free-market economic revolution as a geopolitical instrument. Naomi Kline, *The Shock Doctrine: The Rise of Disaster Capitalism* (New York: Picador, 2008).

39 Kip, "Kip's Story," *Mars Hill Refuge* (blog), March 19, 2012, http://marshillrefuge .blogspot.com/2012/03/kips-story.html.

40 Kip, "Kip's Story."

41 Kip, "Kip's Story."

42 Driscoll, *Campaigns*.

43 Driscoll, *Campaigns*.

44 Driscoll, *Campaigns*.

45 Tony Sampson, *Virality: Contagion Theory in the Age of Networks* (Minneapolis: University of Minnesota Press, 2012), 60.

46 Sampson, *Virality*, 181.

47 Jonathan Dunn, "Appendix B," *Campaigns*, 2011, http://impact.vision/sunday /item/892-campaigns-by-pastor-mark-driscoll.

48 Joel Brown, "Appendix B," *Campaigns*, 2011, http://impact.vision/sunday/item /892-campaigns-by-pastor-mark-driscoll.

49 Ben Anderson, "Affective Atmospheres," *Emotion, Space and Society* 2 (2009): 77.

50 Anderson, "Affective Atmospheres," 79.

51 Anderson, "Affective Atmospheres," 80.

52 This video is no longer available, although footage of this global campaign exists in a different format here, uploaded by Sutton Turner with the title "The Extended Family of Mars Hill Global": https://www.youtube.com/watch?v=5YPmd9vn7V8.

53 "Global and Go: Frequently Asked Questions," originally published in 2014 on the Mars Hill Church website (now defunct), but available at the Mars Hill Church Archive, December 18, 2014, http://marshill.se/marshill/globalfaq.

54 "Global and Go: Frequently Asked Questions."

55 "Global and Go: Frequently Asked Questions."

56 Mars Hill Global Fund memo (2011), evidence of which is available at Warren Throckmorton, "Megachurch Methods: Mars Hill Global Wakes the Sleeping Giant," Patheos, May 14, 2014, http://www.patheos.com/blogs/warrenthrockmorton/2014/05/14/megachurch-methods-mars-hill-global-wakes-the-sleeping-giant/.

57 Mars Hill Global Fund memo.

58 Mike Wilkerson, "Research Survey on Workplace Bullying," Patheos, August 2014, http://wp.production.patheos.com/blogs/warrenthrockmorton/files/2014/08/Research-Survey-on-Workplace-Bullying.pdf.

59 Wilkerson, "Research Survey on Workplace Bullying," 2.

60 Loraleigh Keashly and Brenda Nowell, "Conflict, Conflict Resolution, and Bullying" in Einarsen, et al. *Bullying and Harassment in the Workplace: Developments in Theory, Research, and Practice* (2011).

61 Wilkerson, "Research Survey on Workplace Bullying," 2.

62 Wilkerson, "Research Survey on Workplace Bullying," 13.

63 Wilkerson, "Research Survey on Workplace Bullying," 3.

64 Wilkerson, "Research Survey on Workplace Bullying," 5.

65 Jonna Petry, "My Story," *Joyful Exiles* (blog), March 19, 2012, https://joyfulexiles.com/2012/03/19/my-story-by-jonna-petry/.

66 David J. Morris, *The Evil Hours: A Biography of Post-Traumatic Stress Disorder* (Boston: Houghton Mifflin Harcourt, 2015), 13.

67 Morris, *The Evil Hours*, 15.

68 Morris, *The Evil Hours*.

69 Shoshana Feldman, "Education and Crisis, or the Vicissitudes of Teaching," *Trauma: Explorations in Memory*, ed. Cathy Caruth (Baltimore: The Johns Hopkins University, 1995), 17.

70 Feldman, "Education and Crisis."

71 Morris, *The Evil Hours*, 42.

72 Jonathan Shay, *Odysseus in America: Combat Trauma and the Trials of Homecoming* (New York: Scribner, 2002), 151.

73   Petry, "My Story."

74   Lauren Berlant, *Cruel Optimism* (Durham: Duke University Press, 2011), 10.

75   Berlant, *Cruel Optimism*, 10.

76   Puar, *Terrorist Assemblages*, 174.

77   Berlant, *Cruel Optimism*, 24.

78   Berlant, *Cruel Optimism*, 51–52.

79   Anderson, "Hello, My Name Is Mike."

80   Anderson, "Hello, My Name Is Mike."

81   Donovan O. Schaefer, *Religious Affects: Animality, Evolution, and Power* (Durham: Duke University Press, 2015), 105.

82   Anderson, "Hello, My Name Is Mike."

83   Schaefer, *Religious Affects*, 105.

84   Read, "Ideology and Exploitation."

85   Read, "Ideology and Exploitation," 176.

CONCLUSION

1   Dave Kraft et al., "Statement of Formal Charges and Issues—Mark Driscoll," Patheos, http://wp.production.patheos.com/blogs/warrenthrockmorton/files/2014/08/FormalCharges-Driscoll-814.pdf.

2   After the 2010 earthquake in Haiti, Driscoll partnered with McDonald to found a charity called "Churches Helping Churches," which received donations to rebuild churches in Haiti as a means of "restoring infrastructure in a country through which aid can flow into local communities which so desperately need it" (Johnson 2010). McDonald was also with Driscoll when he "crashed" the Reformed evangelical leader John McArthur's Strange Fire conference in 2013. This publicity stunt was orchestrated in order to pass out copies of Driscoll's new book, *A Call to Resurgence: Will Christianity Have a Funeral or a Future?* while rousing media controversy at an event organized by McArthur, who, as the pastor of Grace Community Church and its affiliated ministries, had criticized Driscoll's use of "vulgar language" from the pulpit (Johnson 2015).

3   Sarah Pulliam Bailey, "Mars Hill Pastors' Letter to Mark Driscoll Blasts Church Leader for Foul Play," *The Huffington Post*, August 2014, http://www.huffingtonpost.com/2014/08/28/pastors-letter-mark-driscoll_n_5731444.html.

4   Leonardo Blair, "Following Paul Tripp, Harvest Bible Fellowship Pastor James McDonald Resigns from Mars Hill Church Board," *The Christian Post*, August 2014, http://www.christianpost.com/news/following-paul-tripp-harvest-bible-fellowship-pastor-james-macdonald-resigns-from-mars-hill-church-board-124219/.

5   Leonardo Blair, "Following Paul Tripp, Harvest Bible Fellowship Pastor James McDonald Resigns from Mars Hill Church Board," *The Christian Post*, August 2014, http://www.christianpost.com/news/following-paul-tripp-harvest-bible-fellowship-pastor-james-macdonald-resigns-from-mars-hill-church-board-124219/.

6 Mars Hill Board of Overseers, "Pastor Mark Driscoll's Resignation," MarsHill
   .com, October 15, 2014, https://marshill.com/2014/10/15/pastor-mark-driscolls
   -resignation.

7 Michael Van Skaik was listed as an unpaid pastor at Mars Hill Bellevue in 2011
   and was involved in "ministry coaching" at the church, though he later moved to
   Oregon, where he had no pastoral role; the second man was Larry Osborne, senior and teaching pastor of North Coast Church, a multisited megachurch of
   roughly 11,000 that meets throughout San Diego County, with its largest campus
   located in Vista, California.

8 Mars Hill Board of Overseers, "Pastor Mark Driscoll's Resignation."

9 Mars Hill Board of Overseers, "Pastor Mark Driscoll's Resignation."

10 Mars Hill Board of Overseers, "Pastor Mark Driscoll's Resignation."

11 Sarah Pulliam Bailey, "Exclusive: Mark Driscoll's Resignation Letter to Mars Hill
   Church," *Religion News Service*, October 15, 2014, http://www.religionnews.com
   /2014/10/15/exclusive-mark-driscolls-resignation-letter-to-mars-hill-church/.

12 Brendan Kiley, "Ex-Mars Hill Insiders Reflect on Pastor Mark Driscoll's Resignation," *The Stranger*, October 15, 2014, http://www.thestranger.com/slog/archives
   /2014/10/15/ex-mars-hill-insiders-reflect-on-pastor-mark-driscolls-resignation.

13 Kiley, "Ex-Mars Hill Insiders Reflect on Pastor Mark Driscoll's Resignation."

14 Kiley, "Ex-Mars Hill Insiders Reflect on Pastor Mark Driscoll's Resignation."

15 Wendy Alsup, "Godly Sorrow Leads to Repentance," *Practical Theology for
   Women* (blog), July 22, 2014, http://theologyforwomen.org/2014/07/godly
   -sorrow-leads-to-repentance.html.

16 Alsup, "Godly Sorrow Leads to Repentance."

17 Alsup, "Godly Sorrow Leads to Repentance."

18 Alsup, "Godly Sorrow Leads to Repentance."

19 Alsup, "Godly Sorrow Leads to Repentance."

20 Sarah Pulliam Bailey, "Mark Driscoll Steps Down as Mars Hill Pastor during Review," *Huffington Post*, August 24, 2014, http://www.huffingtonpost.com/2014
   /08/24/mark-driscoll-mars-hill-_n_5705713.html.

21 Bailey, "Mark Driscoll Steps Down."

22 "Mark Driscoll at Gateway Conference," October 20, 2014, https://www.youtube
   .com/watch?v=2ZVtuOIrrDg.

23 "Mark Driscoll at Gateway Conference."

24 "Mark Driscoll at Gateway Conference."

25 See the Trinity Church website, http://thetrinitychurch.com/.

26 Heather Davis and Paige Sarlin, " 'On the Risk of a New Relationality: An Interview with Lauren Berlant and Michael Hardt," *Reviews in Cultural Theory* 2, no. 3
   (2012): 7–27.

27 Davis and Sarlin, "On the Risk of a New Relationality," 7.

28 Davis and Sarlin, "On the Risk of a New Relationality," 7.

29 Davis and Sarlin, "On the Risk of a New Relationality," 8.

30 Davis and Sarlin, "On the Risk of a New Relationality," 8.

31 Melissa Gregg, "The Break-Up: Hardt and Negri's Politics of Love," *Journal of Communication Inquiry* (October 2011): pre-publication version.

32 Gregg, "The Break-Up."

33 Gregg, "The Break-Up."

34 Gregg, "The Break-Up."

35 On November 19, 2016, the National Policy Institute, a white nationalist "alt-right" organization founded by Richard Spencer, held its national conference in Washington, D.C., where Spencer called for the audience to "Hail Trump, Hail our Victory, Hail our People," and held up his arm in a Nazi salute. See https://www .youtube.com/watch?v=106-bi3jlxk. Milo Yiannopoulos, who wrote for Breitbart News—which is under the helm of Steve Bannon, former chief strategist of the Trump administration—has repeatedly and affectionately called Trump "Daddy," including in a "Happy Father's Day, Daddy Donald" column on Father's Day in 2016, available at http://www.breitbart.com/milo/2016/06/19/happy-fathers -day-daddy-donald/.

36 Trump's executive order indefinitely banned Syrian refugees from entering the United States and for 90 days barred immigrants from several predominately Muslim countries, including Iraq, Syria, Iran, Sudan, Libya, Somalia and Yemen. The order stated that this "extreme vetting" plan intended to keep out "radical Islamic terrorists" while granting Christians and other "religious minorities" priority for immigration. During a signing ceremony at the Pentagon, President Trump stated, "We want to ensure that we are not admitting into our country the very threats our soldiers are fighting overseas. We only want to admit those into our country who will support our country, and love deeply our people." (Michael Shear and Helene Cooper, "Trump Bars Refugees and Citizens of 7 Muslim Countries," *New York Times*, January 2017, https://www.nytimes.com/2017 /01/27/us/politics/trump-syrian-refugees.html?hp&action=click&pgtype =Homepage&clickSource=story-heading&module=a-lede-pack). However, most of the hijackers on the planes that crashed into the World Trade Center and the Pentagon on 9/11 were from Saudi Arabia and other countries that were not on Trump's visa ban list. In addition, recent mass shootings and terrorist violence in the United States, such as the attack on the gay nightclub in Orlando, Florida in June 2016 or the slaughter of African-American parishioners A.M.E. Church in Charleston, South Carolina in June 2015, have been perpetrated by U.S. citizens.

37 Mark Landler and Laurie Goodstein, "Trump Vows to 'Destroy' Law Banning Political Endorsements by Churches," *New York Times*, February 2, 2017, https:// www.nytimes.com/2017/02/02/us/politics/trump-johnson-amendment -political-activity-churches.html.

38 Trip Gabriel and Michael Luo, "A Born-Again Donald Trump? Believe It, Evangelical Leader Says," *New York Times*, June 25, 2016, https://www.nytimes.com/2016/06/26/us/politics/a-born-again-donald-trump-believe-it-evangelical-leader-says.html.

39 Robert P. Jones, "The Evangelicals and the Great Trump Hope," *New York Times*, July 11, 2016, https://www.nytimes.com/2016/07/11/opinion/campaign-stops/the-evangelicals-and-the-great-trump-hope.html.

40 Gareth Davies, "Judith Butler speaks about Vulnerability and Resistance," *Warscapes*, February 16, 2015, http://www.warscapes.com/blog/judith-butler-speaks-about-vulnerability-and-resistance.

41 Davies, "Judith Butler Speaks about Vulnerability and Resistance."

42 Maurizio Lazzarato, "From Biopower to Biopolitics," *Warwick Journal of Philosophy* 13 (2002): 100.

43 Lazzarato, "From Biopower to Biopolitics," 101.

44 Lazzarato, "From Biopower to Biopolitics," 106.

45 Lazzarato, "From Biopower to Biopolitics," 109.

Bibliography

Ahmed, Sara. "Affective Economies." *Social Text* 79, no. 4 (2004): 117–39.

Anderson, Ben. "Affective Atmospheres." *Emotion, Space and Society* 2 (2009): 77–81.

Andrejevic, Mark. *Reality TV: The Work of Being Watched*. Lanham, MD: Rowman and Littlefield, 2004.

Appadurai, Arjun. *Modernity at Large: Cultural Dimensions of Globalization*. Minneapolis: University of Minnesota, 1996.

Asad, Talal. *Formations of the Secular: Christianity, Islam, Modernity*. Stanford: Stanford University Press, 2003.

———. *On Suicide Bombing*. New York: Columbia University Press, 2007.

Attwood, Feona. "Sexed Up: Theorizing the Sexualization of Culture." *Sexualities* 9, no. 1 (2006): 77–94.

Banet-Weiser, Sara. *Authentic: The Politics of Ambivalence in a Brand Culture*. New York: New York University Press, 2012.

Barker, Jennifer. *The Tactile Eye: Touch and the Cinematic Experience*. Berkeley: University of California Press, 2009.

Beller, Jonathan. "Wagers within the Image: Rise of Visuality, Transformation of Labour, Aesthetic Regimes." *Culture Machine* 13 (2012). http://www.culturemachine.net.

Bennett, Jane. *Vibrant Matter: A Political Ecology of Things*. Durham, NC: Duke University Press, 2010.

Benson, Peter, and Kevin Lewis O'Neill. "Facing Risk: Levians, Ethnography, Ethics." *Anthropology of Consciousness* 18, no. 2 (2007): 29–55.

Berlant, Lauren. *Cruel Optimism*. Durham, NC: Duke University Press, 2011.

Bialecki, Jon. "Does God Exist in Methodological Atheism? On Tanya Lurhmann's *When God Talks Back* and Bruno Latour." *Anthropology of Consciousness* 25, no. 1 (2014): 32–52.

Bielo, James. *Emerging Evangelicals: Faith, Modernity, and the Desire for Authenticity*. New York: New York University Press, 2010.

Bivins, Jason. *Religion of Fear: The Politics of Horror in Conservative Evangelicalism*. New York: Oxford University Press, 2008.

Blackman, Lisa. *Immaterial Bodies: Affect, Embodiment, Mediation*. London: Sage, 2012.

Bordo, Susan. *The Male Body: A New Look at Men in Private and Public*. New York: Farrar, Strauss, Giroux, 1999.

Brown, Wendy. *Politics Out of History*. Princeton: Princeton University Press, 2001.

Butler, Judith. *Bodies That Matter: On the Discursive Limits of "Sex."* New York: Routledge, 1993.

Chun, Wendy Hui Kyong. *Control and Freedom: Power and Paranoia in the Age of Fiber Optics*. Cambridge, MA: MIT Press, 2006.

Connolly, William E. *Capitalism and Christianity, American Style*. Durham: Duke University Press, 2008.

———. *Neuropolitics: Thinking, Culture, Speed*. Minneapolis: University of Minnesota Press, 2002.

Cowen, Deborah. "Fighting for 'Freedom': The End of Conscription in the United States and the Neoliberal Project of Citizenship." *Citizenship Studies* 10, no. 2 (2006): 167–83.

Cruikshank, Barbara. *The Will to Empower: Democratic Citizens and Other Subjects*. Ithaca, NY: Cornell University Press, 1999.

Davis, Heather, and Paige Sarlin. "On the Risk of a New Relationality: An Interview with Lauren Berlant and Michael Hardt." *Reviews in Cultural Theory* 2, no. 4 (2012): 7–27.

DeBerg, Betty A. *Ungodly Women: Gender and the First Wave of American Fundamentalism*. Macon, GA: Mercer University Press, 2000.

Deleuze, Gilles. *Nietzsche and Philosophy*. Translated by Hugh Tomlinson. New York: Columbia University Press, 1962.

Deleuze, Gilles, and Felix Guattari. *Anti-Oedipus: Capitalism and Schizophrenia*. Minneapolis: University of Minnesota, 1983.

DeRogatis, Amy. *Saving Sex: Sexuality and Salvation in American Evangelicalism*. New York: Oxford University Press, 2014.

Dowland, Seth. *Family Values and the Rise of the Christian Right*. Philadelphia: University of Pennsylvania Press, 2015.

Driscoll, Mark. *Confessions of a Reformission Reverend: Hard Lessons from an Emerging Missional Church*. Grand Rapids, MI: Zondervan, 2006.

———. "Devout Biblicism and the Emerging Church." In *Listening to the Beliefs of the Emerging Church: Five Perspectives*, ed. Robert Webber, 19–35. Grand Rapids, MI: Zondervan, 2007.

Driscoll, Mark, and Grace Driscoll. *Real Marriage: The Truth about Sex, Friendship, and Life Together*. Nashville: Thomas Nelson, 2012.

Duggan, Lisa. "Censorship in the Name of Feminism (1984)." In *Sex: Sexual Dissent and Political Culture*, ed. Lisa Duggan and Nan Hunter, 29–40. New York: Routledge, 1995.

Ericson, Richard V., and Kevin D. Haggerty. "The New Politics of Surveillance and Visibility." In *The New Politics of Surveillance and Visibility*, ed. Richard V. Ericson and Kevin D. Haggerty, 3–25. Toronto: University of Toronto Press, 2006.

———, eds. *The New Politics of Surveillance and Visibility*. Toronto: University of Toronto Press, 2006.

Erzen, Tanya. *Straight to Jesus: Sexual and Christian Conversion in the Ex-Gay Movement*. Berkeley: University of California Press, 2006.

Faludi, Susan. *Stiffed: The Betrayal of the American Man*. New York: Harper's, 2000.

Featherstone, Mike. "Body, Image and Affect in Consumer Culture." *Body and Society* 16 (2010): 193–221.

Feldman, Shoshana. "Education and Crisis, or the Vicissitudes of Teaching." In *Trauma: Explorations in Memory*, ed. Cathy Caruth, 13–60. Baltimore: Johns Hopkins University, 1995.

Foucault, Michel. *Discipline and Punish: The Birth of the Prison*. Translated by Alan Sheridan. New York: Vintage, 1977.

———. *The History of Sexuality, Volume One: An Introduction*. Translated by Robert Hurley. New York: Vintage, 1978.

———. "Technologies of Self." In *Technologies of the Self: A Seminar with Michel Foucault*, ed. Luther H. Martin, Huck Gutman, and Patrick H. Hutton, 16–49. Cambridge: University of Massachusetts Press, 2008.

———. *Technologies of the Self: A Seminar with Michel Foucault*. Edited by Luther H. Martin, Huck Gutman, and Patrick H. Hutton, 16–49. Cambridge, MA: University of Massachusetts Press, 2008.

Geertz, Clifford. *The Interpretation of Cultures*. New York: Basic, 1973.

Giroux, Henry A. "Private Satisfactions and Public Disorders: *Fight Club*, Patriarchy, and the Politics of Masculine Violence." *JAC* 21, no. 1 (2001): 1–31.

Gregg, Melissa. "The Break-Up: Hardt and Negri's Politics of Love." *Journal of Communication Inquiry* (October 2011): prepublication version.

Griffith, Marie E. *God's Daughters: Evangelical Women and the Power of Submission*. Berkeley: University of California Press, 1997.

Gutterman, David S. *Prophetic Politics: Christian Social Movements and American Democracy*. Ithaca: Cornell University Press, 2005.

Habermas, Jürgen. *The Structural Transformation of the Public Sphere: An Inquiry into a Category of Bourgeois Society*. Cambridge, MA: MIT Press, 1989.

Harding, Susan. *The Book of Jerry Falwell: Fundamentalist Politics and Language*. Princeton: Princeton University Press, 2000.

———. "Representing Fundamentalism: The Problem of the Repugnant Cultural Other." *Social Science Research* 58, no. 2 (1991): 373–93.

Hardt, Michael, and Antonio Negri. *Empire*. Cambridge, MA: Harvard University Press, 2000.

Harvey, David. *A Brief History of Neoliberalism*. New York: Oxford University Press, 2005.

Herzog, Dagmar. *Sex in Crisis: The New Sexual Revolution and the Future of American Politics*. Philadelphia: Basic, 2008.

Jeffords, Susan. *The Remasculinization of America: Gender and the Vietnam War*. Bloomington: Indiana University Press, 1989.

Juffer, Jennifer. "There's No Place Like Home: Further Developments on the Domestic Front." In *More Dirty Looks: Gender, Pornography, and Power*, ed. Pamela Church Gibson, 45–58. London: British Film Institute, 2004.

Kimmel, Michael S. "Masculinity as Homophobia: Fear, Shame and Silence in the Construction of Gender Identity." In *The Gender of Desire: Essays on Male Sexuality*, by Michael S. Kimmel, 25–44. Albany: State University of New York Press, 2005.

Kline, Naomi. *The Shock Doctrine: The Rise of Disaster Capitalism*. New York: Picador, 2008.

Knust, Jennifer Wright. *Unprotected Texts: The Bible's Surprising Contradictions about Sex and Desire*. New York: HarperOne, 2011.

Lakoff, George. *The Political Mind: A Cognitive Scientist's Guide to Your Brain and Its Politics*. New York: Penguin, 2009.

Lazzarato, Maurizio. "From Biopower to Biopolitics." *Warwick Journal of Philosophy* 13 (2002): 99–113.

Lewis O'Neill, Kevin. "Beyond Broken: Affective Spaces and the Study of Religion." *Journal of the American Academy of Religion* 81, no. 4 (2013): 1093–1116.

Loe, Melika. "The Viagra Blues: Embracing or Resisting the Viagra Body." In *Medicalized Masculinities*, ed. Dana Rosenfeld and Christopher A. Faircloth, 21–44. Philadelphia: Temple University Press, 2006.

Lofton, Kathryn. *Oprah: The Gospel of an Icon*. Berkeley: University of California Press, 2011.

Lyon, David. "9/11, Synopticon, and Scopophilia." In *The New Politics of Surveillance and Visibility*, ed. Kevin D. Haggerty and Richard V. Ericson, 35–54. Toronto: University of Toronto Press, 2007.

Maddison, Stephen. "Beyond the Entrepreneurial Voyeur? Sex, Porn and Cultural Politics." *New Formations*, nos. 80–81 (winter 2013): 102–18. doi:10.3898/NewF.80/81.06.2013.

Masco, Joseph. "'Sensitive but Unclassified': Secrecy and the Counterterrorist State." *Public Culture* 22 (2010): 433–63.

———. *The Theater of Operations: National Security Affect from the Cold War to the War on Terror*. Durham, NC: Duke University Press, 2014.

Massumi, Brian. "The Future Birth of the Affective Threat: The Political Ontology of Threat," In *The Affect Theory Reader*, ed. Melissa Gregg and Gregory J. Seigworth, 52–70. Durham, NC: Duke University Press, 2010.

———. *Politics of Affect*. Cambridge, UK: Polity, 2015.

Mazzarella, William. "Affect: What Is It Good For?" In *Enchantments of Modernity: Empire, Nation, Globalization*, ed. Saurbh Dube, 291–309. New York: Routledge, 2009.

McCloud, Sean. *American Possessions: Fighting Demons in the Contemporary United States*. New York: Oxford University Press, 2015.

———. *Making the American Religious Fringe*. Chapel Hill: University of North Carolina Press, 2004.

Mirzoeff, Nicholas. "Invisible Empire: Visual Culture, Embodied Spectacle and Abu Ghraib." *Radical History Review* 95 (spring 2006): 21–44.

Morris, David J. *The Evil Hours: A Biography of Post-Traumatic Stress Disorder*. Boston: Houghton Mifflin Harcourt, 2015.

Paasonen, Susanna. *Carnal Resonance: Affect and Online Pornography*. Cambridge, MA: MIT Press, 2011.

Parikka, Jussi. "New Materialism as Media Theory: Medianatures and Dirty Matter." *Communication and Critical/Cultural Studies* 9, no. 1 (March 2012): 95–100.

Pellegrini, Ann. "Signaling through the Flames: Hell House Performance and Structures of Religious Feeling." *American Quarterly* 59, no. 3 (2007): 911–35.

Puar, Jasbir K. *Terrorist Assemblages: Homonationalism in Queer Times*. Durham, NC: Duke University Press, 2007.

Read, Jason. "The Order and Connection of Ideology Is the Same as the Order and Connection of Exploitation: Or, Towards a Bestiary of the Capitalist Imagination." *Philosophy Today* 59, no. 2 (spring 2015): 175–89. doi:10.5840/philtoday201522059.

Robbins, Joel. "What Is a Christian? Towards an Anthropology of Christianity." *Religion* 33 (2003): 191–99.

Sampson, Tony. "Various Joyful Encounters with the Dystopias of Affective Capitalism." In "Affective Capitalism," special issue of *Ephemera* 16, no. 4 (November 2016): 51–74.

———. *Virality: Contagion Theory in the Age of Networks*. Minneapolis: University of Minnesota Press, 2012.

Schaefer, Donovan O. *Religious Affects: Animality, Evolution, and Power*. Durham, NC: Duke University Press, 2015.

Sedgwick, Eve Kosofsky, and Adam Frank. "Shame in the Cybernetic Fold: Reading Silvan Tompkins." *Critical Inquiry* 21, no. 2 (1995): 496–522.

Shaviro, Steven. *Cinematic Body*. Minneapolis: University of Minnesota Press, 1993.

Shay, Jonathan. *Odysseus in America: Combat Trauma and the Trials of Homecoming*. New York: Scribner, 2002.

Smith, Christian. *The Bible Made Impossible: Why Biblicism Is Not a Truly Evangelical Reading of Scripture*. Grand Rapids, MI: Brazos, 2012.

Stewart, Kathleen. "Atmospheric Attunements." *Rubric* 1 (2010): 1–14.

———. *Ordinary Affects*. Durham, NC: Duke University Press, 2007.

———. "Precarity's Forms." *Cultural Anthropology* 27, no. 3 (2012): 518–25.

Strauch, Alexander. *Men and Women, Equal Yet Different*. Colorado Springs: Lewis and Roth, 1999.

Struthers, William. *Wired for Intimacy: How Pornography Hijacks the Male Brain*. Downers Grove, IL: InterVarsity, 2009.

Van Doorn, Niels. "Digital Spaces, Material Traces: How Matter Comes to Matter in Online Performances of Gender, Sexuality and Embodiment." *Media, Culture and Society* 33 (2011): 531–47.

Ward, Jane. "Gender Labor: Transmen, Femmes, and the Collective Work of Transgression." *Sexualities* 13 (2010): 236–64.

Warner, Michael. *Publics and Counterpublics.* New York: Zone, 2002.

Webber, Robert. "Introduction." In *Listening to the Beliefs of Emerging Churches: Five Perspectives,* ed. Robert Webber, 9–18. Grand Rapids, MI: Zondervan, 2007.

Wellman, James. "The Churching of the Pacific Northwest: The Rise of Sectarian Entrepreneurs." In *Religion and Public Life in the Pacific Northwest: The None Zone,* ed. Patricia O' Connell Killen and Mark Silk, 79–106. Walnut Creek, CA: AltaMira, 2004.

Wicke, Jennifer. "Through a Gaze Darkly: Pornography's Academic Market." In *More Dirty Looks: Gender, Pornography, and Power,* ed. Pamela Church Gibson, 176–87. London: British Film Institute, 2004.

Williams, Linda. *Hard Core: Power, Pleasure, and the "Frenzy of the Visible."* Berkeley: University of California Press, 1989.

Index

atmosphere, 9, 11, 16, 97, 99, 144; affective, 174–77; air war and ground war, 39, 167; Mars Hill, 25, 32, 38, 48, 131, 182; spiritual warfare, 50, 63, 69, 78

attunement, 6, 17, 21, 47, 50, 94, 97

Attwood, Feona, 148

authenticity, 3, 23, 30, 75, 116, 131; marketing of, 39, 143, 149, 159; in *The Hurt Locker*, 98–99

authority: abuses of, 94, 182; church, 35, 83, 90, 92, 173; Driscoll's spiritual and nonspiritual, 2, 7, 12, 29, 32, 34, 39, 85, 105, 131–32, 143–44, 170; ethnographer's, 6; men's, 52, 66, 71, 74, 104; religious, 3, 31, 170; spiritual, 38, 41, 56, 77–79, 83–85, 88–89, 92–93, 95, 146–47

Baja Fresh, 134

Bakker, Jim, and Tammy Faye, 163–65

Ballard, 13, 22, 110, 116, 131; Mars Hill location, 26, 45, 75, 78, 136, 176

Banet-Weiser, Sarah, 143

Bannon, Stephen, 167

Barker, Jennifer, 98

Barnes and Noble, 160, 185

Benson, Peter, 19

baptism, 26–27, 30, 39, 137–42, 144, 147

Baptist Press, 113

belief, 6, 9, 29, 41, 63, 83, 87, 91, 98, 143, 155, 157, 163, 169, 179, 182–84

Beller, Jonathan, 99–100

Bellevue, 15, 131, 178, 185; Mars Hill location, 15, 163, 177

Bentham, Jeremy, 92

Berlant, Lauren, 83, 182, 190–91, 193

betrayal, 2, 102, 163, 179–80, 183

Bettger, Jeff, 94–96

Bible, 1–3, 5, 21–22, 24–25, 28, 30, 36, 41, 49, 55, 57, 66, 70–71, 76, 85, 88, 124, 129, 130, 136–37, 143, 148, 151, 154, 169, 177–78

Biblical Counseling Q&A with Pastor of Biblical Living Mike Wilkerson, 172–73

biblical femininity, 7, 70, 74, 90, 112

biblical gender, 10, 13, 33

Biblical Oral Sex, 6, 122

biblical masculinity, 7, 37–38, 54, 63, 70–71, 74, 90, 120

biblical porn: book, 3, 7, 18–19, 21; definition of, 7–9; political and economic value, 10, 12–13, 18–19, 70, 111–12, 118–25, 128–34, 149, 151–55, 161–62

biblical sexuality, 7, 10, 13, 37, 74, 90, 112–13, 116, 118–22, 129, 149, 151, 154–55, 161

Bigelow, Kathryn, 98–99, 102–3

Biography of a Christian Soldier, 65

biopolitical control, 9, 13, 38, 85, 111, 118, 125, 168, 176

biopower, 7, 9–11, 38, 40, 92–94, 101, 175, 193

Bivins, Jason, 80–81, 87, 97

Blackman, Lisa, 16–17

Blue Like Jazz, 32

Bly, Robert, 52

Boal, Mark, 98, 102–3

Board of Advisors and Accountability, 186–87

Board of Overseers, 186–87

body, 3, 8, 10, 17, 64–65, 67, 182; congregation, 22, 37, 46, 48, 88–89, 162, 169, 173, 175; Driscoll's, 46; entanglements of, 17, 133, 156, 158; event-encounter of, 21; feared, 51, 87, 101; men's, 109, 124; masculine, white, imperial, Christian, 103; network, 53, 57, 70; porous, 156, 181; sensations of, 11, 68, 70, 98, 162; schema, 159; Spinoza's theory of, 140; surveillance of, 123; women's, 7, 72, 105, 111, 122, 124

Bonhoeffer, Dietrich, 188
Book of Acts, 23
Bott, Dick, 113
Bott Radio Network, 113
brain: computer, 116; entanglements, 17, 143, 156, 158; male, 7, 67, 155–56; porn, 157; traumatic injury, 166, 188
Braveheart, 51, 55, 57
Bright, Bill, 62
Broadway, 32–33
Brown, Joel, 176
Brown, Wendy, 9
Bruskas, Dave, 36
Buddhism, 76
Building a City within a City, 48, 77
Bullying and Harassment in the Workplace: Developments in Theory, Research, and Practice, 179
Bush, George W., 166
Bush administration, 72, 158
Butler, Judith, 192–93

Cabriolet, 67
Calvinism: Driscoll and, 30, 134, 140; Mars Hill's relation to, 41, 56, 66, 77
Campaigns: e-book, 39, 167, 168, 170, 172, 174–75; strategy of control, 40, 168, 170–77
Can we _____?, 151
Cape Town, 178
Capitol Hill Gay Pride Parade, 32–33
Case Western Reserve University, 157
celebrity: Driscoll's, 6, 39, 84, 140, 143–44, 147, 165, 191; at Mars Hill, 177; narcissism, 158–59; U.S. evangelicalism in, 12, 144–47, 164
Charlotte, North Carolina, 37
Chicagoland, 186
China, 62
Cho, Eugene, 24

Christian, 1–3, 5–7, 9–10, 13, 19–20, 22–27, 31–33, 35, 42, 47, 50, 54, 56, 59, 61–65, 68–70, 72–75, 77, 81, 87–90, 92, 96, 103–4, 106, 113, 125–26, 129–32, 137, 141, 144–45, 149–50, 155–57, 159–60, 165–66, 169–70, 189, 191–92; cultural nationalism, 166; marriage, 7, 74, 106, 113, 121–22, 125, 129, 149, 159; Right, 165; rock, 177
Christianity, 5, 65–6, 76, 136, 141, 188; anthropology of, 19; evangelical, 114; institutional, 33; muscular, 70–71; political, 165; U.S., 51
Christianity Today, 113, 146
Christian Nymphos, 132
Christian Post, 36
Christian Sex Q&A (Mature Content), 132
Christian Womanhood in a Feminist Culture, 13, 61, 126
Chun, Wendy Hui Kyong, 13, 117–18, 169
Church Leadership, 84
Church of the Apostles, 23
Church or Cult? The Control-Freaky Ways of Mars Hill Church, 93
Central Intelligence Agency, 102
citizen, 139
City, The, 91, 172
CNN, 78
Colbert, 161
Cold War, 13, 101, 165
complementarianism: doctrine of, 61, 182; preached and practiced at Mars Hill, 62, 112, 116
confession: biopower, 90–91, 114, 131–34; commodification of, 12, 74, 115, 117–20, 123–24; communication and practice at Mars Hill, 7, 9, 12, 32, 38, 74, 76, 78, 106, 115, 117, 120, 126–27, 130–33; ethnographic evidence, 40; former pastors', 14–15, 82, 97, 166–67, 182; U.S. evangelicalism, 114, 119, 130, 152

Real Marriage Campaign, 143, 149–50, 153, 157, 160–61, 175

Real Marriage sermon series, 143, 149, 151

Real Marriage: The Truth About Sex, Friendship, and Life Together, 14, 39, 143, 149–52, 154, 158–61, 170, 189

Reborn on the Battlefield, 65

Redeeming Female Sexuality, 125–26

Redemption groups, 172–73

Reforming Femininity, 125–26, 128

Reforming Male Sexuality, 123

repentance, 14, 19, 31, 91, 129–30; instrument of biopolitical control as, 38, 78, 87–90, 128; spiritual, political, and ethnical valences of, 40, 71, 97, 188–89; as weapon, 32–33, 89–90

Repentant Pastor, 2, 15

Republican Party, 165–66

Republicans, 27

resistance, 40, 62, 93, 190, 192–93

resonance, 62, 147, 157; affective, 18; carnal, 7, 82, 95, 104, 110, 156

ResultSource, 35, 160, 178

Resurgence, 35, 65, 133, 167

Righteous, 40–41

Rock, Chris, 28

Rogers, 100–101

Rogers, Matt, 187

Romans, 78

Robbins, Joel, 19

Robertson, Pat, 31

sacrifice, 5, 10–11, 35, 56, 60, 69, 74, 103, 129, 145, 147, 165–67, 184

Safeco Field, 136

Sampson, Tony, 13, 140, 143–44, 149, 175

Sandler, Lauren, 40–41

Satan, 21, 46, 52, 68, 88–89, 104, 106–9, 111, 118, 169

Saving Private Ryan, 69

Saving Sex, 114

Scopes Trial, 164

Seattle, 14–15, 20, 22–24, 27–28, 32, 35, 41–42, 48, 53, 55–56, 63, 66, 77–78, 89, 91, 93, 101, 103, 116, 118, 120, 136–39, 154, 185, 187

Seattle Downtown Library, 49

Seattle Mariners, 136

Seattle Pacific University, 25

Seattle Seahawks, 14, 136–37

Second World War, 165

Sex Rehab, 158

700 Club, 31

scandal, 12, 15, 35–36, 74–75, 163–65, 169, 178–79

Schaefer, Donovan, 18, 68, 183

Schaeffer, Karen, 81

Scottsdale, Arizona, 37, 189

Scripture, 28, 30, 32, 41, 48–50, 61, 70, 84, 91, 111, 129–30, 144, 171, 176, 188

Second Great Awakening, 119

security, 29, 80, 95, 192; domestic, 122; Mars Hill at, 9, 37–38, 45–47, 51, 90, 93, 116, 171–74; national, 18, 65–66, 167, 171

Sedgwick, Eve Kosofsky, 138, 162

Sergeant James, 99, 101

sex, 8, 10, 14, 32–33, 39, 69–70, 72–75, 106–9, 112–13, 118–19, 121, 123, 128–29, 131–34, 172; biblical, 6–7, 115–16, 122–25, 142, 149–55, 159, 161; biopolitics of, 11, 71, 91–93, 161; Driscoll's theology of, 9, 157; immaterial, 8

sexuality, 7, 9–14, 33, 37, 74, 90, 92–93, 112–14, 116, 118, 121–23, 125–26, 149, 154, 156, 161, 185

shame, 9, 12, 17, 21, 39, 80–81, 87, 94, 111–12, 117–18, 121, 125–26, 128, 138, 142–43, 147, 149–50, 152–55, 159, 162

Shaviro, Steven, 99

Shoreline, 35

Simpsons, The, 27

sin, 3, 12, 14, 31–33, 38, 62, 68, 72–75, 83, 85–90, 95, 105–6, 111, 114, 119, 130, 137–38, 148, 173–74, 188–90; sexual, 7, 74, 90–92, 106–8, 112, 114, 116–18, 120, 122, 125–29, 131, 152, 155–57

Smidt, Phil, 36

Smith, Christian, 29

Sober House, 158

Solomon, 122

South Park, 27

Spencer, Richard, 191

Spinoza, 4, 70, 140, 183

spiritual warfare, 3, 5, 46–47, 54, 78, 87, 89, 104, 111, 116, 184; atmosphere of, 50, 62–63, 69, 78; Driscoll's theology of, 87–88, 109; lecture series on, 38, 88, 104, 105–8

Spiritual Warfare Trial guide, 105–6

Spokane, Washington, 178

Stand in the Gap event, 62

Starbucks, 35, 55

subject, 5–6, 8, 17–18, 47, 51, 61–62, 93, 96, 98, 114, 117, 120, 144, 164, 171, 176, 182–83, 192–93

subjectivity, 16, 17, 57, 74, 99, 143–45, 164, 176, 192–93

Song of Songs, 32, 41, 73, 111, 113, 115–16, 124

Spice Girls, 67

Stewart, Kathleen, 6, 18, 47, 50

Straight to Jesus, 114

Stranger, The, 89, 91, 94

Stranger Than Fiction, 26

Strauch, Alexander, 61–62

Struthers, William E., 155–59

Sunday, Billy, 60, 71

surveillance, 8, 10, 12, 46, 78, 81, 87, 92, 99, 109, 114, 117, 120, 123–24, 129, 131–33, 149–51, 168

Sydney, 178

Tacoma, Washington, 178

Talladega Nights: The Ballad of Ricky Bobby, 29

testimony, 114, 127, 181; congregants', 16, 38, 71, 78, 100–101, 105, 128, 141, 150, 153–54, 167, 173, 182–84

Thailand, 62

Thanksgiving, 185

theology, 13–14, 24, 26, 30, 38, 47, 55, 59, 61, 98, 101, 145, 154, 182, 188; of rape, 18, 161; of sex, 9, 113, 157; spiritual warfare of, 87–88, 109

There's No Such Thing as Free Porn, 142

Third Wave Evangelicalism, 46

threat, 11, 18, 29, 36, 46–48, 51, 57, 65–66, 69–70, 72, 75, 79, 86, 88, 91–92, 96, 99, 120, 131, 156–57, 166, 168, 171, 174, 180, 186, 189, 191–92

Thrice, 27

Today Show, 161

Tompkins, Silvan, 138

trauma, 27, 106, 114, 150, 158, 166, 180–82, 190

Trinity Church, 37, 160, 189

Tripp, Paul, 186–87

True Believer: Thoughts on the Nature of Mass Movements, 167

Trump, Donald, 167, 191–92

Turner, Matthew Paul, 89, 93, 107–8

Turner, Sutton, 36, 177–78, 186

Twitter, 36, 175

2016 election, 40, 191

Ungodly Women, 114

United Nation's Human Development Report of 1993, 61

University of Cambridge, 156

University District, 139

University of Washington, 14, 22, 25, 27, 139, 142

UNReformed, 118

CPSIA information can be obtained
at www.ICGtesting.com
Printed in the USA
LVHW081938011121
702142LV00014B/571